THE LOTTERY OF LIFE AND DEATH

By   James K. Schmitt M.D.

"Every man's life ends in the same way. It is only the details of how he lived and how he died that distinguish one man from another."

Ernest Hemingway

TABLE OF CONTENTS   PAGE

3

4

FOREWORD

I never made the same mistake twice.

Sometimes tragedies are our best teachers. This is especially true in the practice of medicine, which is often unforgiving of mistakes. Practically every physician remembers a case where a bad result seared a lesson into his memory forever.

I tell my medical students that they are entering a field where the most important lessons come not from books, but from the lives of real people. Every patient has a history, but he also has "His Story".

Every hospital inpatient in the United States has a wrist band with a barcode. This helps assure that the right medication is given to the patient, that surgery is not performed on the wrong patient, and that the correct patient is discharged.

Despite our best intentions to make life, and medicine, predictable and error- free, random and unpredicted events occur. Occasionally, some totally unexpected, and surprising event saves the day. Instead of causing a tragedy, serendipity may even result in a hilarious event.

"The Lottery of Life and Death" discusses the conundrums that can convert hospitals into places that do more harm than good.

These true stories come from my early career, and my time with the Navy, the Veterans' Administration, and in the Developing World. Interspersed between sobering events are amusing stories, that also have a moral.

Care in Veterans' hospitals presents special challenges which may affect clinical outcomes. These include substance abuse, post-traumatic stress disorder, violence, staff incompetence, disability, and disability fraud, and others.

The stories are self-contained and can be read independent of the other stories. For reader understanding medical information, such as characteristics of opioid abuse, and clinical science, is occasionally repeated.

Identifying information of most individuals has been changed. However, there are heroes in my story. I see no reason to conceal the identities of heroes.

The opinions expressed in this book are those of the author alone, and do not reflect the opinions of the Veteran's Administration, the University of California, Highland General Hospital, the US Navy or Air Force, or the countries of Bhutan, Bahrain, India, Uganda, Senegal or Cambodia.

I am continually telling my students that medicine is a great adventure and they are already having the experiences that in years they can write into their own books. Writing about patients is sometimes more fun than taking care of them.

I am indebted to my patients, students, nurses and physicians, and veterans who have supported me and provided experiences for this book.

I also wish to thank organizations such as SPCA and Richmond Animal League for relieving suffering of God's helpless creatures.

I am especially grateful to my wife Norma who has tolerated my idiosyncrasies, baked bread, raised children, rescued goldfish, kept me honest, and supported me for over 45. years.

James K. Schmitt MD

Richmond, Virginia 2019

CHAPTER 1

THE LOTTERY OF LIFE AND DEATH

Mr. Theodore Mooney looked up from his crossword puzzle at the wall clock. It was 11 AM. Time to get the mail.

Mr. Mooney was a creature of routines. The mail came early at his house, which was a modular structure in a poor area of town. Sometimes neighborhood kids stole the mail. He wanted to reach the mailbox before they got there.

The 65 year -old African American was a retired train conductor. The thin old man wore a red conductor's cap, a memento of his railroad career. What he didn't realize was that this was the last time that he would ever go to his mailbox.

As he walked down the hill, he noticed that the flag was up. The mail had arrived. In the box were several letters and a package.

The package contained medication. He was used to these packages from his pharmacy. At a recent visit with his doctor, Mr. Mooney's blood pressure was elevated. "I will send you a medication for your blood pressure." the physician said. The package contained a medication, quinidine. Mooney assumed that this was his blood pressure medication and began taking it.

Within hours he began to feel weak. He thought he was getting the flu. He went to bed early, hoping that he would be better in the morning.

The next morning his wife couldn't rouse him. His eyes had turned yellow. His breathing was irregular. She called an ambulance and he was taken to an emergency room. In the ER he was found to be profoundly anemic and in kidney failure. He was admitted to the Intensive Care unit and dialyzed. While receiving dialysis he suffered a massive heart attack and died.

Mr. Mooney died because of incredible bad luck.

Quinidine, the medication that he received in the mail, was intended for another patient. It is not for high blood pressure. It is used to control the heart rate. Quinidine had been mistakenly mailed to Mr. Mooney.

In almost every other patient, there would have been no side effects, or perhaps a little diarrhea, but Mr. Mooney suffered from a genetic defect-Glucose-6-phosphate dehydrogenase deficiency, or G6PD deficiency. G6PD is an enzyme which protects red blood cells from destruction by oxidation. When this enzyme is deficient, certain foods such as broad beans, infection, and some drugs, such as quinidine, cause red cells to breakdown. The destruction of red cells can cause jaundice and kidney failure. G6PD deficiency occurs in about 10 per cent of males of African descent.

Mr. Mooney's level of G6PD was very low. This was noted in Mooney's record, but no interaction with quinidine was noted. Had it been listed as an allergy the pharmacy probably would have stopped the delivery of quinidine.

Mr. Mooney, usually a careful man, expected a new medicat' The chance occurrence of a mailing error and an enzyme deficiency resulted in his death.

The practice of medicine is a careful business. It i of forgotten that human lives are at risk. For the pr patients there is a series of checks and balances, such as noting a patient's allergies before prescribing a medication, but sometimes, such as occurred in the case of Mr. Mooney, our best efforts to protect the patient fail.

My wife, Norma, worked for a while as a physician in an outpatient clinic in California. One of her new patients was Mr. Henry Jefferson, a middle-aged African American truck driver. Mr. Jefferson was being treated for hypertension. His blood pressure was difficult to control. Despite the maximum doses of several medications, it was always elevated. Norma also noticed that the man had episodes of rapid heartbeat and sweating.

There is a rare tumor of the adrenal gland, called a pheochromocytoma, which can cause hypertension. The pheochromocytoma makes epinephrine, and other hormones which raise the blood pressure. Epinephrine, (also called adrenaline) also causes rapid heartbeat and sweating, such as Mr. Jefferson had. This rare tumor is sometimes fatal. To diagnose a pheochromocytoma, urine is collected for 24 hours to see if the epinephrine excretion is elevated.

Norma searched her patient's chart to see if anyone had ever measured urine epinephrine. She went through the record looking at the laboratory slips that had been pasted into the record. She found one slip that had been placed in the record upside down. She gripped the chart firmly in both hands and rotated it 180 degrees. It was the sought-after urine epinephrine level. The urine epinephrine level was sky high. In fact, it was the highest level ever recorded by that lab.

Mr. Jefferson had a pheochromocytoma, which was cured by surgical removal. His treatment was delayed because a critical lab test was pasted in his record upside down. His salvation was a physician who took the trouble to rotate the chart and read the number.

Mr. Horace Frazier-Bey knew something was terribly wrong as soon as he got up from the dinner table. The fifty-year old bus driver had agonizing cramps in his abdomen and the urge to defecate. When he sat on the toilet, he passed blood, not stool.

In the Emergency Room he was found to be going into shock. He was given a transfusion and transferred to the Gastrointestinal Suite where a colonoscopy was done to look for the source of his lower intestinal bleeding. The source of bleeding was a diverticulum. Diverticula are small pockets in the wall of the colon. Blood was pouring out from a vein at the base of one of them. The operator quickly stopped the bleeding with a jolt of electricity delivered by electrocautery.

Then he noticed a huge polyp in the colon. A polyp can sometimes harbor malignancy. Under usual circumstances would have been removed. But Mr. Frazier-Bey was too unstable to remove the polyp.

The patient's bleeding was stopped and within a few days he was discharged. His care was transferred to the VA hospital where I became his doctor. A major issue was the huge polyp remaining in his colon.

I requested the Gastroenterology Service to do a repeat colonoscopy to remove the polyp.

But the gastroenterologists declined to do the test until they received the report of the previous colonoscopy. Although I requested the outside report, I never received it. I became diverted by Mr. Frazier-Bey's other medical problems, such as an overactive thyroid gland. This was treated with radioactive iodine.

I again requested a colonoscopy.

I received the reply. "We need to know the results of the outside colonoscopy before we can proceed with one here." Again, I requested the outside report, with no response.

"Mr. Bey could have a malignant polyp in his colon. It has been sitting there for a year and it has not been checked again." I worried. I imagined this polyp becoming massive, spreading and taking over his body. I decided to forget the standard colonoscopy, and perform an alternate procedure that could be done almost immediately.

A virtual colonoscopy is a CAT scan of the colon that evaluates polyps and other abnormalities. I ordered a virtual colonoscopy on Mr. Frazier-Bey.

The virtual colonoscopy showed the polyp, which seemed not to have grown much, but there was another, more important, ominous, finding which would not have been revealed by standard colonoscopy.

The CAT scan showed a large mass on the right kidney. The mass was almost certainly a renal cell carcinoma, a malignant tumor that can spread and cause death. In Mr. Frazier-Bey's case the tumor had not spread. The kidney was removed, and there was no evidence of recurrence.

Months later the gastroenterologists performed a colonoscopy and removed the polyp.

Like many medical students, Lizzy Wong ate a lot of junk food when she was studying. To her horror she discovered that over the year she had gained 50 lbs. She went on a crash diet and lost most of the weight. But then she noticed that when she ate, she got pain in the right upper abdomen. This can be a sign of gallstones. Lizzy went with her husband to a local hospital to be checked.

Lizzy's physician ordered an ultrasound test on her abdomen to look for gallstones. Sure enough, the ultrasound showed a gallbladder that was full of stones.

"So, you are a medical student?" asked the smiling ultrasound technician. "Let me show you how this works." He moved the probe from Lizzy's abdomen around to her back. When he got to the right kidney he stopped and stared.

"I see something. Don't worry. I will have the doctor take a peek." A minute later the radiologist arrived and looked at the image revealed by ultrasound.

"Yes, there Is something." He turned to Lizzy. "Don't worry. We see something on your kidney. To be on the safe side I would like to do a CAT scan." Lizzy grimaced, then gave a chipper smile.

"OK"

The CAT scan showed a mass on the left kidney, consistent with a renal cell carcinoma.

A few days later Lizzy's kidney was removed. A stage 1(the earliest stage) renal cell carcinoma was found. There was no evidence of spread.

Renal cell carcinoma is the most common malignancy of the kidney. It may present with abdominal pain, blood in the urine, or a flank or abdominal mass. When it is diagnosed early, it has a high cure rate, but often, by the time it is diagnosed, it is advanced. The first clue that cancer of the kidney is present may be pain from a metastasis to the bone.

In the case of Mr. Frazier-Bey, the difficulty in obtaining a colonoscopy led to a virtual colonoscopy, a CAT scan, which unlike the standard colonoscopy, revealed a renal cancer.

The fact that Lizzy Wong ate junk food, and was a medical student resulted in early detection of a potentially lethal tumor.

Were it not for this lucky happenstance, Lizzy and Mr. Frazier-Bey might have died years later from widespread cancer.

Sometimes luck favors the patient.

CHAPTER 2

A BUG'S VIEW

The fly buzzed along in the hot August air.

It was held up by the currents rising from the roofs of the overheated buildings. The large black insect was looking for food. Suddenly, he sensed something below him. It was the odor of fresh blood. The smell was coming up from an open skylight of a building. It was open to provide some relief from the sweltering August heat. The overworked air conditioner had broken down.

The fly swooped down toward his meal.

Far below him masked figures dressed in green hovered around a table. Lying on the table was an unconscious man. His brain was exposed, revealing a huge clot.

This was an operating room. The patient was an alcoholic.

I was a student at the University of California at Berkeley where I had spent three years studying astronomy and the thoughts of great men. Then a new and troubling thought entered my brain. "In order to eat I will have to make a living." Whereas, many people with degrees in the humanities are unemployed, virtually every physician has a job.

In a near panic, I abandoned the elegant, tidy, world of physics and mathematics for the chaotic field of blood, poop, disease and death. I decided to go to medical school.

Many medical students produce a curriculum vitae that reflects a lifelong interest in becoming a physician. I needed to, within weeks, retool my career so that it looked like I had a long commitment to becoming a physician.

In short order I enrolled in premed courses, shaved off my beard, bought a pair of white buck shoes (they made me look clean cut), and tried to join a fraternity. The fraternity wouldn't have me.

I got a volunteer job in the Student Health Pharmacy putting pills in bottles.

Upstairs from the Student Health Service was Donner Pavilion. Donner Pavilion housed patients who were receiving radiation at the giant atom smasher that dominated the hill above the university. I soon moved from the pharmacy upstairs to taking patients for walks.

Three physicians worked at Donner.

Dr. Jack Linfoot, the Director, was a pleasant little man who was part Sioux Indian. He loved telling funny stories.

"Jim, there are two traits that make a doctor an iconic physician." He once remarked.

"What are they?" I took the bait.

"Gray hair and hemorrhoids. Gray hair to make you look distinguished.......and hemorrhoids to make you look concerned!"

Dr. Linfoot sometimes took me with him on house calls. He was perfect example of the kind, principled, dedicated physician that books are written about.

"He knows." said a visiting nurse to me admiringly as he visited the home a woman who was dying of breast cancer. Dr. John

Linfoot, for me, made Medicine into a noble profession. He was an example to me throughout my career.

Another physician who worked at Donner was Frank Lafferty. Dr. Lafferty was a scholarly man in thick rimmed glasses who loved expounding his theories, using a piece of chalk, on the blackboard in his office.

One of his interests was the treatment of pain. "Untreated pain leads to death, by suicide and other causes." he said. "To prevent disease and even death from pain we need to use much larger doses of narcotics than are recommended." He illustrated his theory by a graph which he drew on the blackboard.

Many years later I googled Dr. Lafferty to see if he was still alive. In his eighties he had lost his medical license for inappropriate prescribing of narcotics, which resulted in at least three deaths. Here was a picture of him standing in front of the Medical Board, defending his theories. He used the same graph that he showed me 40 years earlier.

Dr. Donald French was a neurosurgeon who sometimes saw patients at Donner. The overweight young man with the blond crewcut liked having an audience, and took me with him when he did surgery in the community. The gregarious physician talked and joked during surgery. He sometimes even sung to his patients while operating on them.

So here I was in an operating room at Alta Bates Hospital in Berkeley, on a sweltering summer day watching Dr. French remove a blood clot from an alcoholic's brain.

Alcoholism shrinks the brain away from its leathery covering, the dura. Veins running from the brain to the dura become stretched. Relatively minor trauma places tension on the overstretched veins, and may rupture them, causing a clot on top of the brain.

This clot is called a subdural hematoma. The clot presses on the brain, and if it is not removed, may cause death.

The surgical team was removing the clot to save the man's life.

The functions of the brain are distributed over different areas. Moving the arms and legs is controlled by the frontal lobe which is in the front of the brain. Behind the frontal lobe is the parietal lobe which controls sensation. At the sides of the brain are the temporal lobes, which store memory. The patient's blood clot was on his left temporal lobe.

The team was so intent on saving their patient's life that they were unaware of the fly buzzing around the room

"Little old man with blood on your brain. You drank too much alcohol. That is clear. Be it wine, be it whiskey, be it beer." the heavily perspiring surgeon sung with a lilting voice, as he cut through the tough dura to expose the clot.

At first the insect that had dropped in through the skylight flew at the edges of the room avoiding the walls. Then it sensed the warm blood at the center of the room. It began circling above the exposed brain. Each orbit was smaller as it dropped toward its prize.

The surgeon was intent on removing the clot in the overheated operating theatre. Beads of sweat formed above his surgical mask and he breathed heavily as he leaned over the patient. He had been up late the previous night removing a malignant brain tumor, and he was feeling the fatigue. He held a sucker, which he used to remove blood from the brain. Just as the sucker touched the clot, the fly landed on the brain, three inches from the surgeon's hand.

Everyone standing around the table gasped as the sterility of the operative field was broken by this creature that feeds on garbage and feces. Dr. French stared at the fly for a few seconds. Then he sighed and looked across the table at his assistant.

"Mrs. Cooper, please spray that fly with antiseptic solution" he said with a bit of whimsy.

The insect flew off and the surgeon resumed removing the clot.

Perhaps the fly had destroyed his concentration. He inserted the sucker a little too deep. With the suction he removed not only the clot, but also a piece of the underlying temporal lobe, the memory place. The exhausted surgeon sighed again as he realized his mistake. Then he spoke.

"Oops! There goes High School! "

CHAPTER 3

THE SPIRIT IN THE LAKE

The great adventure of my teenage years began in the Oakland, California Greyhound bus station.

It always occurred in the summer. Standing among other passengers with my backpack I felt like a famous explorer. A red bandana was wrapped around my neck to ward off the sun, making me look like a frontiersman. I noticed teenage girls looking at me with what I imagined to be admiration. I was a brave hero going to explore the wilderness. I stood up straight and smiled.

Many hours later, after driving through the hot farm country of the Central Valley and through the foothills of the Sierra Nevada, the bus arrived at Yosemite. In front of me was Half Dome, a granite sphere that thousands of years ago was cut in half by the glacier that dug this valley. I shouldered my pack and walked east, past hotels and tent cabins, to the back of the valley. Then I began the steep climb up the side of the valley.

Always to my left was the stream that flows into the mighty Merced River. The spray wetted my face, which is why this is called the Mist Trail. I reached the first fall of the Merced, Vernal Fall. I continued up the steep trail, finally, at about sunset, reaching the top of Nevada Fall. At the top of the fall the trail goes through rocks polished by the movement of glaciers. The river becomes calmer and invites swimmers. But its looks are deceptive. Many hikers have taken a swim in the river, only to be swept over the falls to their death.

The river now flows from a forested area known as Little Yosemite Valley. I rolled out my sleeping bag. This is a common place for hikers to spend their first night. This fact is known only too well by bears.

One night the silence was broken by a scream coming from up the river. The yelling reverberated from camp site to camp site. A marauding bear was raiding the camps. Campers came running through the darkness with flashlights. Finally, the culprit was discovered. Sitting on a rock in the middle of the river, staring defiantly at the angry hikers, was a huge gold colored bear, holding a loaf of pumpernickel bread that he had stolen.

After several days of walking along the river I retraced my steps back down to the Yosemite Valley. I was always starving when I reached the valley floor. I wolfed down Coke and candy and ice cream. The most thrilling part of the entire trip was the ice cream and candy I ate at its end. I boarded the bus for the long trip home. My father picked me up at the bus station in his International Harvester pickup truck and I spent the rest of the summer regaling my family with stories of my adventures. I exaggerated the danger. It made a better story.

When I got interested in women my annual pilgrimages to Yosemite took on added meaning. They became a courting ritual. I wanted the girl to see me as an outdoorsman who could cut trail and would take care of her in the wilderness. Numerous women trekked through Yosemite with me, their back breaking with an oversized pack, sleeping on rocks and pine needles, and eating undercooked dehydrated food. They smiled through chapped lips saying they "loved the wilderness." Usually, a backpacking trip with a woman marked the end of my relationship with her.

Near the end of the first year of medical school I went on a blind date. My roommate, Don, who played the saxophone, invited two women from our class to see him play in a performance of "The Mikado". He asked me to be their escort while he performed. In truth, he was interested in Norma McKenzie, a pretty, auburn-haired woman with hazel eyes. Don's plan was for me to pair up with Vivian, the other girl. Norma and Vivian didn't know who I was. When they looked me up in the class pictures, they recognized me. "He's the one who has shaving cream on his ear in the elevator." one of them remarked.

One of the things that attracted me to Norma was her practical nature and her coolness under stress. While I and other students panicked and crammed the night before an exam, Norma calmly remarked "In the long run it doesn't matter". Then she went into the kitchen and began baking bread. Soon, the soothing aroma of baking bread permeated the apartment.

Somehow Norma and I clicked. My way of finding out if I turned a woman off was to pretend that I had fallen asleep with my head on her shoulder. If she didn't seem to mind I knew that she wasn't totally disgusted by me. Norma didn't seem to mind my attentions.

That summer Norma and I drove her aged Peugeot sedan to Yosemite Valley. This was going to be my standard, macho, hike.

That night we camped in Little Yosemite Valley. I made a wood fire in a rock fireplace that a previous hiker had built. I was delighted to show my fire building skills and to be able to protect "my woman". I totally ignored the small gas stove that was hidden in the bottom of my pack.

The following day we followed the Merced River on a soft carpet of pine needles on a gradual climb up to Merced Lake. That night we camped at Merced Lake, a large lake from which the river sprang."

To protect the food from the many bears that inhabited the area there were metal "bear boxes". But I ignored the boxes. I threw a rope over a high tree branch, then tied our packs to the end of the rope and pulled them up the tree where the bears couldn't reach them. It would have been simpler just to put our perishables in the boxes, but less macho. I wasn't sure if Norma thought I was being a savvy frontiersman, or just stupid. It boiled down to what she thought the purpose of the metal boxes was. She just sat on a log and smiled sweetly.

The complete "I can take care of the woman and impress the heck out of her" experience entails living off the land. To accomplish this, I brought my fishing pole. Three miles above Merced Lake was Washburn Lake, a smaller lake where the fishing was good. The next morning Norma and I walked along the trail that led to the upper lake. The trail went along a steep granite embankment that was above the river where I could see trout. My bait was red worms which I carried in a container of dirt. Norma followed me carrying a book.

When I caught a fish I proudly showed it to Norma. I planned to cook the fish that night in front of my admiring companion.

As we walked along the granite embankment changed into a swampy area. This told me that we were getting close to the lake, Suddenly, up in front of us we heard loud shouting. "Help! Help!" Norma and walked up the trail toward the sound. A totally naked man appeared in front of us. He was about 30 years of age, fit looking with a black beard that reached to his chest. His bare feet were bleeding from running down the rocky trail. "You'd better stay back." I told Norma.

I approached the man. "My girlfriend and I were climbing up the rock face. She fell in the river!" the man screamed in anguish. "Can you help me look for her?" I followed the distraught man up the trail to the lake. On the northern side of the lake was a steep cliff overlooking the river. "We were climbing up there." the man said pointing to the rock face a hundred feet or so above the water. "My girlfriend slipped, and she fell into the river." He was naked, without ropes or protective gear. I assumed that his female companion was naked too, but I didn't ask the question.

The stretch of the river below the cliff flowed fast. It was interrupted by large boulders that stuck out of the water. There was no sign of the woman. I guessed that she hit the rocks, then was washed away in the current. I winced at the thought of bare flesh colliding with the sharp rocks. Her body would be washed down the stream toward Washburn Lake.

I ran down the stream. My progress was hampered by rocks and brush. I covered perhaps half a mile looking in rocky pools and in brush for a woman's body. It was possible that she was still alive and just injured, but there was no sign of her. It was apparent that I could not, by myself, search every possible place where her body had come to a rest.

I made it back to the naked man who was sitting on a rock crying. "You stay here." I told him. "I will get help." I headed down toward Merced Lake. Norma was sitting at our campsite wondering what was going on. "A woman fell into the river!" I shouted. Then I left her and ran down the trail toward the Yosemite Valley. About a mile down the trail I came upon three hikers coming up to Merced Lake. "A woman fell from a cliff into the river!" I yelled. "We need help to find her. Go down to the valley to get help."

One of the hikers turned around and headed back toward the valley. The others followed me. I ran back up the trail to the naked man who was sitting dazed on a rock. "I will keep looking." I said and once again ran down the stream. I was afraid that the woman was still alive and that she had been washed up against a rock by the current. Every minute counted. I continued for a mile down the stream looking in every pool and every pile of brush for the woman.

It began to get dark. I walked back up the stream to the naked man. He was now covered by a blanket that a hiker had given him. A helicopter hovered over him. The backpacker had gotten help.

"I want to thank you for what you did." The naked man said weakly as he offered me his hand.

I walked back to our camp at Merced Lake where Norma retreated when I told her about the naked man. I had brought corn meal to cover the trout when they were fried. Norma had contrived a Dutch oven from a cooking pot and made corn meal bread. She was a better wilderness chef than I was.

I told her about the woman who fell from the cliff.

That night we slept on the shore of the lake in our sleeping bags. I had trouble getting to sleep. I thought about the woman and her poor boyfriend. By now he must be in a hospital. He would have to call the woman's parents and tell them what had happened to her. She was probably dead.

Finally, I got to sleep. I dreamed.

In my mind I crossed the lake in the darkness. I traveled up the stream running into the lake. I moved over rocky pools and ripples and piles of brush. Then I crossed the second, smaller lake and ran into the river. About two miles up the river I stopped. I spotted something in the water. It was the form of a woman held under the water by a large branch. The woman had long blond hair that waved in the strong current. The naked body glowed in the dark.

Then, a ghostly shape left the body. The phosphorescent body began moving through the murky river following its downstream course. The spirit arrived at Merced Lake. It began moving through the night across the lake. The apparition reached the shore near where I was sleeping and came up on the land next to me. I heard a tinkling sound. I woke up.

A deer had come into our camp and was licking one of our cooking pots. That was the noise.

I looked over at Norma's sleeping bag. She was already awake. "You will never guess the dream I had." I said.

"You saw the body of the woman in the water."

I gasped. Norma continued.

"And it was being held under the water by a big branch."

"Yes." I was astounded by this surprising revelation.

"The woman had blond hair."

"That's right!"

"And she was right below a small waterfall."

"Yes, there was a waterfall." I continued to be amazed.

"And I could see some sort of glow leaving her body and coming down the creek. It washed up on the shore."

We had the same dream.

In my dream there were specific clues to the location of the body. It was about two miles upstream, below a small waterfall, under a branch. Perhaps I had seen the body when I was searching but it had not registered. Then, at night, my subconscious produced the dream.

That morning I told the searchers about my dream. Two miles up the stream, under a log, they found the body.

I could explain my dream, but not Norma's. She had not gone down the river looking for the body. Did the poor woman's soul come out of the lake and invade both of our sleeping brains?

My previous track record dictated that this hike would end my relationship with Norma. But, she still dated me and even continued to go on backpacking trips with me. At the time of our marriage in 1973 she informed me.

"I still will go hiking. I love hiking, but I won't sleep on the ground."

CHAPTER 4

" THE PSYCHIATRIST AND THE PARROT

"I'm paying eighty dollars an hour to breathe smoke."
I thought, as I inhaled the nutty fragrance that was being blown at
me. The source of the smoke was the bearded man in the tweed
jacket sitting across from me.

I was near the end of my second year of internal medicine
residency at Highland General Hospital in Oakland, Calif.   Every
fourth day the resident worked a 24hour shift, taking care of
every sick patient who came in the door. If a hospitalized patient
stopped breathing or began vomiting blood, the resident and his
two interns took care of him too.

 At 8 am the resident presented his cases to the Attending
Physician in a room near the cafeteria. While the senior
physician munched on his scrambled eggs and biscuits, the
resident and his interns told the Attending about the events of the
prior evening. Sometimes the Attending seemed to be more
interested in his breakfast than in the cases, only occasionally
looking up from his eggs and grunting. If a mistake had been
made, even if a patient had died because of that mistake, the
resident was informed at breakfast.

 But the shift was not over. For the remainder of the day the
resident and interns worked to get their patients off to tests. By
the time they went to bed they had worked thirty- two hours.

On Saturday morning was held Morbidity and Mortality Conference, which was commonly referred to as Death Rounds. At Death Rounds the sadistic Chief of Medicine, Dr. Scout Raker, mercilessly tormented the residents for their mistakes. The resident, and only the resident, was held responsible for the patient's fate.

It seemed as if Dr. Raker looked at the resident's call night as a test, to see if he could get through the night without making a mistake. He believed that the thirty- two- hour shift benefited the patient because it provided "continuity of care". The image of their little bald Chief, who would crucify them for their mistakes, haunted sleep deprived interns and residents as they staggered from patient to patient.

Years later it was recognized that residents should have direct supervision and that a physician who worked thirty- two hours without sleep was not safe to care for patients. Now when criticism is meted out at Morbidity and Mortality Conference, it is the Attending Physician who supervises the resident who receives it, not the resident.

At Highland General Hospital in 1971 patients literally died for the resident's education. You were too busy taking care of the next patient to dwell on a mistake. If you killed a patient, you hoped that what you had learned would prevent you from killing the next patient.

The stress of the year was catching up with me. I began to have almost constant headaches. I wondered if I had a brain tumor. I fidgeted and seemed distracted. I felt guilty about my patients who had died.

In the midst of the mental trauma and noise and terror and death at Highland Hospital there was a guardian angel, almost a mother figure, who noticed that people were suffering and tried to help them. This benign presence took the improbable form of a female pathologist, Dr. Sonya Hess. She was a pert little woman aged about 45. When she spoke. you detected her European origins in her accent.

One day she pulled me aside and whispered. "People are noticing that you are stressed. "HE is noticing that you are stressed."

"HE" had to be Dr. Raker. Whatever else happened I didn't want to fall apart in front of Dr. Raker.

"Now I know a psychiatrist, Dr. Kessler. He is very good. I will call him. You can see him. He will help you."

It was rumored that Dr. Hess, a Jew, had been in a concentration camp during WWII. If a psychiatrist could help her, he could help me. Maybe he could make my headaches go away.

So here I was a week later sitting in the second- floor office of Dr. Harvey Kessler.

To be honest, I liked the smell of his pipe smoke. It was soothing. Perhaps that was part of the therapy. Dr. Kessler was a thin, athletic looking man. His full black beard was beginning to show white hairs. The office was sparsely decorated. On the left was a shelf that contained a few books and a statue of Buddha. In front of the psychiatrist was a small table. There was no writing pad. Dr. Kessler did not take notes.

He looked like pictures I had seen of Sigmund Freud. This made me think he was probably a Freudian psychiatrist.

I knew that Freud believed that psychiatric disorders stemmed from stresses that occurred during childhood. One of those stresses was competition between a child and his father for his mother's affection. Another stressful time was toilet training. Psychoanalysis involved discussing these earlier stresses and deep -seated conflicts.

"I never wanted to have sex with my mother." I began.

The psychiatrist nodded and took a puff of his pipe.

"And I didn't hate my father. I loved my father. He took me fishing." I glanced at Kessler, looking for his approval.

He took another puff and nodded.

"Sometimes when I was little, I wet the bed. I was a sound sleeper. I had a rubber sheet." I was especially ashamed of the sheet, but thought that my doctor needed to know everything. "But by the time I was six I was toilet trained and didn't have any more problems." I glanced at Kessler for a look of approval, but his bearded visage was in a cloud of smoke.

"I was ashamed of my parents. They were simple working people. When I graduated from Medical School they showed up. When I was talking to some friends, my father said he had to leave because he had a rental car. I was so embarrassed." At that time the man across from me removed his pipe and spoke. "You couldn't stand it."

My weekly sessions in the upstairs office on Telegraph Ave pretty much consisted of my talking about everything to make Kessler happy, and him saying nothing except interjecting an occasional "You couldn't stand it."

"My mother got cancer and was in the hospital dying. She died when I was working. I was the only one in my family who wasn't with her. In a way I am glad that I wasn't there. I can tolerate seeing a patient die. But my mother was different."

"You couldn't stand it."

I was very anxious about seeing a psychiatrist. Telling the psychiatrist everything about your life is supposed to be therapeutic, like telling him that you wet your pants in school when you were eight. For physicians to do their job, the patient must have total confidentiality.

If a small- town minister develops chest pain and goes to the Emergency Room, he needs to be able to disclose the fact that he used cocaine without being exposed. Cocaine causes heart attacks and rhythm problems. Treating them appropriately can save the minister's life. If there is the possibility that the information may be turned over to the newspapers and police and ruin his career, the minister may remain silent and die of a cardiac problem.

Privacy is one of the pillars upon which the profession of medicine is founded. This is particularly important in the field of psychiatry.

In 1971 a violation of privacy occurred which shook the belief in the right to privacy and disgusted the medical world.

Daniel Ellsberg, who was a consultant to the Pentagon, discovered instances of fraud in US policy toward Viet Nam. Whereas, officially we were involved in Viet Nam to defend a friendly ally, in fact, our real goal was to limit the expansion of imperialist China and to avoid the embarrassment of a humiliating defeat.

Ellsberg released the so-called "Pentagon Papers" to the New York Times to be published. The Nixon administration did everything that it could to discredit Ellsberg, who they labeled as a traitor. At one time President Nixon made the statement "If the President orders it, it is not illegal." A group known as the "Plumbers" broke into the office of Ellsberg's psychiatrist, Dr. Henry Fielding, to photograph his medical record.

The perpetrators were caught and sent to prison for a violation of Ellsberg's fundamental rights.

As I sat looking at my pipe puffing physician, I wondered where this information was going. Was he speaking into a recorder after I left? Was he writing everything down? When he retired what would happen to my record? If he died would his son come to the office and find my medical record and use it to blackmail me?

A few weeks later, at my weekly session with Kessler, something seemed to be different. Kessler puffed his pipe and nodded as usual. The beard and tweed coat were unchanged. The Buddha on the shelf had not been moved.

Then I noticed something that I never expected to see in a psychiatrist's office. Sitting on the small table was a parrot. It was a full- grown parrot, a huge bird with a bright red head, a curved yellow beak and blue tail that seemed to go on forever. For a moment I thought that it was a statue. Then the bird began to preen its chest. I wondered how long it had been there- perhaps for weeks. Was I so intimidated by Kessler that I hadn't noticed the big bird? I decided not to mention the animal. That might not be polite. I got back to the business of psychotherapy.

"I didn't own a car and couldn't drive anyway. When I took a girl on a date my sister Irene drove us to the movie. I was humiliated."

I looked at Kessler, then at the parrot, then back at the psychiatrist. I half expected the parrot to say. "You couldn't stand it." But both the bearded man and the bird were silent.

Finally, my curiosity got the best of me.

"Dr. Kessler, I couldn't help noticing the parrot."

"Yes, what do you think of him. Why do you think he is here?" He managed a little smile. This was the first time I saw him smile.

"You use him as a decoration. The room is kind of dull and grey. The parrot brightens it up. Is that why you have him?"

"No." Kessler extended his wrist and the bird stepped on it.

"Well, maybe it is therapeutic. Animals relax people. Like rescue dogs, or tropical fish in a nursing home. Animals make people feel more comfortable."

"No, that's not why he is here."

Then a more ominous thought crossed my mind. I thought of the Daniel Ellsberg case.

"A tape recorder is hidden in his feathers. You are recording everything I say."

Kessler smirked and puffed twice on his pipe. "No."

"Well, Dr. Kessler why do you have a parrot in your office?"

The psychiatrist took another puff, then removed his pipe and spoke.

"If I leave him home, he craps on the carpet."

CHAPTER 5
MISSED OPPORTUNITIES

Mrs. Hum enjoyed the smell of her doctor's small walkup office, which was located in San Francisco's Chinatown.

The aroma was a combination of odors from the Chinese restaurant next store, and the pungent herbs that her elderly Chinese physician used in his practice.

Dr. Lin trained in Traditional Medicine in China when he was a young man. Traditional Chinese medicine teaches that the body's energy circulates through channels to the organs of the body, and that disease is due to a disorder of this energy flow. Traditional Medicine relies on herbs, acupuncture, and massage.

When he came to America Dr. Lin obtained a degree in modern medicine. He combined both medical disciplines in his practice. But he found that his patients, especially those who were old or had been born in China, preferred Traditional Medicine to modern American medicine. His practice became more of a Traditional Medicine practice than a modern practice.

All around Mrs. Hum on shelves were jars that contained medicinal herbs and roots and minerals. In some jars were what appeared to be dried animal parts.

Mrs. Hum, a petit 35 year- old woman, noticed increasing fatigue since the birth of her third child two years previously. She lacked the energy to care for her family, and sometimes dozed off in the middle of the day. As opposed to her other children, she did not breast feed, but fed this baby with a bottle. This was, in part, because she had little milk production. Often, she was too tired to hold the bottle to the infant's mouth and her teenage daughter fed the baby. She now had three daughters and wanted to try for a son, but her menstrual periods had become irregular, and she couldn't conceive.

Dr. Lin asked Mrs. Hum a series of questions about her health. Then he examined his patient.

"Open your mouth." he asked. He studied Mrs. Hum's tongue. Then he sniffed to detect any body odor. He put on his stethoscope and listened to her lungs. Finally, he felt her pulse in her wrist. He noted that it was weak and slow.

There is a teaching in Traditional Chinese Medicine that in the neck resides a source of the body's energy. This is in remarkable agreement with the modern scientific finding of the thyroid gland in the neck. The thyroid is necessary for normal energy levels. Traditional practitioners increase their patient's energy by rubbing the neck with coins.

The old man reached into a drawer and retrieved an ancient Chinese coin. He vigorously rubbed the woman's neck with it, so hard that he made bruises. She grimaced in pain. Perhaps this would wake up Mrs. Hum's lazy thyroid gland.

The healer went to a shelf and picked up a bottle that contained a yellow powder. This was dried human placenta, a remedy for infertility. "Take a little of this every day to help you conceive." he said in Mandarin to the woman.

Dr. Lin was also aware of modern science. He sent Mrs. Hum to a lab to get a test of her thyroid hormone level.

The thyroid hormone level was low. Her thyroid was not working properly.

The aging Asian physician referred Mrs. Hum to the University of California Thyroid Clinic for further treatment. These were the experts on thyroid problems.

In Thyroid Clinic Mrs. Hum was seen by a resident physician. He noted her puffy features and absence of the outer parts of her eyebrows and her coarse hair. These were signs of low thyroid hormone levels. or hypothyroidism. This diagnosis was confirmed by the low thyroid hormone level obtained by the Chinese physician.

Scattered throughout the body are the endocrine glands. The thyroid gland is necessary for energy. The ovaries and testes produce sex hormones. The adrenals produce cortisol, a steroid which helps the body respond to stress.

The pituitary gland is a ball of specialized cells which sits at the base of the brain. It is called "The Master Gland". This is because the pituitary sends out messenger hormones to stimulate other glands in the body. Thyroid stimulating hormone (TSH) stimulates the thyroid gland to produce thyroid hormone, Adrenocorticotropic Hormone (ACTH) stimulates cortisol, (cortisone) release by the adrenal gland, Follicle Stimulating Hormone (FSH) stimulates the ovaries and testes.

Elevation of these pituitary hormones provides evidence that an endocrine organ is failing. For example, a menopausal woman whose ovaries are failing will have an elevated FSH.

The pituitary is a bit like the thermostat in your house. There is a feedback loop. When someone leaves your door open, letting in the cold, the thermostat senses this and turns the heating up. When a gland, such as the thyroid, stops working, the pituitary increases the messenger, in an attempt to wake up the ailing gland.

The vast majority of cases of hypothyroidism are "primary hypothyroidism". This means that the thyroid gland has been damaged by antibodies, surgical removal, or some other process. In primary hypothyroidism the healthy pituitary sends out a messenger to try to wake up the sleeping thyroid. The resident therefore ordered a TSH level. He fully expected the TSH to be elevated. It would take a week for the TSH value to return from the laboratory.

In only 1/1000 cases of hypothyroidism the thyroid fails because of damage to the pituitary gland. The pituitary can't send out signals to thyroid gland. The clue to this rare condition would be that the TSH in the hypothyroid patient is not elevated. This uncommon condition is "secondary hypothyroidism."

The youthful resident physician wrote a prescription for thyroid hormone. "You will start feeling better in a few weeks." he told his hopeful patient. "We will see you back in two months."

But Mrs. Hum felt more fatigued and weaker. She felt dizzy when she stood up and twice passed out. While visiting her cousin she developed abdominal pain and collapsed. The Rescue Squad was called, and she was taken to a nearby Emergency Room.

The Emergency Room was busy. In two beds were elderly men with chest pain. In two more beds were an alcoholic man with pancreatitis, and a spinal cord injury patient who needed his bladder catheter changed. In yet another bed was a man with a fish hook stuck in his hand.

Mrs. Hum was placed in a bed next to the spinal cord patient and the curtains were closed. A nurse took her blood pressure. "Its 80/60!" she shouted. "Let's give her some fluids." A bottle of saline was started and allowed to run in as fast as it could. A few minutes later a physician walked in and asked some questions.

Then he did a physical examination. Although Mrs. Hum complained of abdominal pain, her abdomen seemed relatively nontender. Blood was drawn, and a urine specimen was taken. "Her blood pressure is now 100/60." said the nurse, happy at the improvement.

Thirty minutes later the labs returned. Mrs. Hum had white blood cells and bacteria in her urine, signs of a urinary tract infection. Her blood work showed her to be anemic. The white blood count was slightly elevated. This finding, combined with the patient's fever of 101 degrees Fahrenheit, supported the diagnosis of infection.

A surprising finding was the huge number of little pink cells, eosinophils, in Mrs. Hum's blood. Perhaps it was because the patient was from China and she might have parasites which increase eosinophils. Or perhaps the overworked physicians never noticed this abnormality.

The diagnosis of a urinary infection was made. Gentamycin, an antibiotic that kills bacteria that infect the urine was administered by vein and Mrs. Hum was admitted to the hospital.

Mrs. Hum seemed to be improving in the hospital. Her blood pressure increased to 110/70. However, an hour later she became more anxious. Her blood pressure plummeted to 60/40. Fluids were given to resuscitate her. Her blood pressure continued to drop, and she went into cardiac arrest. She could not be resuscitated.

Because she died so soon after entering the hospital an autopsy was performed.

The female pathologist shook her head as she looked at the Asian woman lying on the autopsy table. Like her, Mrs. Hum was a mother of three.

The chest was opened first. The patient died in shock. It was important to see if the heart had failed. The heart was normal. An embolism to the lungs can cause shock, but the lungs were normal.

The pathologist then opened the abdomen. The intestines were unremarkable. But when the kidneys were exposed, she noticed something unusual. The adrenal glands, which sit on top of the kidneys, normally look like mushroom caps. Mrs. Hum's adrenals looked like flattened wafers. They were atrophic, sick. But why?

The pathologist, turning her attention to the brain, opened the skull. She was now particularly interested in the pituitary gland. At the base of the brain is the pituitary gland, the Master Gland of the body that controls several glands, including the thyroid, adrenals, and sex glands. A normal pituitary gland is the size and shape of an olive.   Mrs. Hum's pituitary looked more like a shriveled pea.

The mystery of what killed the Chinese woman was solved. Mrs. Hum had Sheehan's Syndrome, which was described in 1937 by Dr. Harold Sheehan, an English pathologist.

During pregnancy the pituitary gland enlarges and can outstrip its blood supply. If, during delivery, the woman loses too much blood and goes into shock, the pituitary is injured and can die. As a result of this catastrophe, the glands controlled by the Master Gland can stop working. The thyroid fails, causing fatigue and the sex organs fail, causing infertility.

But the most ominous consequence is failure of the adrenal glands. The adrenal glands make cortisol, a steroid hormone that helps the body survive stress.   Without cortisol, a stress such as a urinary infection, or just initiating thyroid hormone, can cause irreversible shock and death.

The case of Mrs. Hum unraveled further as physicians who had seen her were informed of her death. Her Chinese doctor, who found that she was hypothyroid, was told by Mrs. Hum that she no longer menstruated. This indicated that the ovaries were no longer functioning.

The pituitary also makes prolactin, a hormone necessary for milk production. The Asian woman's inability to nurse her baby was additional evidence that her pituitary was destroyed at the time of delivery.

Her TSH was reported to the Thyroid Clinic as "normal". In most cases a "normal" finding is reassuring. The resident forgot that his patient was hypothyroid, and he expected the TSH to be elevated. A normal or low TSH in a patient with a failing thyroid has ominous implications. It indicates that the source of TSH, the pituitary, is destroyed, and other glands controlled by the pituitary, such as the adrenal may also be failing. It is a "red flag" that tells the physician that his patient is in trouble and needs cortisone to survive.

Someone whose pituitary gland is failing is a bit like a hibernating bear. Their metabolism has shut down. When the resident physician started Mrs. Hum on thyroid hormone it placed increased demands on a sick body. It was like forcing a heart patient to run a marathon. He collapses and dies. But the mother of three still could be saved.

Mrs. Hum was taken to an Emergency Room. The emergency physicians were not aware of Mrs. Hum's endocrine problems. She had fever, abdominal pain, low blood pressure and evidence of a urinary tract infection. These are common symptoms seen in emergency rooms. They treated her with fluids and antibiotics and admitted her to the hospital. Was there any clue that something more ominous was going on with the Chinese woman?

Her blood work, surprisingly, showed a high eosinophil count. One cause of elevated eosinophils is damage to the adrenal glands, such as Mrs. Hum had.

Stress raises cortisol. Cortisol suppresses eosinophils. The fact that a person in shock had an elevated eosinophil count, should have sounded the alarm that life threatening adrenal insufficiency was present,

The emergency room doctors were distracted by other patients who seemed to be sicker than the 35- year old mother of three.

Simply injecting 100 mg of hydrocortisone into her intravenous line might have saved her life.

Giving Mrs. Hum thyroid hormone, without also replacing her adrenal hormone, was like leaving the front door open to the bitter cold when the thermostat is broken. Disaster can occur.

The resident physician in Thyroid Clinic assumed that his patient had the common variety of low thyroid function, not the rare form that Mrs. Hum had. The odds were on his side, but this time his luck ran out. The medication, rather than curing her, led to her death.

There are many hopeless cases in the practice of medicine; the terminal cancer patient, the patient with a gunshot to the head who is brain dead, the Alzheimer's patient who is no longer eating.

But there are other patients, like Mrs. Hum, whose lives can be saved by a few dollars-worth of medication.

Her Chinese doctor's instincts were sound. However, multiple clues were ignored by other physicians, and she was lost in the busy environments of academic and emergency medicine.

COMMON THINGS HAPPEN COMMONLY

RARE THINGS HAPPEN RARELY- -

BUT THEY HAPPEN

CHAPTER 6

A TRUE-BLUE STORY

A short walk across the Employee Parking Lot at the Richmond VA Hospital takes you to a large one- story building that is partially hidden by trees and bushes

It has a brick and wood facade, and an A- frame entrance. It is partially surrounded by a wrought iron fence. Near the building, in bowers of plants, are tables and chairs, sitting areas for patients and their families.

This is Sitter-Barfoot, a nursing home. It is named for Sitter and Barfoot, two Congressional Medal of Honor winners. Carl Sitter received his Congressional Medal of Honor for service in the Korean War, and Van Barfoot received his medal for heroism in World War II. Both men died in Richmond, Virginia. Sitter-Barfoot is not a part of the Veterans Hospital, but it was built for veterans.

One Sunday afternoon I was working in our Emergency Room. A call came from Sitter- Barfoot. "We have a patient who is cyanotic. His name is Benjamin Towne. We want to transfer him to the Emergency Room immediately!" an excited nurse relayed to one of our nurses.

Cyanosis means that the patient is turning blue. The hemoglobin in the blood carries oxygen. When the oxygen content of hemoglobin is too low, the color of blood changes from red to a blueish tinge and the patient may appear blue.

Conditions that decrease oxygen delivery to the blood cause cyanosis. These are life threatening conditions like heart failure, cardiac arrest, massive infection, overwhelming pneumonia, or a massive clot to the lung that blocks delivery of oxygen to the blood.

"Send him over." I said.

A few minutes later we received a radio message from an ambulance. "We have a cyanotic patient on route to your facility. His blood pressure is 110/80, his pulse is 100, his respirations are 20 per minute."

A patient who is turning blue is clinically unstable and may already be in cardiac arrest. We prepared for the worst.

The nurses prepared bed 6 for this patient who might be on the brink of death. A bottle of saline was hung on a pole near the bed and an intravenous line prepared so that the patient could be given fluids as soon as he arrived. The IV was also a conduit for drugs that could stabilize his heart rhythm. A plastic tube was connected to the oxygen outlet that was near the bed so that we could deliver lifesaving oxygen as soon as the patient arrived. And a "crash cart", the cart that has a defibrillator that can shock a lethal rhythm such as ventricular fibrillation into a more stable rhythm, was moved near bed 6.

A siren blared. Our patient had arrived. I quickly put on a pair of rubber gloves. This was for my protection, just in case the patient was bleeding or had something contagious. The nurses and I stood around the bed nervously eyeing the automatic door between room 14 and room 15. He might be in cardiac arrest and we would have to begin CPR.

A moment later the door burst open and EMTs (emergency medical technicians) pushing a stretcher rushed in. The patient already had an IV running. An oxygen mask covered most of his face. "Bed 6!" shouted one of our nurses. The EMTs took the patient to bed 6 and nurses and EMTs lifted him onto the bed. I ran over to see if the patient needed to have a tube inserted into his trachea to help him breath. He was an elderly man, about 70.

He was breathing normally. He looked up at the people surrounding him, seeming curious about what was happening to him. I touched his skin. It was warm and dry. He was not perspiring and clammy like someone in shock. I felt for his pulse in his groin. It was strong and regular. I relaxed a bit. The nurses talked to the patient and measured his vital signs. An oxygen probe was threaded on to one of his fingers to measure the oxygen concentration in his blood. In a cyanotic patient this would be low.

Within a few minutes, these vital numbers would appear in the patient's computerized record. I sat down next to computer and watched the nurses do their work.

I pulled up his record. Yes, here were the vital signs. Our nurses are efficient. His temperature was 97 degrees Fahrenheit. So, he probably didn't have pneumonia. His blood pressure was 110/80 and his pulse was 80. He wasn't in shock. His respirations were 20 per minute. He wasn't breathing hard like somebody who was suffering from lack of oxygen.

My eyes moved down to the "pulse ox" reading, which told the oxygen saturation of his blood. "Per cent saturation-99 per cent." was the reading. This meant that 99 per cent of his blood oxygen receptors, almost all of them, carried oxygen. The patient was getting plenty of oxygen. He wasn't cyanotic now. I was surprised at this finding, but maybe he was blue at the nursing home.

I thought "The nurses at Sitter-Barfoot saw that he was blue, and they gave him oxygen which made him better and the oxygen was continued in the ambulance. Yes, that was probably it." In certain conditions, such as emphysema and asthma, a small amount of oxygen can have a dramatic effect.

I looked over at the patient. The X-ray technician had arrived to do a chest X-ray. In a cyanotic patient a chest X-ray is especially important to rule out pneumonia and other conditions that block delivery of oxygen from the lung to the blood. The young Hispanic woman slipped a metal film holder behind the patient's back. Then she positioned her machine in front of his chest. "Step back!" she commanded, not wanting to expose the nearby nurses to radiation. But they were already moving out of the way. She pushed a button and the X-ray was taken. She left the Emergency Department with her machine. Within minutes the X-ray would be developed and read.

I walked back to bed 6 to examine Mr. Towne. "Mr. Towne, I am Dr. Schmitt. How do you feel?" I asked. With his good blood oxygen level, I felt that it was safe, at least for a few minutes to remove the mask. The man seemed to be in deep thought for a minute, then he replied "OK." His thinking seemed to be slow, consistent with his diagnosis of Alzheimer's Disease.

"What brought you to the Emergency Room?" I asked.

"I don't know. An ambulance. They just brought me here."

"Did you get short of breath? "

"No"

"Did you get chest pain?"

 "No"

"Do you smoke?"

"No"

48

I noted that even with oxygen discontinued for a few minutes his pulse ox was 98 per cent saturated; After a few more questions I put the oxygen mask back on Mr. Towne and examined him.

He was a relatively fit looking white man. He had apparently been healthy except for his Alzheimer's disease for which he had been placed at Sitter-Barefoot. His lungs were clear, without wheezes which might be present in asthma or emphysema. And there were no rales, the crackling sounds that indicate the presence of fluid in the lungs, which may occur with pneumonia or heart failure. The remainder of the exam, with the exception of mental slowing, was normal.

The technician came back with Mr. Towne's chest X-ray. She thoughtfully put it in the view box.

A chest x ray is like a photograph negative. Fluid in the lungs blocks radiation, making the image lighter. Mr. Towne's lungs were a healthy black color. There was no fluid from pneumonia or heart failure. His lungs were totally clear, yet he had been cyanotic, blue.

I was becoming more and more puzzled. A massive pulmonary embolism lodging in a pulmonary artery could block oxygen delivery, yet not show up on a chest X-ray. A patient in a nursing home, such as Mr. Towne, was at high risk for a pulmonary embolism. This commonly would cause shock, chest pain, and strain to the right side of the heart. Heart strain would show up on the electrocardiogram. But Mr. Towne's EKG was normal, and he had never been in shock or had chest pain.

I was stymied by this patient who appeared healthy, and yet had become blue at Sitter-Barfoot. I wondered if he really needed extra oxygen at all.

"Let's take him off oxygen for 15 minutes and do a pulse ox." I asked the nurses. After 15 minutes the pulse ox was repeated. "98 per cent!" shouted the nurse. Mr. Towne was not cyanotic. His oxygen level was fine.

I racked my brain for a plausible explanation for what had happened. "Maybe he had a massive pulmonary embolism at the nursing home. He turned blue. Then the clot broke up and he became a healthy pink." I wondered. I had heard of this happening. But this didn't seem plausible. I decided to do another physical exam.

Mr. Towne was lying quietly in bed, happy that the uncomfortable oxygen mask had been removed. His lungs still sounded clear. His heart exam was still normal. I hadn't overlooked any faint murmurs. I knew that blood shunting from the right side to the left side of the heart, bypassing the lungs, can cause cyanosis. But this would often be revealed by a heart murmur, a swishing sound with each heartbeat. I pressed on his ankles. There was no edema, such as there might be in heart failure.

I was about to return to my desk when I noticed something strange about Mr. Towne's lips. At the edge of the thick pink part, called "the vermilion border", of his lips was a thin blue line. "Did you eat anything just before they brought you over here?" I asked

"Yes"

"What was it?

"A popsicle."

"And what color was that popsicle?"

"Blue"

The mystery was solved. Mr. Towne had eaten a blue popsicle.

Very soon after that the nurse who was caring for him noticed the blue color of his face. Seeing her patient turn blue, she assumed the worst and the alarm was sounded.

The crisis was resolved. Mr. Towne could return to Sitter-Barfoot. I wetted a paper towel and wiped the blue pigment from his lips. I didn't want there to be any further speculation that he was cyanotic. I wrote a diplomatic note to the staff of Sitter. Mr. Towne was placed in a wheelchair to await transportation.

Getting him back to Sitter was more involved than I thought it would be. It was Sunday afternoon. His health insurance would only accept certain ambulance services. The Emergency Department clerks worked the phones trying to find an appropriate carrier. But after an hour they were unsuccessful. The Richmond area was experiencing an unusual number of emergencies, tying up several of the carriers.

The old man sat in a wheelchair next to bed 6 waiting to get a ride to his home which was only a few hundred feet away. Another hour passed without locating transportation. My patience reached its limit. "Enough of this! Come, let's go. I am taking him back to Sitter."

"I don't know if that would be appropriate." said one nurse who was a stickler for the rules. "It's not protocol."

"It's OK. Let's go. Mr. Towne I'm taking you home." I told the old man who smiled faintly. "Call Sitter-Barfoot and tell them we are coming.

I reached down and buckled his seat belt. A very obese female LPN (licensed practical nurse} was quickly appointed to accompany me.

I pushed the wheelchair through the automatic doors and into the hallway of the main hospital. Within a few minutes we were passing through the Spinal Cord Injury Service. Then we exited the hospital into the parking lot. At this point I accelerated. I was almost running. I reveled in the physical activity. The poor nurse who was running beside us sweated and gasped for breath, her white dress blowing in the breeze.

Mr. Towne was laughing. Up ahead the entrance to Sitter-Barfoot, his home, loomed. He was getting the ride of his life, at least of his elderly life.

"Whoopee!" he shouted.

CHAPTER 7

A BEAGLE ON A BLUE BLANKET

One of the surest ways of getting admitted to a Veterans' Administration Hospital is to go to the Emergency Room and say you are going to commit suicide.

Threat of suicide, like chest pain, frightens emergency room physicians. You don't know how serious the problem really is, but if you ignore it, and the patient dies, you are in deep doodoo.

Many patients who claim they are suicidal, are not, really, suicidal. They do this, so they will be admitted to the hospital where they will receive a warm bed, three meals a day, and a color television to watch.

One afternoon a man presented to the Front Desk, stating "I am going to kill myself."

The woman sitting at the desk recognized the man as a "frequent flyer", someone who had presented multiple times with the same complaint. It was clear from the man's inpatient psychiatry history that he was not suicidal, that he just wanted to get a place to stay. The clerk, a 60 -year old grandmother, was fed up with the patient's shenanigans.

"All right. I am tired of this. Let's get it over with!" she shouted. She reached into her desk drawer and pulled out a pair of scissors which she handed the man. Do it right now. Try not to get any blood on the carpet!"

The startled patient stared at the clerk in disbelief. His mouth fell open. He looked down at the scissors, then back at the clerk. He was not ready for this new information which he seemed to have trouble processing. He glanced at the sharp pointed scissors, then dropped them on the desk and recoiled from them in terror. He eyed at the clerk who was glaring at him. Finally, he spoke. "You're mean!" Then he turned around and walked out into the parking lot.

In 2008 our Emergency Department got a new chief, Dr. Frank Gardner. Until 2008 the Director of the Emergency room was an internist. Dr. Gardner, a balding man of 45 who stayed fit by riding a bicycle, was the first Emergency Medicine Board Certified Chief. The arrival of a new Chief caused considerable anxiety among the Emergency Room staff. There might be a shakeup in the Emergency Room and people would lose their jobs.

A person who was especially worried about getting a new boss was Marie Felton, a physician assistant. She always wore a white dress and was frequently mistaken for a nurse. Her large size, and white apparel, made her resemble a giant marshmallow. She worked on the Nonacute side of the Emergency Room seeing relatively minor problems such as colds and insect bites, and medication refills. Marie had a good grasp of the myriad of problems that are seen in the Emergency Department, but there had always been a problem with her productivity. The target number of these relatively trivial patients was four per hour, but Marie averaged less than three per hour.

Within a few weeks Marie's fears were realized.

"She sees WAY too few patients." Gardner said as he pointed to a spread sheet with Marie's name on it. If nothing else, the new chief was a bean counter.

"I am her friend. I will talk to her." I replied I waited until Marie had finished seeing her patient, then took her into room 14 where we could have some privacy.

"Dr. Gardner doesn't think you see enough patients." I began.

She frowned, but didn't reply.

"You don't have to watch the IV running into the patient. You can move on to the next patient."

By this, I meant that in the Emergency Room, you must take care of several patients at once. After you have started intravenous fluids on the dehydrated patient in bed 9 you can move on to bed 10 and treat the spider bite. I was giving Marie advice to help her productivity. I left her to go back to her patients, hoping that she found my remarks useful.

That afternoon I worked in the Emergency Room with a medical student. A patient presented with pain in the scrotum. The vascular surgeons had used the femoral artery, the large artery in the groin, to insert a catheter and remove clots from a leg that was turning blue from poor circulation. In the process of doing this they traumatized the scrotum.

"You see the scrotum." I told the medical student as I handed him the chart. Nearby Marie and a nurse talked to patients.

The following morning my boss, Dr Vinnekova, asked me to come and talk to her. Dr. Vinnekova trained in Russia before she came to the US. She was a warm, motherly person, but she also was an astute clinician. One time I described working for her like "working for the heroine of a Russian novel." But today her usual disarming smile was gone. She had a pained look on her face. I wondered, what could be the matter.

"Marie Felton has accused you of sexual harassment."

I was stunned.

For an instant I felt myself mouthing the "F" word, but stopped short of uttering a profanity on Federal property.

Dr Vinnekova continued. "She says, you said 'Marie Loves Scrotums'. She says she told you to stop, but you kept doing it." Dr. Vinnekova paused for a moment, then she spoke softly. "Apologize to her."

I wondered if Marie's accusation might be true. I try to reduce the tension of work in the Emergency Room with light banter and humor. Perhaps I had crossed a line. I felt that my medical career might be coming to an end. One of the penalties for sexual harassment is dismissal.

I went back to the Emergency Room and quickly pulled three female nurses and a female clerk into a small room used for family counseling. "Is there anything that I do that offends you?" I asked. "Do I ever do anything that offends you…. sexually?"

"No Dr. Schmitt. You are fine." one of the nurses said. The other members of the group nodded in agreement. I thanked them and went to talk to Marie who, at the moment, didn't have a patient. She followed me into room 14.

"Marie, you never told me that I offended you." I began. She nodded her head, then moved her right hand as if she were dismissing that claim.

"Dr. Schmitt, you can retire any time you want. I can't do that. I need to keep my job."

Her claim of sexual harassment was made to block her imagined dismissal from the Emergency Room. She heard me tell the student to "see the scrotum case." From the word "scrotum" she concocted the phrase "Marie loves scrotums." and spun it into a sexual harassment case.

However, this wasn't enough to make a claim of sexual harassment. For a claim of verbal harassment to stick, the perpetrator must continue his abuse despite pleas for him to stop. Marie added the fictional statement that I refused to stop "despite multiple pleas for me to do so."

At the time of this writing the "Me Too" movement is in full blossom. Many famous men have been ruined by accusations of sexual harassment. I almost always believe the women, but this time I was the injured party.

I felt professionally injured, contaminated, scandalized by Marie's claim, even though I knew it wasn't true. That is the nature of lies. My reputation was already damaged.

"Marie I've been here a long time and I've never known a physician assistant to be fired."

"Dr. Schmitt, I can't see 16 patients a day like the people in Primary Care Clinic."

I was stunned. This slander on my character wasn't even to save her job. She just didn't want to be required to work harder.

I went back to Dr. Vinnekova and told her what had transpired with Marie.

"Well maybe she was having a bad day." the Russian woman said.

Marie never apologized to me.

Norma, my wife, was incensed at Marie's accusation. She quoted the Bible's injunction against "bearing false witness." "She didn't apologize because that would require her to take responsibility for doing something evil." Norma said angrily.

I had a different take on what happened. In the Federal Service it is common practice to throw a monkey wrench into personnel actions by claiming some form of discrimination, such as racial or sexual. Marie's complaint was not meant for me to take personally. She was just doing "business as usual."

I never again brought up her productivity in the Emergency Room.

The second crisis resulting from Dr. Gardner's appointment as Chief of Emergency Services occurred on a Saturday morning.

At 7 AM Norma awakened me. "Our answering machine is going off downstairs." she said.

I ran downstairs. There were two messages. One was from Frank Gardner. "Jim, please call me." it said, but there was no phone number given. The second message tersely stated. "Call the Emergency Room." I called the Emergency Room, and learned that Dr. McGee, who was supposed to work, was sick, and I was his substitute. I had to be there by 8 o'clock to relieve the night doctor.

Stark naked I went to the laundry room to get a pair of slacks out of the dryer. We were dog sitting for my son's beagle, Scout, who followed me everywhere I went.

Next to our laundry room is an outside door. Just as I reached inside the dryer there was a loud knocking on the door.

"Norma went out to get the paper and she locked herself out." I thought. I pulled a small blue blanket from the drier and modestly wrapped it about my loins, then opened the door.

Standing in front of the door with a look of surprise and horror on his face was Dr. Gardner wearing his Spandex uniform. Because I had not answered his call, he had ridden his bike over to my house to tell me I had to work in the Emergency Room. "I got the message Frank!" I said, humiliated that I was standing before my boss, practically naked. He stood staring at me with his mouth agape, not uttering a single word.

At that point Scout ran out the door and up the hill toward the street where he might be hit by a car. "Scout!" I shouted. Just as Scout did a 180 degree turn to the left and came running down the hill back to me, Gardner turned to his left and walked back up the hill. Scout and the Emergency Room Director almost collided.

I made it to the Emergency Room with five minutes to spare.

The first person that I ran into was Emmy, a tall auburn -haired nurse known for her droll sense of humor. I breathlessly told her what had happened, and she philosophically assessed the events of the morning. He blue eyes twinkled, and she smiled.

"Dr. Schmitt, from now on your family crest should be a blue blanket with a beagle on it!"

CHAPTER 8

THE KILLING FIELDS

It was the King's birthday.

I was working at Sihanouk Center of Hope Hospital in Phnom Penh, Cambodia, as a medical volunteer.

But today was the King's Birthday, a national holiday. I had the day off and I was now a tourist.

When I donated to charities, I was never quite sure what how the money was spent. When I came to a poor country and rolled up my sleeves and cared for patients, I knew that I was helping.

I was standing in front of a tower. The tower was perhaps thirty feet high and enclosed with glass. It had a kind of symmetry as it reached toward the sky. And there was a stark simplicity, like many pieces of art that I had seen in museums. What was unusual was the material out of which it was made.

The grey tower was made entirely of human skulls.

In 1975 Cambodia was taken over by the Khmer Rouge, a fanatical Maoist group. The leader, Pol Pot, a Hitler-like figure, wanted to convert Cambodia to a Communist agrarian society. All that were required were two million people to establish this society. Everyone else was expendable. The Khmer Rouge especially resented educated people, foreigners, and religious people, such as Buddhist monks. A systematic process of extermination was undertaken. The story of the Cambodian extermination has been told in the movie "The Killing Fields".

Just having soft hands revealed that the owner had not done hard labor. The individual was summarily executed, sometimes by putting a plastic bag over his head and allowing him to suffocate. It was estimated that, by the time the Vietnamese routed the Khmer Rouge in 1978, two million Cambodians were exterminated. Especially hard hit were doctors. It was estimated that the Khmer Rouge executed all but four of the doctors in Cambodia.

I met one of the physician survivors.

"I was working in the fields planting rice." the middle- aged woman told me in halting English. "I knew people were sick. I wanted to help them. But if I helped, the Khmer Rouge would know that I was a physician and kill me. And so, I did nothing." she sobbed. The she added. "If I tried to help people, they would have killed me anyway, and I would have been of no use. But I am alive today, and can help people today."

The monument marks the site of Choeung Ek, an extermination camp where the remains of 8985 people were found. They were usually bludgeoned to death to save bullets. Children, who were swung through the air by their feet, had their heads bashed in on a nearby tree.

In 2007, the time of this visit, Cambodian medicine was still suffering from the genocide of the Khmer Rouge. There was a shortage of physicians. All specialists, such as cardiologists, pulmonologists and gastroenterologists had been trained in other countries. The hard core of medical educators was killed by the Khmer Rouge.

Cambodia is the poorest country in Southeast Asia. A major benefactor has been Japan. But recent disasters, such as the tsunami, have damaged the Japanese economy. This has resulted in a reduction in aid to Cambodia. Some hospital wards have been closed.

My major job at Sihanouk Center of Hope Hospital was teaching.

An important means of transportation in Cambodia is the motor bike. Whole families are seen on a motor bike. The father drives. A child sits in front of him. Behind the father is the mother holding a smaller child. And behind the mother, holding on for dear life, is still another child.   Often, no one is wearing a crash helmet.

The major cause of death in young adults in Cambodia is not malaria or HIV or suicide. It is motor vehicle accidents. When I was in Phnom Penh the monks had a special service for the victims of motor vehicle accidents. Therefore, my lecture on spinal cord injury was extremely popular.

I also made rounds on the internal medicine wards and in the Emergency Room. The chief of medicine was Dr. Tom Meng, a quiet, thoughtful, man, aged about 40.

As a child Dr. Meng and his family escaped the Khmer Rouge hiding in the container of a milk truck. His wife's parents were killed by the Khmer Rouge. His wife, who happened to be out in the country visiting her grandparents, survived.

Rounds on inpatient wards were made every day.

A common diagnosis was rheumatic heart disease. A streptococcal infection, such as a strep throat, results in the body making antibodies to fight the infection. Certain species of streptococcus resemble the tissues of heart valves. The antibodies attack both the bacteria and heart valves, gradually destroying the valve after several years. If antibiotics, such as penicillin, are given to fight the infection, the chance of valve destruction decreases. In the United States antibiotics are so commonly used that the incidence of rheumatic heart disease has decreased dramatically.

62

But in Southeast Asia, strep infections are not so aggressively treated, or not treated at all.

An 18year old boy was in one of the beds. He was gasping for breath. Sitting up helped him breathe. His feet were swollen with edema fluid. On a viewing box nearby was his chest X-ray. The heart was dramatically enlarged, and the lungs were congested with fluid.

The mitral valve, the valve between the upper and lower chambers of the left side of the heart was critically narrowed from rheumatic heart disease. The dilated atrium. the upper chamber. had begun fibrillating, causing blood to back up in the lungs. The result was edema in the lungs.

Back pressure in the lungs, in turn, increases pressure in the veins of the legs. This was why the unfortunate young man had swollen legs.

The treatment of choice for this condition is a procedure called "mitral commisurotomy". A catheter is threaded into a groin artery and up to the left ventricle. Then it is popped through the narrow mitral valve, and a balloon inflated. The balloon is then dragged back through the narrow valve, opening it up.

Unfortunately, the hospital had no catheterization lab. The only treatment for the young man was medications, such as diuretics, to remove fluid, and digoxin, to slow the heart

"In the US we would do a commisurotomy." I mentioned on rounds.

"Yes. I know that would be done in the US." Dr. Meng said with a pained look on his face. He knew his medicine well, but he knew that in Cambodia only certain things were possible. We both knew, that if nothing more was done, this young man would be dead in a couple of years.

I decided to avoid using the phrase "In America we would do it this way." The Cambodian doctors knew what the standard of medicine was. They also were aware of the painful truth that in Cambodia, medical care doesn't come up to the standards of the Western World.

Cambodia is a Buddhist country.

At one time in India there were two main forms of thought.

Some people practiced self-indulgent preoccupation with pleasure.

On the other extreme was Jainism which was founded by Mahavira in the Sixth Century B.C. Jains believed that way to escape the endless cycle of birth, death, and reincarnation, was extreme physical denial, leading to death and oblivion. Jains believed that it was wrong to destroy any life, even insects and worms. A Jain might walk sweeping with a broom to avoid stepping on an insect or worm, and wearing a mask to avoid inhaling small flying creatures. Jains had little or no clothing, pulled their hair out by hand, leaving a bloody scalp, and, ideally, died of starvation.

Jains were forbidden to farm, because a plow might kill some creature buried in the earth. They were also proscribed any work which involved contact with animal products, such as leather working.

Jains were allowed to work with money. Therefore, some of them became wealthy bankers. I am told that their path of denial, leading to death, might entail giving up their Mercedes and gradually, over the years downsizing to a used Civic.

Also born in the Sixth Century B.C. was Siddhartha, the founder of Buddhism. Buddha taught a "Middle Way" between the extremes of self-indulgence and Jainism. Buddhist monks live simple, virtuous lives. They wear orange-colored robes, shave their heads (instead of pulling their hair out), and may beg for food and shelter and money. (When I took a photo of two monks, they proffered a cup to ask for a dollar donation}.

Buddhist monks are not obliged to starve to death.

Buddhists believe in reincarnation. But there are also traditional beliefs that impact on the practice of medicine.

Because of a belief in ghosts, families were sometimes afraid come into the hospital to remove the body of a deceased relative. To counter this problem, terminal patients were sometimes discharged from the hospital just before they died. When they died at home, the terrified family immediately removed the ghost-ridden body from their home and had it cremated.

Cambodians tend to be thin and eat a low-fat diet. Yet they have a relatively high incidence of coronary artery disease and diabetes mellitus.

One explanation for this has been the theory known as "The Programming Hypothesis."

This idea is that, when children are developing in utero, factors such as malnutrition of the mother "programs" the development of the fetus. The coronary arteries of the fetus of a starving woman may be underdeveloped and narrow. This would predispose the adult to heart attacks. During the reign of the Khmer Rouge, many pregnant women starved.

I spent time in the Emergency Room supervising the resident doctors. An 18 year- old man came in with weight loss. His heart beat was rapid and irregular. His eyes were bulging in a stare and there was a huge mass in his neck. One of the doctors showed me his EKG. The young man was in rapid atrial fibrillation. He had an overactive thyroid gland which was driving his heart. Enlarged eye muscles were pushing his eyeballs forward in a stare. This condition is known as Grave's Disease.

The mass in his neck was an enlarged thyroid gland. The normal thyroid gland weighs 15 grams. This thyroid gland weighed at least 100 grams. A substance called LATS (long acting thyroid stimulator), was stimulating his thyroid gland to grow and produce thyroid hormone. The thyroid hormone was stimulating his heart. Without treatment he would die.

The treatment was simple. A beta blocker was given to slow the heart, and the drug propylthiouracil was given to turn off production of thyroid hormone. In the US you might never see a thyroid gland this big. It would be treated earlier.

When you go to the Developing World you may become frustrated because of the lack of resources to treat common diseases. However, you get to see diseases at their extremes. And sometimes a very simple treatment makes the difference between life and death. This is satisfying.

A thirty-year old woman came to the Emergency Room complaining of severe abdominal pain. The pain had started 4 months ago. She visited the monks who tried prayers, massage therapy and herbal medicine. But the pain worsened. She was a Buddhist who believed that suffering improved her karma. She did not fear death, and knew that if she died, she would be reincarnated. But the pain worsened. She finally could bear it no longer and came to the Emergency Room.

The woman was lying on a bed grimacing in agony and her abdomen was swollen. Morphine was given to relieve her pain. A needle was inserted into her abdomen to remove fluid to learn the cause of the swelling. The fluid in her abdomen looked like blood. Her abdomen contained an inoperable malignancy.

The cause of the malignancy could be found in the market where she bought fish for her family's table. In some fish, under the scales, resides a kind of worm. In the intestine of the human host the worm changes into a liver fluke. The fluke migrates from the duodenum up the bile duct to the liver. The fluke grows in the bile duct, lays eggs, and causes scarring and cancer. In western Cambodia and eastern Thailand is the highest incidence in the World of cholangiocarcinoma, a cancer of the bile ducts.

The eggs of the liver fluke pass out in the human's feces. If they land in water a snail eats the eggs. From the eggs comes the worm. The worms leave the snail and swim to the fish where they take up residence under the scales. When the poorly cooked fish is eaten, the life cycle is completed.

To the east of Phnom Penh is Lake Tonle' Sap, the largest lake in Southeast Asia. On this lake, groups of boats come together in floating villages. Livestock, such as chickens and pigs are kept on some of the boats. In certain areas fish, such as the rainbow fish, are kept in underwater pens to be harvested and taken to market.

There are no toilets on these fishing boats. Human waste goes back into the water carrying the lethal eggs.

Many dishes in Cambodia contain fish. Amok Fish, which has fish, curry and other ingredients, and is wrapped in banana leaves, is the National Dish. After seeing the poor woman in the Emergency Room, I always made certain that my fish was well-cooked.

In the middle of Phnom Penh is the Tuol Sleng museum. It was once a high school, but in 1975 it was converted by the Khmer Rouge into a center for detention and torture. It was known and Security Prison 21 (S-21).

Like the Nazis, the Khmer Rouge meticulously recorded their victims. The walls of the museum are covered with many hundreds of pictures of the murder victims, many of them children.

Standing in front of the museum I found three men. One of the men was missing a leg, one an arm, and one had a terribly mutilated face. These were victims of land mines that were placed during the wars in the 1970s. There are still many unexploded mines in Cambodia, and every so often, some unfortunate person steps on one.

In doctor's offices and in store windows and in other places are posters of Princess Diana. One of her charities was land mine victims. The money from the sale of the posters goes toward these victims. I gave each of the men a dollar for permission to take their picture.

A short flight across Lake Tonle' Sap is the city of Siam Riep, which means "Death to Siam." This refers to the wars with Siam which occurred in this area.

I was greeted at the airport by a young man driving a white Buick. For 60 dollars he agreed to be my guide for the weekend.

The gem of Cambodia is Angkor Wat, the largest religious building in the world.

My driver parked at the beginning of a causeway that ran across moat that led to the structure. I was immediately besieged by children. Some of them carried books, such as guides to Cambodia and Phnom Penh. Others just proffered their hands for money. "Buy from me. Buy from me. You buy from me." they begged. I reflexively put my hands on my wallet and my passport to protect them.

"I am going into the temple." I said. "Maybe I will buy something when I come out." I walked down the causeway which was decorated with stone images of huge mythical snakes, called "Nagas".

I am usually not enthralled by buildings and works of art. I take little time with them. Several years earlier, while visiting Paris my wife and I arrived at the Louvre a half hour before quitting time. We ran through the museum, just taking a second or two to glance at masterpieces. I, at least, was satisfied with the experience.

But Angkor Wat overwhelmed me. This was in part because of the size of the monument.

In many corners of the huge building monks sat burning incense. Here and there were statues of Buddha, many of which had been beheaded. This was the doing of the Khmer Rouge, who detested any form of religion.

I was approached by a young man. "I am going to college. Would you contribute to my studies?" he asked with a smile.

"I would like to help you, but I am almost out of money." I said.

A half hour later, the same young man approached me. "The Khmer Rouge killed my whole family. Please help me." he pleaded, changing his story.

When I walked out of Angkor Wat and down the long causeway the children were waiting.

"You said you would buy from me, you promised." said a boy who was about 10.

Other children pressed in on me. "You promised, you promised!" they shouted.

"I did not promise." I said.

To protect myself from the children I got in the car and closed the window. Some of the children were selling illustrated guides to Angkor. I took a twenty- dollar bill from my wallet and opened the window. "How much for the books?" I asked.

Without hesitation, one of the boys reached inside the window and grabbed at the bill. It tore in two. I closed the window.

"Let's get out of here!" I told my driver. He was only too happy to oblige. We drove away as fast as we could.

A few minutes later I spied a motor scooter coming up on our left. On the back of the scooter was the boy who had grabbed for the money. He realized that without the other half of the bill, his half was worthless. So, he was in hot pursuit of me. And I knew that my half was just as worthless. The boy motioned to me from his seat.

"Pull over." I told the driver.

"What will you give me for my half of the bill?" I asked the boy

He held up an "Illustrated Guide to Angkor". It had a lot of pictures and probably was worth twenty dollars. The deal was made. I was careful that I had the book in my hand before I gave him the other half of the twenty.

I was tempted to lecture the boy on the wages of sin, that what he was doing was wrong. Then I thought back to the sign in the lobby of my hotel.

"No one younger than 18 will be allowed in the rooms." it said. It referred to child sex,

Cambodia is the child sex capital of the world. Pedophiles come to Cambodia from all over the world. Desperate families will sell their children's bodies to survive. They almost have no choice. Unwashed and starving children wander the streets of Phnom Penh begging. I had firsthand knowledge of people dying because of lack of money. The situation here was grim.

The boy was just doing what he needed to do to survive. I dispensed with the lecture.

As we drove, we passed a hospital. I noticed a sign. The sign read "Kantha Bopha" hospital. We need blood."

Kantha Bopha hospitals were founded by Beatacello Richter, a Swiss physician. He was a world renown cello player who gave performances to benefit his hospitals. The hospitals were especially for children. One year, Dr. Richter was named "Outstanding Swiss Citizen."

This part of Cambodia was in the middle of a dengue fever epidemic. Dengue fever is transmitted by the bite of a mosquito. The first case of dengue fever is like the flu, with fevers and muscle aches. But with repeated exposure to the virus, especially in a child, a more ominous condition occurs, hemorrhagic dengue fever.

The body's immune response triggers a cascade of inflammation which contributes to the death of the virus. However, each year the virus changes slightly, so although inflammation occurs, the antibody is not perfectly tailored to the virus, and the virus survives. Inflammation continues unchecked, resulting in leaky capillaries and hemorrhage. This can cause death. This was the reason the hospital was calling for blood donors.

Dr. Richter had an admonition for tourists who came to Cambodia. "If you are old give money. If you are young give blood."

The next day was Sunday. My driver drove me to more ruins.
He would let me off at the beginning of the ruin, and I walked
through it. Signs warned that automobiles could come no closer
to a ruin than 100 feet. When I reached the opposite end of the
ruin, I walked the required 100 feet to the car.

After several hours we arrived at the last ruin. I had already paid
the young man and given him a tip. After this he would drive me
to the airport. When I got to the edge of the ruin my driver was
waiting with his car.

"How did you get so close?" I asked.   "The rules say you can't
get closer than 100 feet?"

"I told them my client had broken his leg." he said with a smile.

That young man will go far.

CHAPTER 9

CHEDDY RAT AND THE RACCOON

The nurse had been knocking on the restroom door for 10 minutes.

"Are you OK in there, sir? Are you alright?" There was no response. Finally, he decided to use has master key. Sitting on the toilet was a dazed young man. On the floor was a syringe.

"Are you OK, sir?" the nurse asked. The man grunted and slid off the toilet on to the floor.

"Call a Code Blue!" shouted the male nurse.

"Code Blue Yellow Clinic Waiting Room!" blared from the overhead paging system a few seconds later.

Within 3 minutes the Waiting Room was filled with doctors and nurses pushing a gurney and a crash cart, the cart that carries a defibrillator and drugs used for treatment of a cardiac arrest. A doctor knelt near the man on the floor and touched his neck. "He's got a carotid pulse. He's breathing!" shouted the physician. With that news, the team relaxed.

"OK, let's take him to the Emergency Room" someone said.

Four people lifted the young man on to the gurney and he was wheeled over to the Emergency Room and transferred to Bed 6. An intravenous line was started, and a physician examined the patient. "His pupils are pinpoint. His respirations are slow." The tiny pupils were a clue that the patient had overdosed on a narcotic, such as heroin. "Let's give him one amp of Narcan IV." Narcan is a blocker of the effects of narcotics and can be life-saving in cases of a narcotic overdose. The nurse squirted the medication into the man's IV line. Instantly the man opened his eyes and glanced around the room.

"Tom, you are in the Emergency Room." his nurse said. The patient glanced at his arm. Then he slid down to the edge of the bed, disconnected his IV from the bottle and ran out the door with his intravenous line still in his arm.

Mr. Jensen was my clinic patient. Why was he injecting heroin into his arm in the bathroom in the clinic, at this particular time? I reviewed his record. He had no appointments at the hospital on that day.

There was one shocking explanation. This was where he got his heroin.

A month later, when Tom Jensen came to my clinic, I asked him about what had happened. "I have to wonder. Did you get your heroin here? Where did you get it?" When he wasn't strung out on drugs, he was an amiable young man who was anxious to please.

"I got the heroin on Hull Street." Hull street was just a few blocks from the hospital. "When a white man walks down Hull Street, they know he wants drugs."

Zip codes where there are Veterans Administration hospitals are the zip codes where there are the highest rates of death from prescription drug use. These deaths occur not only in veterans, but also in nonveterans living in these areas.

Veterans Administration hospitals are often built in poor area where land is relatively cheap. Near the Richmond VA Hospital are houses where crack is smoked, and heroin is injected. One night a man overdosed in one of these crack houses. His fellow users were considerate enough to bundle the man into a car and drop him off at the nearby emergency room.

Narcotics are commonly traded for cocaine. A clue that this is occurring is the finding that the patient fails to show narcotics, such as oxycodone, in his urine, but does have cocaine.

I have heard that some employees go out to their cars at night and shoot up heroin or snort cocaine. When they return from the parking lot, they are noticeably happier.

One afternoon the police caught a kitchen worker sitting in her car in the parking lot injecting heroin. The policeman noticed the woman shoving something, possibly evidence, into her vagina. The middle- aged women was brought to the Emergency Room in handcuffs.

The woman was still in the middle of a drug induced high when she was placed in Bed 8. Her right hand was handcuffed to the metal side rail of the bed. A hospital security policeman stood at the woman's head. The woman cooperated by opening her legs. The female nurse standing to my right, handed me a plastic speculum which I inserted into the vagina. I noticed a piece of paper near the cervix. Using a forceps, I retrieved the piece of paper and put it in the evidence bag.

I was slated to testify at the woman's trial, but at the last minute she copped a plea and I was excused.

The desert of crack houses surrounding the VA hospital is nourished by a river of prescription narcotics that flows from the hospital.

I have been told that some patients pick up their pain meds from the pharmacy, then go out to the Parking Lot and trade them for heroin and cocaine. One dealer is reputed to be a person known as "The Woman in the Red Wheelchair." I have looked for this shadowy person, but up to this point, have never seen her.

One day I received an anonymous note. "Mr. Thad Cummings is selling his Percocet at the bus stop and in the smoke boxes." (Percocet is a combination of oxycodone and acetaminophen). Smoke boxes are the small rooms positioned outside of the hospital to permit smokers to smoke while being protected from the elements. Mr. Cummings was a felon with several drug offenses.

With a pharmacist and a plain- clothes policewoman I devised a "sting" operation to catch Mr. Cummings in the act. When he came to the Pharmacy to pick up his Percocet, the pharmacist called me. I called the policewoman and she followed the patient, hoping to catch him in the act, but this time Cummings just walked off the hospital grounds with his Percocet.

Narcotics relieve pain by binding to a receptor, called the "mu" receptor, which is located on nerves. Use of narcotics for acute pain, such as might occur with a broken leg, produces dramatic pain relief. But with chronic use of narcotics, such as might be seen in a patient with chronic low back pain, the analgesic effects dissipate. The "mu" receptors decrease in number and narcotics become less effective. Chronic use of narcotics can produce dependence and addiction. When the patient stops them. he can go through withdrawal.

I received first -hand knowledge of the effects of narcotics from my wife, Norma. She is a "bird nut", who has set up feeders and houses all around our home. Her most valued "tenant" is the bluebird, which has the triple threat of an attractive appearance, pretty song, and that it consumes annoying bugs. Norma keeps her bird seed in a teak box on our deck.

One morning, when she opened the box, she was startled to see an unwelcome visitor, a full- grown raccoon which had eaten a hole in the back of the box and was feasting on seeds. Norma yelled and fell backward, striking her left shoulder on the edge of our hot tub. She gripped her shoulder and screamed in pain.

I took her to a nearby emergency room where an IV was inserted. Hydromorphone, a narcotic was injected. As the drug was running in, Norma's body relaxed, and she smiled. "Like mana from heaven." she said, delighted that the pain was gone. An X-ray of her shoulder showed what is known as an impacted fracture. The upper part of the arm was jammed into the shoulder, thus holding the bone together. Therefore, the bone didn't need to be set. Norma was discharged with a sling, and hydrocodone, another narcotic, for pain.

As the weeks passed the hydrocodone became less and less effective for pain relief. After a month Norma remarked "Advil gel caps are twice as effective as the narcotic."

The receptors had decreased with chronic use and the narcotic was no longer effective.

My own wife was an "experiment" which showed me how narcotics work. They are good for acute pain, but not for chronic pain. In the past few years this concept has been echoed by prominent scientists. It is increasingly becoming a factor in National policy toward narcotics.

This receptor phenomenon sometimes results in death.

When an addict goes into Rehab, he stops narcotics, and his mu receptors increase. If when he leaves Rehab, he injects his usual dose of heroin, he is more sensitive to it and may die of an overdose. This explains stories of famous personalities dying of overdoses soon after they leave Rehab.

Short acting narcotics such as oxycodone, and hydrocodone produce an acute high. This is the reason they are sought so aggressively for drug abusers and traffickers. One Percocet is worth up to 80 dollars on the street. A patient receiving 180 Percocet per month can reap an income of over `$14,000 per month. There is therefore a tremendous incentive to fool the urinary drug screen.

When I was supervising a resident physician, we received a call from the lab. "We think Mr. Hall's urine specimen is tap water with a few drops on lemon juice in it." the savvy lab technician said.

We asked Mr. Hall, a chunky man of about 50 wearing ball cap, to submit another specimen, this time with the young male resident watching. The second urine specimen was positive for cocaine. "We have to stop your Percocet." I told the patient.

In spite of this, Mr. Hall treated me with respect. "Thank you." he said as he shook my hand. Then he turned to the resident and snarled. "No thanks to you!"

On another day the lab reported that the urine of Mr. Seigel, a truck driver, contained cocaine. I called my patient. "Mr. Seigel, your urine has cocaine in it. Cocaine is an illegal drug. The VA rules are that use of illegal substances disqualifies you from getting narcotics. I'm sorry."

I listened to the heavy breathing on the line. Finally, Mr. Seigel spoke.

"Was there any marijuana in my urine?"

"No there wasn't."

"Well I was using marijuana too. That can't have been a very good test!"

One night while I was working in the Emergency Room I looked up from the computer and was surprised to see Mrs. Wright, one of our nurses, crying. This was especially unusual because Mrs.

W. seemed to be a "hard as nails" person, who exhibited little sentimentality. She was even reported to pack a firearm, when she was not on Federal property. In her right hand she held an object. It was a pill bottle. The label read oxycodone-acetaminophen. The bottle had contained Percocet. A closer look showed that the bottle was covered with the chew marks of a carnivore.

"This woman said her dog chewed on the bottle and ate the Percocet." the nurse sobbed.

"What happened to the dog?" I asked.

"It died."

Mrs. Wright had one weakness. She loved dogs. The dog had died of a narcotic overdose. I too was stunned by the death of a beloved pet. A tear ran down my cheek. "I will refill her Percocet." I said without a second thought.

But after a few minutes I regained my composure. The patient had a history of cocaine abuse. Percocet is commonly traded for cocaine. In my personal experience eighty per cent of the time, when a patient reports that his dog has eaten his medication, the medication is a narcotic. And the culprit is not always a dog. A woman once reported to me that a bird had flown off with her bottle of pain meds in its mouth after she placed it on her kitchen window sill.

"Is all that you have to do to get $8000 worth of narcotics is to put some gravy on the bottle and let the dog chew on the bottle for a while, then take it to the Emergency Room and say the dog died?" I wondered. When a patient signs a narcotic contract, it is stipulated that a lost narcotic will not be replaced for any reason.

When I thought of the bottle, I remembered that the plastic was not broken and there was a safety cap. I could not see how the dog had gotten the pills. I cancelled my prescription for Percocet, instead giving the disappointed patient a prescription for Motrin.

But the most interesting nonhuman narcotic thief was not a dog, or a bird, but a rat.

Mr. Bradley was a Viet Nam war veteran who was taking Percocet for back and knee pain.

The saga of Mr. Bradley and Cheddy Rat was recorded in an Emergency Room note at 2 AM one morning.

"Cheddy Rat is a special rat." the corpulent and bearded patient told the drowsy physician. "Most rats are only worth 10 dollars, but Cheddy Rat is worth $6000. That is because Cheddy Rat is smart, even brilliant. He will fetch things that you throw. He will ride on a rolling ball. He will play basketball. He will put a ball right through a hoop. Cheddy Rat was even on TV one time." The emergency room physician nodded with understanding, then quickly jerked his head up, as he felt himself falling asleep.

"Well, one night I was sitting in my living room in my easy chair. My Percocet and my heart medication were in a plastic bag. Cheddy Rat was sitting in my lap. I fell asleep. When I woke up, Cheddy Rat and my medications were gone. I looked everywhere, and I couldn't find him. Then I heard some squeaky sounds in the wall. It was Cheddy Rat, and he was in trouble.

My son and I broke through the drywall. We found Cheddy Rat and the empty bottles. Cheddy was barely breathing. My son and I performed CPR with our fingers. It is kind of hard with a small animal like a rat. Then we took him to the vet. The vet did some more CPR and injected something into Cheddy. I told the vet that Cheddy cost $6000.

But the vet couldn't save him, and Cheddy died. Cheddy was only a rat, but in his heart, I believe he was a Christian. My friend built a small wooden coffin, and he painted the insignia for my army unit, the 32nd Airborne, and a cross, on the lid. I paid him $10. We buried Cheddy in a Christian ceremony. He is buried in my back yard."

Mr. Bradley's amazing story had driven the urge to sleep from the physician's brain.

"I will give you a few Percocet to tide you over. But tomorrow you will have to see Dr. Schmitt if you want any more." Then the physician, looking at the wall clock which showed 3AM, and the Emergency Room which was empty of patients, realized that he was exhausted and -went into the Call Room and lay down.

The next morning Mr. Bradley repeated the story of Cheddy Rat to me. He was not a bright man and spoke with sincerity. As I studied his puffy pink face, which was surrounded in a halo of white hair, I saw nothing but innocence. I didn't think he was smart enough to invent such an elaborate story. It probably was true. But even if it wasn't true it was the most creative story of lost narcotics that I had heard in my career. That deserved something.

I rewrote Mr. Bradley's Percocet prescription.

CHAPTER 10

WHY CAN'T PETTY OFFICER SANDERS COOK?

A father who could breast feed his children would be a useful parent indeed. There are, actually, reports of men producing milk and nursing babies.

Prolactin is a hormone made by the pituitary gland that stimulates milk production. Some men with prolactin secreting tumors produce milk. Other situations, such as constant stimulation of the male breast by sucking, can induce prolactin secretion and milk production. But, in the vast majority of men, the nipple is just a useless decoration

Enlargement of the male breast is called gynecomastia, which means "female breast." Since hormones such estrogen cause the breast to enlarge, men with gynecomastia often seek the care of an endocrinologist.

On one of my Naval Reserve weekends I saw two men with enlarged breasts.

Petty Officer Gomez was a fit looking young Hispanic man. As I stared into his brown eyes, I wondered why he needed an endocrinologist

"My breasts are large." I glanced at his chest. His newly pressed khaki blouse was covering a muscular chest. It seemed to be no different than the chests of many other buff young men. The Navy encouraged physical fitness and many sailors worked out. He sat straight in his chair, almost at a brace, as if he were undergoing a military inspection.

"Your breasts are large?"

"Yes." He chose his words carefully.

"How much alcohol do you drink?"

The liver destroys estrogen. Liver damage, such as occurs with heavy alcohol intake, may result in high estrogen levels which make the breasts larger.

"I don't drink."

"Do you take any medication?" Some medications, such as digoxin, a heart medication, can cause the breasts to enlarge.

"No." he replied with a shake of his head.

"Do your breasts make milk.?"

"No."

"Even when they are stimulated?"

"No."

 Petty Officer Gomez blushed at this question. When he opened his mouth to speak, I noticed a flash of silver which I guessed to be a filling. His dark handsomeness and good health seemed to be marred by just this one defect.

"How long have you noticed that your breasts are getting large?"

"About 6 months."

"And what brought you here now. What concerns you about your breasts." He paused for a second, then spoke."

 "I am afraid that people will look strangely at me. That they will notice my breasts when my shirt is off. Like at the pool or in the gym. It's embarrassing."

83

"OK. Please go into the examination room and take off your shirt." Petty Officer Gomez disappeared inside the adjoining room. I answered a phone call, then followed him in. He had already removed his blouse.

His muscular abdomen attested to the countless abdominal crunches that he did every day. His large biceps muscles had resulted from doing 100 pull ups on weekdays at the base gym.

My eyes moved to his chest area. There was no hair on his chest. It had been shaved. His pectoral (chest) muscles were also large, as befitted a man who lifted weights.

But what startled me was not any overgrowth of breast tissue, or milky discharge, but something that I had never seen while performing a physical exam.

Passing through each nipple, right where it attaches to the breast, like earrings in a woman with pierced ear lobes, were gold rings.

"And he was worried about people noticing his breasts!!" I thought with amazement.

After a minute I regained my composure. I rubbed the breasts to try to produce milk. The nipple rings made this process difficult. There was no milk.

I decided to do a more complete exam. "Please open your mouth."

PO Gomez opened his mouth. I received my second shock of the day.

Piercing his tongue was another ring. This one was huge, much larger than those in his nipples. I felt like I was about to have a heart attack. I winced at the thought of the pain entailed in inserting this ring. Why would someone do this to himself?

As with the nipple rings, I didn't comment on his tongue ring. Somehow, I thought that would be intrusive and rude. There was something going on here that I didn't recognize, some aspect of human behavior that I should have known about. I left the subject of body rings alone.

Later I learned that rings in various parts of the body were the new fad. They were partly decorative, partly sexual. Rings in the tongue, I was told, improved oral sex.

The last part of the physical would be my examination of the genitalia. But after the rings in the breasts and mouth, I was afraid to go there. What would I find? I might have a seizure. I might drop dead. I deferred the genital exam.

On this day I had lost my innocence, at least as far as body piercings went.

"Your breasts are fine." I told Petty Officer Gomez as he put his blouse back on.

When I returned from lunch a tall, lean young man was in the Waiting Room. I noticed that his arms seemed to be especially long. He was wearing the black working uniform of an enlisted man. This was Petty Officer Herman Sanders.

Petty Officer Sanders was perplexed and frightened. For much of his life he wanted to be a chef.

"I love creating new flavors." he said. "It's like being a chemist."

He attended the Navy's finest cooking school and did well on the written testing. "I got honors in baking cakes." he said proudly. He could perform routine tasks, like frying an egg.

But when it came to more complicated dishes, especially dishes that required sauces, such as spaghetti, he failed miserably. His cooking just tasted bad. There were so many complaints about his cooking that he was placed on administrative leave until the problem could be fixed. There is a tradition in the Navy that when someone is not performing satisfactorily, he gets a physical exam.

"Have you had any trouble with the law? Have you ever used drugs or alcohol?"

"I have a beer, once in a while. I have never been in trouble."

"Have you had any medical problems? High blood pressure? Heart problems? Stomach problems?"

"No."

"Are your parents alive?"

"Yes."

"Do they have any medical problems?"

"No. They are healthy." Grateful that his parents were healthy, he smiled.

I then began my physical exam.

I noticed that PO Sanders had almost no hair in his armpits. He also had sparse pubic hair.

"How often to you shave?" I inquired as I looked at his smooth face.

"I don't shave."

"You don't shave your armpits either"?

"No."

His breasts were enlarged. They contained firm breast tissue, not just fat. He had true gynecomastia.

I reached down to examine his testicles. Normal testicles for a man are at least 3.5 cm in diameter. His were less than 1 cm and they were soft. His penis was small and infantile appearing, like you would find on a little boy. My next question was awkward.

"Uh, Petty Officer Sanders. Do you…date? Uh, have you ever had sex?"

"No." He answered immediately and frankly.

The medical mystery of PO Sanders was being solved. He had male hypogonadism, which means failure of the development of the testicles. Development of the testicles is controlled by pituitary hormones, called gonadotropins. The testicles make testosterone, the major male hormone. Without testosterone, sexual development is retarded, and the breasts enlarge.

But why couldn't the patient cook? That was why he was here.

"What dishes are you especially bad at preparing?" I asked. He thought for a moment.

"Those with sauces. Complicated dishes, dishes that require me to taste them to see if I need to add more spices."

"How is your sense of smell?"

"Not very good."

"Close your eyes. I am going to try something." He closed his eyes. I took a pinch of instant coffee from a nearby jar and rubbed it between my fingers.

"Can you smell this? What is it?" I placed my fingers under Sanders' nose.

"I can't smell anything."

Petty Officer Sanders had anosmia, an inability to smell things.

"He has Kallmann's Syndrome!" I thought, excited to make a diagnosis.

The parts of the brain that control sex hormones and sense of smell and are very close together. Every perfume manufacturer is aware of that fact.

In Kallmann's syndrome, named after Dr. Franz Kallmann who discovered it, the patient is born without the ability to smell or to have normal sexual development. It occurs in both men and women. A male becomes an awkward, immature looking young man who can't smell things and is embarrassed to go to the gym.

If the patient decides to become a cook, he is even more unfortunate. The sense of taste is closely related to the sense of smell. PO Sanders couldn't taste to see if more spice or salt or lemon or other additives were needed. Therefore, he failed as a chef.

I explained my findings to PO Sanders. I started him on monthly testosterone injections. He developed more body hair, his voice became deeper, his muscle enlarged, and he began dating women.

Regrettably, I could not improve his sense of smell or taste. He gave up cooking and went into Naval Intelligence.

CHAPTER 11

A WAKE IN THE WOODS

Hannibal McNabb was angry. His roommate had told him to turn off the radio.

Hannibal was a patient in the VA hospital. He was on ward 1E, a psychiatric ward, being treated for bipolar disorder.

Hannibal was a Viet Nam war veteran. At first his symptoms were felt to be due to posttraumatic stress disorder (PTSD), but then the diagnosis was changed to bipolar disorder.

In bipolar disorder the patient has wide swings of mood, from depression to elation and sometimes anger. Hannibal had been placed on lithium, a drug that smooths out the swings in mood.

He was a huge man, six feet six tall. Until recently he worked on his father's farm and stayed fit, but his episodes of mania caused him to eat more and he stopped working. His large frame had been taken over by fat. His hair was black and greasy and much of his face was covered with a thick black beard. In spite of his size, his facial features, when he wasn't angry, were delicate, giving him an almost sweet and innocent visage.

But this morning he was angry. The object of his wrath was the black man in the bed at the opposite corner of the room. His roommate, who was also a Viet Nam veteran, was being treated for depression. The antidepressants made him drowsy and he just wanted to sleep. Hannibal's radio, which was loudly playing

Country and Western music, was the object of the roommate's concern.

"Turn off that God damn radio! I need to sleep." the black man shouted.

Hannibal's anger boiled over. He picked up the small radio and flung it across the room with all his might. The radio barely missed the black man's head, and struck the wall with a loud crack. The parts of the radio, electronics and all, fell onto the pillow of his bed.

"This guy's trying to kill me!" he screamed. A nurse stuck her head inside the door to see what was happening. "Call a Code Atlas!" she shouted. Code Atlas was the signal that a patient is violent and needs to be restrained. An instant later, the overhead paging system blared "Code Atlas Ward 1E! Code Atlas Ward 1E!"

Within 5 minutes the room filled with the Code Atlas Team. These were muscular orderlies, policemen, physicians, nurses and psychologists. They had been trained in the ways of calming and subduing patients without violence. It was also hoped that their sheer numbers would coax a disruptive patient to behave.

The group made a semicircle around Hannibal's bed.

"OK Hannibal. You are OK." reassured a female nurse who was a member of the team. Hannibal looked around at the members of the team. He didn't like being penned in. He tried to push his way through the group.

"OK, Mr. McNabb, we are going to give you something to make you feel better." said a psychiatrist with a soothing voice. As the psychiatrist was talking, a nurse was filling a syringe with a concoction euphemistically known as "The Hammer". The Hammer consists of a mixture of Valium, a medication that sedates, Benadryl, which calms and puts the patient to sleep, and Haldol, an antipsychotic which controls abnormal thoughts and behavior.

His psychiatrist's reassuring words calmed Hannibal and his rapid breathing slowed.   Then he turned and saw the nurse holding the syringe. He again became agitated and tried to break through the group.

"Ok, let's give him the shot." someone said.

The group pushed the big man to the floor, like a throng of ants climbing on a beetle. The nurse, being careful not to inject a member of the Atlas Team, thrust the needle into McNabb's thigh and pushed the plunger.

 Within thirty seconds the tension left the huge man's body and he became calm. Seeing this, the members of the Atlas Team relaxed and smiled at each other.

"He's not breathing!" someone shouted. The big man's chest wasn't moving. "And he doesn't have a pulse." shouted a man who was feeling for the carotid pulse in the man's neck. "Let's start CPR." A policeman began compressing the chest.

"Do we have an ambu bag?" asked a psychiatrist. A nurse returned with the bag. The mouthpiece covered the patient's face and the rubber bag was rhythmically squeezed to deliver air to the patient.

For the second time in less than half an hour the overhead pager summoned a Stat team to ward 1E. "Code Blue 1E! Code Blue 1E!" came the call.

The Code Blue Team arrived. They were younger and trimmer than the Dr. Atlas Team. They were also more colorful. An anesthesiologist wore a flowery cap to keep his hair out of the operative field. A nurse wore a pink cap that contrasted with her green scrub suit.

A resident relieved the policeman who was doing CPR.

The anesthesiologist studied McNabb's chest for a moment. "He's not moving air very well. I will intubate him." Using a metal laryngoscope, the anesthesiologist skillfully inserted a rubber tube through the nose and down into the trachea. He then inflated the balloon that held the tube in place. Now, with each inflation of the ambu bag, the chest moved.

EKG leads were placed on the chest.

"It is sinus rhythm." shouted a nurse.

The electrical activity of the heart was now normal.

"He has a pulse." said a physician.

It seemed that that the only problem with McNabb was that he had stopped breathing. Now that oxygen was delivered his heart had recovered.

He was moved to the Intensive Care Unit and placed on a ventilator to move his lungs. All systems were go-his heart and lungs and kidneys and liver, all systems but one, the brain. Had the lack of oxygen during his respiratory arrest just stunned the brain, or had it killed it? Time would answer that question.

After a few days it was found that Hannibal was breathing on his own. But that was as far as it went. There was no sign of waking up. The brainstem, the lower part of the brain, that controls breathing and heart function, was working. Above that there was nothing. The patient was in what is known as "a persistent vegetative state."

In the Intensive Care Unit, a tracheostomy, which is a hole in the trachea was placed. Periodically the nurses put a catheter through the opening and down in to the lungs to suction secretions. This would help prevent pneumonia.

To provide nutrition, a tube was inserted through a hole that was made in his abdominal wall and continued into the stomach.

Intensive care units treat acute problems, such as shock and overwhelming infections, in hope that the patient's life can be saved by careful monitoring of his vital signs, and meticulous nursing care. It became apparent that McNabb didn't have an acute problem that could be made better by intensive care.

Availability of intensive care unit beds controls the flow of patients into a hospital. If all of the ICU beds are occupied, critically ill patients can't be admitted from the Emergency Department. Ambulances carrying patients with life threatening problems are diverted to another hospital if there are no ICU beds. There is tremendous pressure to move patients out of the ICU to the medical ward as soon as possible.

McNabb's brain damage was not reversible. He would spend the remainder of his life in a nursing home, fed through a tube in his stomach.

But there were two caveats in his case. He was young, only 38. And his brain injury was caused by something that had been done to him in the hospital- giving him a huge dose of sedatives.

And there was his family.

Hovering around his bed was a scrawny, deeply tanned, little woman of about 60 years. "Hannibal, I am here." she said as she leaned into her son's bed. When she noticed something that she thought needed to be attended to, like a gurgling in her son's tracheostomy tube, she frowned and turned to the nurse and asked her to attend to the problem. The obedient nurse ran a tube into the trachea and suctioned up the mucus.

Sometimes the little woman was accompanied by an equally diminutive man of the same age. This was Hannibal's father. He wore a broad brimmed straw hat and his face had the leathery appearance of someone who has spent his life working in the sun. He was a farmer.

The little man said very little. But whenever the mother spoke, he nodded in agreement. I was surprised that such small parents had produced such a giant.

The ICU Waiting Room was frequently occupied by Hannibal's sisters and assorted cousins and uncles and aunts who were continually inquiring about his condition.

Hannibal's family talked about suing the hospital. He had stopped breathing because of a medication that the hospital gave to him. This was probably the major reason that the big man remained in the ICU for weeks after he had received the maximum benefit of intensive care.

Finally, the family was convinced that Hannibal didn't need intensive care, and he was moved out to the medical ward.

When one could be found, a special- duty nurse cared for Hannibal during the day. This involved suctioning him every hour, turning him on his side every two hours to prevent bedsores, and bathing him every few days. His diaper was changed several times a day, and food and water were infused into his feeding tube. The Nursing Service was often short-staffed, and it was difficult to meet their large patient's needs.

The physician responsible for Hannibal was the Ward Attending. He directed the resident and interns in the patient's care. Every month there was a new Attending Physician.

Hannibal's angry family was not happy with his nursing care. There were frequent meetings with the family, the nursing staff, and the Attending Physician.

"He is lying in his own filth!" the mother would say, upset that the pad on her son's bed was not being changed when it was dirty.

The Attending Physician usually sided with the nurses. After all, Hannibal was "brain dead", and "brain dead" is practically the same as being "dead". This dead person was taking up a hospital bed and stretching the overworked nursing staff to its limits.

These meetings often resulted in raucous anger with the various parties shouting at each other

Another issue was what to do if Hannibal stopped breathing. People who are brain dead, or near death from a terminal illness, have no quality of life. It is considered most merciful to allow them to pass away quietly. They are not considered worth salvaging with cardiopulmonary resuscitation. Families sometimes don't agree with this. They want everything to be done for their loved one, even to allow his heart to beat a single extra beat before he passes away.

When physicians disagree with the family's wishes, the demands of the family can be overruled by an order "Resuscitation Not Indicated" or "RNI". This requires two physicians to write a note in the patient's chart that the patient is terminal, and that resuscitation is not likely to improve quality of life. The hospital has an Ethics Committee which deals with such difficult situations.

Months passed.

Despite the nurse's best efforts, Hannibal developed a bed sore on his buttock, and he got a pneumonia which responded to antibiotics. He became gaunt. The skin of his face developed a scaly rash. The slowly dying man took on a wraithlike appearance. His parents continued to hover around his bed.

One month I became McNabb's attending physician, and very soon there was family meeting.

The mother spoke in a drawl commonly heard in people who lived in the western part of Virginia.

"My son ain't being kept clean. His diapers ain't being cleaned. He's a lying in his poop and pee, and that is why he is getting them bedsores." When Hannibal's mother spoke, you could see that she had a missing front tooth.

Her words were directed toward the Nursing Supervisor, a graying African American woman who was sitting next to me. Hannibal's father nodded his support with his wife. The nurse spoke.

"We are giving your son VIP, very important person care. I check him personally once a day. I have never seen waste in his bed. Our nurses are sometimes overwhelmed, but they are giving your son excellent care."

The mother shook her head.

Hannibal's parents were simple country people. They could not understand how their living son had come to the hospital and been converted to a lifeless zombie. Perhaps they thought that if everything was done right, if their son did not get pneumonia, if he did not get bedsores on his bottom, and he didn't get dehydrated, he would recover and be their son again.

These simple people reminded me of my own parents, my nearly deaf father who was a plumber, and my country girl mother who had not been to high school.

"I know how hard the Nursing Service works." I began. The supervisor nodded and smiled. "But I too have sometimes noticed that his bed was dirty and wet."

The old couple, sitting across from me, looked at each other, then smiled at me and nodded their thanks. It was decided that the Nursing Service would pay extra attention to McNabb's hygiene.

I had bonded with the family who now trusted me. I decided that it was now time to discuss what would happen if their son died.

"We are doing everything that we can for Hannibal, but he is deteriorating. The part of his brain that controls his personality, his ability to speak, is dead. He will never be the way he was before. I am sorry."

The parents seemed touched that someone would take the time to explain to them what was happening with their son. "I am sorry for your loss. I know what you are going through."

I paused for a minute, then continued. "If we find him not to be breathing, we would like permission to leave him in peace. Pounding on the chest of a patient like Hannibal seldom brings him back. Death is natural. We would like permission to leave your son in peace, should he pass on."

Hannibal's parents were devout Baptists. They believed that their son would go to Heaven when he died. They accepted that when he his heart stopped he would be left in peace.

Three days later Hannibal McNabb died. I was surprised that this happened so soon. I felt awkward when I saw his parents. I searched my brain for something comforting to say. "I'd like to come to the funeral."

The sadness on the couples faces turned, first to surprise, and then to gratitude. They were genuinely moved that a physician would come to their child's funeral. They wrote down directions to the church where the funeral was going to be held.

Four days later I drove north on Route 95 to Stafford County to Hannibal McNabb's funeral. I was leaving the hospital late and it was already getting dark. I hoped that I would get to the funeral before it was over.

After about 70 miles I turned onto a side road. After another 15 miles I made a left turn onto another road. I looked for a small one- story church, but all I saw were hay fields, small houses, and darkness. At one place, a large bull standing in the road blocked my way. In a minute he moved to the side of the road and I gingerly drove past him.

I took another road hoping that I would find the church, but all I saw were fields of hay. This road wasn't even paved. I turned again, hoping that my luck would change. It was now close to 9 PM. The funeral was probably over. I just wanted to go home.

Now I was driving through a maze of corn fields. I heard a loud screech in front of the car. A large animal had dropped out of the sky and was in my headlights. It was an owl grabbing a rat that had strayed in front of my car. Before I could hit the brakes, the huge bird ascended back into the sky with its prey in its talons.

I came to the end of the corn field. Off to the right I saw a barbed wire fence. Beyond the fence was a small house with a single light. I stopped my car, climbed over the fence and walked toward the house. At one corner of the house was a screened porch where a man and a woman sat. I hoped that they would be able to give me directions.

98

I heard dogs barking. The barking was getting louder and louder. I realized that the barking was becoming louder because the dogs were coming at me. There were at least two. I turned and began running. As I neared the fence, I heard the dogs yapping and breathing very close to me. One of their teeth grazed my heel. In another second, they would be on top of me.

Suddenly a voice came from behind me. "Tom come back. Lucy come back. You! Come back!" I turned and looked behind me. The dogs had stopped chasing me, and now were running back to the house. I could see that one of the dogs was a hound and the other was a pit bull

Silhouetted in the light of the house was the figure of a man. He was carrying a rifle.

"What are you doing here?" he asked.

"I am just looking for directions. I am lost. I am a doctor. I am looking for my patient's funeral."

"Lost, eh? OK come forward."

I walked toward the house. The man with the rifle was about 50 years old. He wore a light jacket which showed a fit looking torso. Even in the faint light, I could see that he wore a patch over his right eye. As soon as he got a good look at me, he relaxed and lowered his gun. I didn't look dangerous. "I'm looking for a funeral. I am lost." I repeated.

"OK. Come on inside. Maybe I can help you."

Inside the house was a sturdy woman whose blond hair was beginning to turn grey. She was surprised to see me. "This man is lost. He is looking for a funeral." her husband said. Hearing this, the woman smiled broadly. "Would you like a cup of coffee?" As I drunk the coffee her husband looked in the phone book for directions to any nearby churches or funeral parlors.

"There is a little church about 12 miles away. You have to cross over a little bridge and take another road after you get back on the road that you took. It may be hard to find in the dark. If you keep going for another twenty miles you will hit Route 95."

My host wrote some directions on a slip of paper. He noticed me staring at the patch on his eye.

"I got this when an automatic garage door hit me in the face. I lost the eye. I have a glass eye which I use on formal occasions, but this patch is more comfortable. Besides my grandchildren like it. They say it makes me look like a pirate!" He grinned.

The man walked me across his field to my car, with his dogs running in front of us.

It was now after 10 PM.

I decided it was too late to go to a funeral. I didn't like the idea of being lost in the dark in an unfamiliar area. I just wanted to get back on Route 95 and go home. I headed toward the highway.

Off to my right I noticed a light. Through the trees I saw a white one-story building. In front of the building was a grey van. It could have been a hearse. I stopped my car and walked into the building. People stood in small groups talking and drinking coffee, as if they were at a party.

At the center of the room was a large coffin. It was painted in the finest white paint and almost looked like it was made of ivory. The coffin was open. I cautiously peaked inside. What I saw astounded me.

It was Hannibal McNabb, but he had been transformed. He was wearing a tuxedo. His hair was neatly trimmed and the only hair remaining on his face was an elegant mustache. The embalmers magic had changed his pasty color to the rosiness of health. He wore a faint smile and the look on his face was of total peace.

As I stared at my patient, I felt someone touching my left elbow. It was Hannibal's mother. "Looks pretty good for what he has been through, don't he." she said. Behind her was his father wearing a white dress shirt and a string tie. He grinned and shook my hand. Then he called out to people in the room. "Here is Hannibal's doctor." Men and women came up to me to shake my hand.

"It is an honor to meet you." said a plump woman in an apron, and she pumped my hand. A man come up behind me and clapped me on the back.

"Doc, do you know what this thing is?" asked the corpulent minister who officiated at the funeral. He pointed to a crusty lesion on the back of his hand. It looked like a wart.

It was as if I had fashioned a miraculous cure for my patient, and he wasn't lying dead in a bed of silk 10 feet from me.

Hannibal's father patted me on the back. "Do you want to come up to the house for a cup of coffee?" he asked. It was close to midnight and I dreaded the two-hour drive home. "No thank you. I have to drive home." Hannibal's parents walked me to my car. His mother hugged me, and I got into the car for my long drive in the dark.

Hannibal's family did sue the hospital for his death. Dozens of people were named on the suit, including the Hospital Director, the Chief of Staff, the Chief of Nursing, many nurses, and every physician who had contact with him.

One name was significantly absent from the suit. The name was mine.

CHAPTER 12
THE LEGACY OF PHIDIPPIDES

I moved swiftly and quietly as I searched for my prey. Man's primitive ancestors evolved to walk long distances to follow an animal. Then, as they got within striking distance, they sprinted to thrust their spear into a mammoth or moose.

In the distance I saw what I was searching for. At first it was just a small white dot. I accelerated and gained on my prize. I closed the distance to within a hundred feet. Now I could see it clearly.

The white spot was the head of an old woman wearing a tee shirt, running shorts and Nikes. She was breathing heavily and wobbling with fatigue. I came up beside her and slowed my pace. I smiled disarmingly. "Hello" I said.

"Hi." she gasped, almost unable to speak.

"I'm a doctor." I said with concern. "Are you OK?" She nodded, barely glancing toward me. She was determined to finish the race. "I have some Tylenol if you want it."

"No, thanks I am OK."

"Well, good luck." I accelerated my pace and moved away from the woman. A smile crossed my face. "Now, at least I won't finish dead last!"

I was running the Richmond, Virginia, Marathon. Well, not exactly running. I was mostly power walking. The race began almost three hours ago. It was a cold November morning, but the mass of moving humanity was packed so tightly that their body heat probably raised the air temperature a few degrees. As time passed, the pack spread out. I fantasized that I was doing well and was ahead of hundreds, or even thousands of runners.

Then, I heard an ominous sound behind me. I looked back. An ambulance was moving slowly, only 10 feet behind me. There could be only one explanation. "I was dead last in a field of twenty thousand runners!" The ambulance took up the rear of the runners. The not too subtle connotation of the emergency vehicle is. "If you are so slow that you see an ambulance, you are too frail and slow to be in the race, and you should get off the course."

I glanced back at the ambulance and shook my head. I walked faster, even sprinted a bit. I knew that tomorrow morning the Richmond Times Dispatch would publish the times of the finishers. It would be embarrassing to be dead last and have everyone in Richmond reading about it as they ate their breakfast. But thanks to the old lady that I passed, I would avoid that humiliation.

When I neared a water stop, that was manned by a pretty young woman, I sucked in my stomach and ran. I accepted the paper cup of water or Power Aid from the woman and gave a manly grunt of thanks. Without stopping, I drained the cup, then forcefully crushed the cup and tossed it on the street with thousands of other cups. When I was out of sight of the young lady, I let out my stomach and resumed walking.

The first marathon was run in 490 BC by a Greek named Phidippides.

The Persians were preparing to attack the Athenians on the plain of Marathon. The Athenians sent Phidippides, their best runner, to Sparta to get help. The Spartans said they would help, but only after a religious holiday had passed.

The Athenians defeated the Persians. Phidippides ran the 26 miles to Athens in 3hours, wearing armor. He relayed the news of the victory, then died.

In modern times the marathon was introduced as a 26- mile race.

Doing a marathon has become a symbol of health and overcoming health problems. Signs on the backs of runners announce this. "Cancer survivor." some say. "I overcame breast cancer." says another. Some people run in memory of those who have died. The name, and sometimes the picture of the deceased, is embossed on their tee shirt. Other runners have had heart attacks and even bypass surgery. By completing the "ultimate" cardiac stressor, the runner proves that his heart is now normal and, perhaps, thinks he is spitting in the eye of disease and death. Many runners have the belief that doing a marathon is good for their body, a rejuvenator, a "Fountain of Youth."

During the race their body burns hundreds of calories. The runner can almost see the cholesterol being burned out of his arteries as he runs. The marathon cleanses the body of impurities. "No one who has completed a marathon has died of a heart attack." I once heard an aficionado of running say. Some participants are obese, even morbidly obese. I wonder if they think that running 26 miles will burn off their extra weight.

"If I can do a marathon it means that my coronary arteries are ok." I thought as I attempted my first Richmond Marathon in 1999. Many people my age get a stress test just to check their heart out. The problem with the stress test is that, often, the results are "equivocal." There is a minor abnormality of uncertain significance. This triggers a cardiac catheterization.

Doing a marathon would be my physiological stress test. If I got through it, my coronaries were fine. It did occur to me that if my coronaries were not "fine" I might drop dead. In my defense, I promised myself that if I got chest pain, I would stop immediately.

The marathon starts on Broad Street, then makes a huge loop, and eventually crosses back over the James River. At the 16 mile point you cross the Lee Bridge back into downtown Richmond. When I saw the city buildings I was thrilled. My thighs and calves began to ache. From now on it was just a matter of fighting pain.

The problems in my life were driven from my brain by physical pain. My entire universe was this narrow course. My reason for existence was getting to the Finish Line.

At about a mile from the end I saw a friendly face. Norma had come to see me to the finish line. Now every step was agony. I crossed under the banner that marked the finish line and my foot hit the chip timer. I staggered into the arms of a young woman who was holding a medal. Then someone else gave me a mylar blanket to prevent hypothermia.

Norma took me wrapped in my blanket into the nearby Marriot Hotel to buy me a beer. I gulped down the cold yellow nectar.

"I love you." I told the young man who was my waiter. "I know you prayed for me." I was becoming delirious. The surprised waiter stared at me.

"My wife is a minister." he said.

"Well I know she prayed for me too."

A few years later I found myself sitting in the upper levels of a hospital amphitheater weeping. Sitting around me were perhaps fifty other people. Some of them were crying. The center of our attention was a young woman sitting on a chair in the place where the lecturer stands. She was Asian, and her protruding abdomen showed that she was in the last stages of pregnancy.

Four days early, her husband, Charchi Kasirapa, a 34- year old cardiologist, while training for the Richmond Marathon, dropped dead.

The woman reached down and turned on a tape recorder. "I wanted his son to know what people said about his father."

A man stood up.

"I was the one who found him. The expression his face was peaceful. He didn't suffer." he reassured the widow.

Then Dr. Nelson Bernardo stood up. Dr. Bernardo, also a cardiologist, was a good friend of the victim. When Dr. Bernardo heard that his friend was being resuscitated in a nearby Emergency Room he went there to help.

Dr. Bernardo spoke in Chinese. He looked at the dead man's parents who sat in the front row. They had flown in from the Orient. Sometimes he broke down and sobbed.

Despite his youth, an autopsy showed that Charchi had extensive coronary artery disease. He died from a heart attack.

Running a marathon subjects the body to unusual physical stresses. Silent coronary artery disease announces itself. If the young cardiologist never ran a marathon, he probably would have lived a normal lifespan. What people sometimes forget, is that Phidippides, the first marathoner, died during the run.

One spring I decided to do the Charlottesville Marathon. Charlottesville is a university town about 70 miles to the west of Richmond.

The marathon started at 7AM near its headquarters, an athletic store called "The Charlottesville Running Company." Charlottesville is in the mountains, and spring mornings are cold.

Runners stamped their feet and ran in place to get warm. A huge arc of blue and pink and white balloons marked the starting line. The slower runners, like me, were placed at the back of the pack.

"Go!" the starter gave the command and the group lunged forward. An electronic chip was tied to the laces of my right shoe. A rubber pad covered the device that registered the runners' times. When my foot hit the pad, the timer rung. My race had begun.

The huge throng moved through downtown Charlottesville. As it moved along, the concentrated mass of humanity thinned out. Soon the slow runners and walkers, like me, took up the rear. After a while we moved through the grounds of the University of Virginia. Then we went through a residential area where the front of each house was resplendent with huge azaleas. Pretty soon, the route went along a narrow country road. I passed the six -mile marker.

Without warning, a huge man stepped out from behind a tree, blocking my path. He wore a baseball cap, and he was so fat that with his outstretched arms I couldn't run around him. "You're going too slow. I'm taking you off the course." he said.

"What do you mean. I registered as a walker. I am doing 15 - minute miles. I am going to finish in 6 and a half hours. That's what I said I would do when I registered on line." I was upset that my race was being ended so early.

The big man thought for a moment. Then he spoke. "Well that was a typo. Maybe next year we will open it up to walkers. We can't close this road to traffic all day."

In my mind I saw my coveted marathon medal flying away. I tried to think of a way to salvage this experience. "Can I convert to the Half Marathon? I have gone 6.5 miles. I just have to turn around and go back and I will be doing a half marathon."

The big man thought for a moment, then spoke. "Well, OK."

I turned around and began retracing my steps. I went back down the road. Then I was moving through the neighborhoods whose houses sported azaleas in their spring glory. Their colors reminded me of the colored balloons at the starting line. As I moved along, I wondered if I would get a medal. I wasn't even sure if they gave a medal for the half marathon. This symbol of athletic achievement was extremely important to me. I moved back through the University of Virginia. "You are doing great! Keep it up!" shouted a young woman when she saw my runner's bib.

When I left the university campus, I noticed people lining the streets to cheer the runners. A smiling old man in a sweater came up to me. He was holding a Styrofoam cup which he offered to me. It was cold beer. "Thanks, that hit the spot." I said as I patted him on the shoulder. Looming in front of me was the arc of blue and pink and white balloons that marked the finish line. I was going to finish. I accelerated my pace. "Am I going to get a medal? Do they even give a medal for the half marathon?!"

People lining the route shouted and cheered. These were the loudest cheers that I had ever received in any marathon. And I was just walking it.

I crossed under the arc of balloons. My right foot, with its electronic timing chip, hit the rubber pad. I had finished. Up in front of me was a smiling young woman holding a ribbon. Hanging from the ribbon was a medal.

"Congratulations!" she said as she looped the ribbon around my neck.

I drove home, delighted that I had acquired yet another athletic medal to hang on the wall of my study.

"How did you do?" Norma asked as soon as I came through the door. "I finished." I said calmly as I flashed the medal. Norma disappeared up the stairs to check the marathon website.

Five minutes later Norma reappeared. Her mouth was half open, and she stared at me with confusion and amazement.

"You WON the Charlottesville Marathon for your age- group!" Then she took a deep breath and continued. "How did you do it?! That's the best time you ever did."

I was surprised and thrilled. For a few minutes I believed that she was right, that I won the Charlottesville Marathon. I was proud of my athletic prowess. I searched my mind for a reply.

"That big guy scared the heck out of me. I ran like I never did before."

For the first time in many years my spouse was impressed by my athletic prowess. Not since we were dating, and Norma was awed by my ability to swim the length of an Olympic size pool under water, had this occurred. I was not going to let this go easily.

I thought back to the race.

The Richmond Marathon is electronically sophisticated. They need to be sure of the runners' times. Winners can qualify for other marathons, including the prestigious Boston Marathon, which may lead to a spot at the Olympics, and they can win thousands of dollars. The Richmond Marathon has a chip timer at the beginning, another at the 13.1mile point, and another at 20 miles.

The Charlottesville Marathon is not so electronically sophisticated. There is just a chip timer at the starting line. It knows only when you started and when you finished.

I registered for the Charlottesville Marathon as a 26- mile runner. Nothing had changed that. When the fat man let me turn around, my distance changed to 13 miles, but no one told the chip timer. It still thought that I was doing the whole marathon. This was why I received such an ovation when I neared the finish line. The bystanders thought that I was the winner.

For several months I let Norma believe that I won the marathon for my age class. I didn't want to part with this newly found adulation. Then my need to tell a story eclipsed my desire to be an athlete, and I told Norma the truth.

I still enter marathons and half marathons, even though there is no data to indicate that running marathons makes you live longer.

As I move along the course, I imagine blood coursing through healthy coronary arteries. Otherwise I couldn't be doing this.

CHAPTER 13

PERVERSE INCENTIVES

Chief Petty Officer Lucille Clinton was worried

She had just undergone her Navy physical, and she was called back to discuss her lab results. She wondered what could be wrong. Was it something serious?

Chief Clinton was the single mother of two teenage girls. If anything happened to her, who would care for them? Three years ago, her best friend, Clara, was called back because of abnormal labs. They found that Clara had leukemia. Clara died two years later. "Do I have leukemia too?" the chief wondered. "Could I have HIV? I have only had sex four time in the past year, and he used condoms?" she thought about her sometimes boyfriend Jeff. "At least I thought he used condoms. I should have checked. Could I have AIDS?"

A nurse practitioner motioned her to come into the office. The chief trembled as her medical report was read. "Your blood sugar is high. It was 118. It's not diabetes. Diabetes is when it is above 126. But it is prediabetes. It can go into diabetes. You are a little overweight. If you watch your diet and exercise you can make it go away and reduce your chance of getting diabetes."

The chief grimaced at the thought of becoming a diabetic. Her aunt had diabetes and had just had one of her toes amputated. "I don't want to lose my foot." The muscles in her neck tensed up and she thought of her aunt. Then something crossed her mind and she relaxed. "I will get on top of this." she said with a smile.

I met Chief Clinton 3 months later in the Endocrinology Department at Portsmouth Naval Hospital. I reviewed her record. Instead of losing weight she was 3 pounds heavier. Her fasting blood sugar had increased to 130. It was now in the diabetic range.

Blood sugar is maintained within the normal range by secretion of insulin by the islet cells of the pancreas. Insulin decreases glucose production by the liver and increases muscle uptake of glucose. Obesity causes resistance to insulin. To keep the blood sugar normal, the pancreas responds by raising the insulin level. Eventually, the overworked islet cells can fail, and the sugar rises. The patient has developed type 2 diabetes, the most common form.

"Have you been exercising?" I asked, as my gaze flitted from her brown hair, to her blue eyes and down at her flabby midriff.

She hesitated and then replied. "Not as much as I should."

"Have you been sticking to the diet?"

"Not really."

"Well, your sugar is creeping up. Now you are in the diabetic range. You can still bring it down with diet and exercise. You don't want to get diabetes, do you?"

The chief stared into my eyes for a few minutes as she formulated an answer to my question. Finally, she spoke.

"You are a naval reservist. You are a civilian. I can tell you the truth. Right?"

To her I wasn't a regular naval officer. I was just a civilian, a "reenactor", who posed as a naval officer two days a month.

"What you tell me is confidential."

"I am a single parent. I am not a doctor or nurse or a pilot. I have no marketable skills. I am a master chief. When I retire in two years, I may have trouble finding a job. I have two daughters. My retirement pay won't be enough. "

"Go ahead." I nodded.

"I need to get all of the disability that I can. Prediabetes is a disability. I will get several hundred dollars a month for it. Now that I have diabetes, I will get thirty per cent of my base pay as disability. I need the money."

"But diabetes can cause complications and shorten your life. You want to be here for your daughters."

"It takes a long time for diabetes to kill you. By then my girls will be out of college. If I exercise my diabetes will go away and I will be out money. And by the way, if my sugar gets worse and I need to go on insulin my per cent disability will go up to 50 per cent of my base pay."

The chief had done her homework. I racked my brain to dispute her reasoning, but could think of nothing.

On another day I met another patient.

The red- haired young man in the green flight suit seemed out of place in a medical clinic. He was trim and fit. He had a confident smile on his face and seemed to exude good health. I wondered if he had gotten lost and had wandered into the wrong building. "Diabetes Mellitus" was the only condition listed on the Problem List.

Commander Lance Titcomb was the pilot of an A6 fighter jet. A year earlier he noticed that he was fatigued and losing weight.

Laboratory testing showed the reason. The commander's blood sugar was over 200. He had diabetes.

Complete lack of insulin causes a more severe form of diabetes, called type 1 diabetes. Absence of insulin allows the liver to produce acids, called ketones. High sugar and acid levels in the blood cause a life-threatening condition called diabetic ketoacidosis. Without treatment with insulin, the patient dies. Because this condition commonly presents during childhood, it is also called juvenile onset diabetes.

Since the commander's ketone level was normal and he didn't seem to be sick, he was classified as a type 2 diabetic. In type 2 diabetes we give various medications to wake up the failing pancreas and help what insulin remains to work better. Sometimes type 2 diabetes progresses to type 1 diabetes. The young airman was started on glyburide, a medication that causes the pancreas to secrete more insulin, and metformin, which helps insulin work better. Technically he did not require insulin treatment. This was especially important for the commander, as he knew that taking insulin disqualified him from flying a jet.

Commander Titcomb wanted to be a pilot for most of his life.

Military pilots have often told me that it is the best job in the world. Some pilots are almost addicted to flying. I often have observed pilots sitting in the clinic while they are waiting for their flight physicals. They speak happily about their flying adventures, sometimes moving their hands to mimic the maneuvers of a jet.

And now Commander Titcomb was in danger of losing this.

The commander read about diabetes. His body was making a small amount of insulin. Sugar is taken up by exercising muscle. He reasoned that if he exercised, his muscles would increase in size, his insulin would work better, and his sugar would fall.

Each morning at 5 am he got up and ran. Within two months he had increased the distance to 10 miles. After he ran, he did pushups to build up his upper body. Over time, this increased to 100 pushups per morning. Then he did 50 sit-ups. At noon he went the base gym and lifted weights. In the evening he ran an additional 10 miles and did more pushups. He restricted his calories to 1500 calories per day. Within six months his body fact decreased to 5 percent. He was all bone and muscle. His blood sugar fell to the normal level. "You don't need insulin." he was told by a nurse practitioner at his follow-up appointment.

But 3 months later, despite his exercise regimen, the commander's blood sugar was again above 200. "You need to go on insulin." I told him at his first appointment with me.

"Wait. I can exercise more. As long as I am not on insulin, I can fly. Give me another chance."

I empathized with the young man as he looked hopefully into my eyes.

"Well OK." I said, "But we will need to see you in another month."

I wondered if I was doing the right thing. In truth, the commander had a kind of diabetes between type 1 and type 2, and his was likely that he would eventually become type 1 and require insulin.

Commander Titcomb began running three times a day. He ran 10 miles in the morning and evening and an additional 5 miles at noon. He spent most of his evenings in the gym pumping iron. Flying was the center of his existence, and he didn't want to give it up.

Unrecognized by Commander Titcomb, but suspected by me, was that something ominous was occurring deep in his abdomen. The insulin secreting cells of his pancreas were being attacked by antibodies. Soon they would be destroyed, and he would need to go on insulin

When he returned a month later, I was horrified at his appearance. He weighed only 140 lbs. All his body fat was gone. His bones were covered by muscle. He looked like a muscle- bound wraith, a concentration camp victim who spent his time in the gym. His blood sugar was 230. I knew he had lost his fight. I needed to start insulin. I should have begun it months earlier. My empathy for the young man had clouded my clinical judgment.

"You fought the good fight. I am proud of you." I said as I hugged the commander. He began crying.

I started him on four units of NPH insulin, an intermediate acting insulin. Normally a man of his size would require at least 40 units of insulin. But his fitness program made him so sensitive to insulin that this trivial amount was enough to bring his blood sugar into the normal range.

The intrepid commander could no longer be a pilot, but he hoped that he could move over to the second seat in the A6 fighter and become a bombardier navigator. I wrote a letter trying to get the Navy to give him a waiver, but they declined, and he was grounded

Health problems create perverse incentives.

Chief Clinton was motivated by a disability check. An elevated blood sugar gave her a financial advantage.

Commander Titcomb needed to be healthy to fulfill his passion, flying. He did everything he could to cure his diabetes, even to endangering his health. But time and his body were against him.

Many of the Commander Titcomb's flying partners distinguished themselves in Operation Desert Storm.

To me, Commander Lance Titcomb, was also a hero, just as much of a hero as his friends who flew over Iraq.

CHAPTER 14

THE DOG PARK

"That woman can't be married, or probably even have a boyfriend." Norma mused.

" She says that big brute sleeps in her bed. There wouldn't be room for anybody else." Norma chuckled.

We were sitting on benches in a dog park, a fenced- in lawn where people brought their dogs to play with other dogs. The object of our attention was a woman standing about 30 feet from us. She was a young brunette, no more than 25, and pretty, with delicate facial features, pale blue eyes and a slightly upturned nose. Her tight- fitting blouse and designer jeans showed her figure to good advantage.

The woman smiled at her companion who was standing to her left, a huge creature that seemed almost to resemble a horse more than a dog. Its long legs supported a massive body and head whose ears reached up to the woman's shoulder. The body was pale white, and the eyes were an odd pink color. The albino Great Dane had an almost supernatural appearance. It reminded me of the description of the "Hound from Hell" in the Sherlock Holmes mystery "The Hound of the Baskervilles." Hanging from its neck, near the license, was a sign that read "Deaf Dog." Despite this, the woman spoke softly to her friend who eyed her lovingly. Perhaps he could read lips.

I tried to imagine the dog sleeping at the foot of the bed. It would be a very wide bed. Maybe he slept next to her under the covers. I laughed at that picture. I glanced at her left index finger. There was no ring. Maybe Norma's suspicions were right.

All around us was the panoply of the dog park. Excited dogs ran with groups of other dogs.

Sometimes the whole pack changed direction in unison, like a flock of birds wheeling in the sky. This was the pack instinct of their wolf ancestors coming out. Occasionally a dog was out of step and he was trampled by the running hoard. No one seemed to get hurt. There were dog toys scattered over the grass. Sometime a dog would pick up a toy and taunt the others to chase him and take it away. Our little beagle, Happy, particularly liked this game. When another dog tried to take a toy, Happy grabbed it, and a growling tug of war ensued.

There was a kind of etiquette in the dog park.   First, mounting was strictly forbidden.   When Happy mounted another dog we were chagrined, and we pulled him off with an apology to the owner.

Second, aggressive dogs that fought with other dogs, were banned from the park.

Third, and most important, the dog's owner picks up his pet's poop. For this purpose, little plastic bags were provided at the gate.

One day a young man brought his German Shepherd to the park. When the dog squatted and pooped in the middle of the field, the man ignored it.

"You need to pick up your dog's waste." one of the owners chided him. But he just looked at the ground and didn't budge. Twenty pet owners stared angrily at the man. "You have to clean up after your pet. Read the sign!" shouted the old man, who owned the basset hound.

The young man just shook his head and stared at his feet. Maybe he was afraid to touch feces, even with a glove. Finally, the lady who owned a black cocker walked to the middle of the field, a plastic bag in her hand, and removed the poop, glaring at the young man all the while.

Applause erupted as people stood and smiled at the woman. For some reason, the young man and his dog were never again seen at the dog park.

Just as the dogs socialized, so did the humans.

A very fat man came to the park with his four beagles. He had a long white beard and wore coveralls. As the dogs frolicked nearby, he smoked a cigarette. Periodically, one of the beagles broke off from the pack and ran up him. It wagged its tail, then ran back to the pack. One of the dogs that he identified as the female ran up and jumped on the bench and sat next to him. "This is the Penny. She loves me. Yes, she does" he said with emphasis as he petted her ears. Then she put her head on his lap. He took a drag on a cigarette and announced. "They all sleep with me. These cold nights they keep me warm."

I pictured the fat man lying in bed, his large body half covered with beagles. It reminded me of a scene from the movie "Tom Jones" where the uncouth Squire Western finishes a night of drunken feasting lying in a pile of dogs who appreciate the bones that that he has left them. The squire even wipes his mouth on the fur of one of the dogs.

As the fat man left the dog park with his loving brood in tow, one thought entered my mind. "I hope he stops smoking. If he drops dead those dogs will be devastated. Who will take care of them?"

A chunky woman aged about 40 came in with her setter. "She is always taking about her marriages and her divorces." Norma whispered to me. The woman came up to me and stared for a moment.

"I didn't know Happy's daddy was such a handsome man." she said with a seductive smile. Then she walked across the field and sat on the bench on the other side, her dog following her.

"Do you mind if I go over there and sit next to her for a while?" I teased Norma.

One of Happy's favorite friends was Baxter, a spotted hound. Like Happy, Baxter loved to run, and they gleefully cavorted around the field.

Baxter's master was a grey- haired man of about 50. His first name was Bill. Bill always wore a baseball cap and carried an electronic cigarette which he frequently sucked on. Bill never smiled. He just stared sadly at the ground and out at the dogs. Bill was a loner. He had been married once, a long time ago, but that marriage had ended badly.

"My wife got the house, and most of my money… and she got the boy." He said bitterly. "And now the boy is 22 and in jail for selling drugs. I never see him. He doesn't want to see me. She poisoned him against me. I have no friends. I barely get by on my VA pension. And with all the corruption in Washington, the Government is going to fall, and I won't even get my pension."

Norma and I, sitting on the bench next to him, nodded in sympathy. Bill stared at the ground, then sighed and took a drag on his electronic cigarette. The only time that Bill smiled was when he looked out on the field and saw Baxter playing.

"Baxter was a rescue dog. The people who had him before me abused him terribly. He was nothing but skin and bones when I got him, and he growled at me. But that changed. I fed him up and now we are friends. He knows that I saved him and." Bill choked back tears… "he loves me." Seeming to prove the point, Baxter broke off from the pack and ran over to Bill and sat down in front of him wagging his tail.

A young black woman in long dreadlocks walked into the park. She wore jeans and a yellow tee-shirt with the words "VCU Rams" embossed on it. The Rams are the basketball team for Virginia Commonwealth University.   She carried a bottle of water and a notebook.   The water was not for the woman, but for the dogs. She poured her donation into a bucket near the fence, smiled at us, and sat down and began studying her notebook. I surmised that she was a college student.

Her companion was a large black dog. It had the body shape of a Labrador retriever, but its hair was longer and curly. The hair on its face gave it the appearance of having a beard and moustache. Its tail was bobbed short.

At first the animal ignored the other dogs and sat on his haunches in front of his mistress. She looked up from her book, said something, and the animal walked over to us and began wagging its tail. This dog preferred people to other dogs. The woman looked up and smiled. "He's friendly. His name is Winslow." Then she began writing in her notebook.

Winslow looked directly into my eyes and opened his mouth a bit, as if he were smiling. His moustache was wet from his having just drunk water. He wagged his bottom, not just his tail, but his whole bottom, in an enthusiastic greeting. He acted like he knew me. Winslow reminded me of someone that I knew a long time ago-Rigel.

Rigel was the first of three dogs that Norma and I owned together. Rigel's mother was a pedigreed Viesla , a short haired retriever. She was named Sheeba. There is no doubt about that. The identity of his father is uncertain.

The curly puppy looked like a little black lamb with floppy ears.

His feet were too big for his body. We tried to think of a name. In the constellation of Orion, the Hunter, is a bright blue star, marking one foot of the giant hunter. The Arabic name for this hot star is Rigel, which means "The Foot of the Giant." Thus, he was named Rigel.

Norma and I were busy medical students in San Francisco. Her mother and father cared for Rigel much of the time in their ranch style house in Concord thirty miles to the east.

Their tiled family room was separated from their open kitchen by a step. Rigel was allowed in the family room but not the kitchen. So long as he kept his hind feet in the family room, he was legal. He stretched his little body as far into the kitchen as possible, when he smelled food, but kept his back feet in the family room. Sometimes he barked in frustration, but always kept his hind feet in legal territory.

"Don't you sass me!" Norma's mother snapped in mock anger. She was a practical woman who had grown up on a farm in Nevada. Animals were to do work or be eaten. Pets were a luxury.   But she loved Rigel.

As Rigel grew, he continued to keep his feet in the family room. Within a year his large body stretched half way into the kitchen, his hind feet never leaving the family room. This made a comical picture. He never forgot the lesson from his puppy days.

Norma's father was an easy- going Scotsman. The one time he spoke harshly to me was when I was trimming Rigel's toenails. I cut too deep and drew blood. Rigel yelped in pain. "Be careful with what you are doing!" her dad snapped. I was hurting his friend.

Norma and I began our medical internships at Highland General Hospital in Oakland, California on July 1, 1971.

County hospitals are often built in depressed, crime- ridden areas of the city. This is because real estate is cheaper.

Norma lived in a small house across the street from the hospital. As her protection she brought Rigel. Rigel, who slept next to her at night, was a deep sleeper. When Norma heard a noise, she shook Rigel awake.

One time, Norma looked across the street and saw a curious sight. A man was standing on top of a car. Down on the street she spotted the reason. Rigel, standing at the base of the car, had cornered man who had strayed into her yard.

During her year of internship Norma's house was never robbed, probably because of Rigel. And who knows? Maybe he saved her life.

Toward the end of internship Norma and I took a vacation in Oregon, taking Rigel with us.

While we were driving back to California, we stopped, and Norma called home. When she got back into the car her skin was ashen and she was trembling. Without saying anything, she resumed driving. After a few minutes she spoke. "My father is dead." Now I could see tearing in her eyes. "He went out to coach the Little League team. It was the first time since his heart attack. He collapsed on the field. They took him to the Emergency Room, but they couldn't bring him back." She didn't take her eyes off the road. Then she sobbed. "My father is dead. My mother said "Don't hurry. There is nothing you can do now."

When we reached the house, a neighbor lady opened the door. Neighbors had arrived to give their support and condolences. Norma's stoic mother came and hugged Norma. Her face betrayed almost no emotion. But then she saw Rigel. "If that dog begins looking for Norm, I don't know what I will do." her voice beginning to crack.

Rigel, smiling and wagging his tail, began running from room to room looking for his friend. But his friend was no more. Her mother began weeping.

Rigel made it to fourteen, old for a dog, especially a big dog. His joints were giving out and he seemed to be in constant pain. He was weak. His health was rapidly declining. He may have had cancer. "Maybe we should have him put to sleep." said Norma's mom, glancing at the dog lying on the family room floor. She loved Rigel because her husband had loved him, and maybe she thought there was a part of her late husband in the dog. But she didn't want the animal to suffer.

Rigel looked up and wagged his tail to show that he was OK. "You know what we are talking about." the woman said gently as she looked at the dog.

One day when I was away at a meeting, I called home. "Rigel died today." said Norma. He just went outside and lay down under a tree and passed away. We are taking him to one of those animal places where they will dispose of the body. He had a good life." I began crying and I could hear Norma crying at the other end.

Our next dog was a pedigreed golden lab which we bought when we moved to Virginia. He was our only purebred dog. He was registered as "Schmitt's Magic Mist". We called him Magic. Magic was the alpha male of his litter and therefore was stubborn and rebellious. He sometimes ran away and refused to come when we called him. He came back when he was good and ready.

But Magic was a great retriever. One Sunday morning we were startled to see a pile of newspapers on our porch. Magic had retrieved every Sunday paper in the neighborhood.

Magic reached the ripe old age of 14 and his health, primarily his joints, declined. It became difficult for him to walk.

We went on summer vacation, leaving Magic in a kennel. When we returned, we picked him up at the kennel. He was lying on the floor, unable to stand. When he saw me, he wagged his tail.

At home he lay on the family room floor, whining in pain. I knew he was near the end. His suffering needed to be ended. I decided that it would be better if Magic died at his home than in a vet's office.

I searched for something that would provide a painless death. A patient had given me a bottle of 80 proof whiskey. Whiskey makes humans drunk, but enough can stop breathing.

I mixed some whiskey with milk than offered it to Magic. He listlessly licked the brew up. I gave him some more. He seemed relaxed and was no longer crying in pain. Perhaps he was getting drunk and mellow and dreaming about chasing squirrels and rabbits. I poured some more whiskey into the dog's mouth. He swallowed it without choking. This I repeated several more times, then waited. After an hour, Magic's respirations stopped.

I wrapped Magic's body in a white sheet and buried him in a wooded area of our lot. I meant to plant a dogwood tree over his grave as a monument to him, but never got around to it. But I did cover his grave with bricks, so the raccoons wouldn't dig it up.

A few years later we sold the house to move to a house on the lake. The buyers called with an unusual request. "Our dog has just died. We would like permission to bury her on the property before we take possession." the woman asked.

"Of course, you can." replied Norma. "Our dog Magic is already buried there."

"I feel better now. Dixie will be buried next to another beloved pet." the woman said with a quaver in her voice.

The next day a woman, a man, and a little girl drove up in a car. They carried a small box. I watched the man dig a grave next to Magic's and inter the box. The man and girl were silent, but the woman was crying loudly. Perhaps the dog had been hers before she got married.

Now Magic would have a friend beside him. That was better than a dogwood.

As Norma and I watched Happy run around the dog park we were like proud parents. Packs of dogs ran together, sometimes chasing the dog that had a toy in his mouth. Happy loved this keep away game. Although he was not as fast as some of the big dogs, he could turn on a dime and outmaneuver them. We were reminded of the days when our boys were in Little League. When our son, Brian, caught a fly and ended the baseball game we were thrilled. When Happy outran the other dogs, we were likewise excited.

Happy was found starving and cold in rural Virginia. We guessed that his fear of loud noises and deformed feet disqualified him as a hunting dog, and he was let out to die.

"Happy, when we got you, you had worms, and kennel cough, and you were afraid of men. You didn't even know what stairs were. They kept you outside in the cold. You were afraid of loud noises. But now you are healthy and happy." Norma says conversationally.

Happy responds by putting his head on her lap.

We have come to look upon Happy like we would look upon a traumatized child that had come from an abusive family. He represents the suffering animals and people in the World. We may not be able help all of them, but at least we can make his life better.

One afternoon I noticed a man sitting in my Waiting Room crying. Ms. Stanberry, my nurse, seeing his distress, took him into her office and took his blood pressure. "Please see this man as soon as possible." she said as she dropped the chart in my box. The complaint written on the chart was "Back Pain."

The sobbing man was about 60. His name was Joseph Lombardo. He was trim, almost skinny. His hair was jet black and his skin was light brown.

Mr. Lombardo looked at me to see if I was listening.
"My brother died. He had lung cancer. He smoked. He coughed
up blood six months ago and the cancer went to his brain and he
died last week." I nodded.

"And my dog Fred died." He sighed, his voice cracked, and
unable to go on he began crying again. After a minute, he took a
breath and continued. "Fred was a pug. He was seven years
old. He started bleeding, all of a sudden, and the vet couldn't
save him.

I have a sailboat. I take disabled veterans sailing. But it got too
cold. So, I stopped taking people out. Fred loves to go out in the
boat. Something told me that Fred wasn't going to live very long.
So, I took Fred out in the rain. He stood on the bow with his fur
blowing in the wind. He loved it! But then he died.

My brother and I weren't very close. I saw Fred every day. Fred
loved me. I was never sure about my brother. Should I feel guilty
that Fred's death bothers me more than my brother's?"

"No. Dog or no dog, you were closer to Fred than to your brother.
You need not feel ashamed." I said. "To be honest, I like dogs
better than a lot of people I know."

The man relaxed. He reached into his pocket and pulled out his
cell phone. "Look at this."

He showed me a picture of a green field. At the edge of the field
was woods. "Now look at the next picture." It was the same
field, the same woods, but at the very edge of the woods was a
small white dog. It was a pug-nosed bull dog. "See that, see the
dog?"

"Yes, I see it. It is a dog. Is that Fred?"

"Yes, that is Fred. Look at the next picture." In the next picture I saw the same field and woods, but the face was gone. "See the dog is gone." Mr. Lombardo remarked. Now look at the next picture I took a few minutes later." The bulldog had returned.

"That's Fred again?"

"Yes, that is Fred."

"It's nice that you have pictures to remember Fred by. I bet you have better pictures. When were these pictures taken?

"Doctor Schmitt, these pictures were taken **after** Fred died.

CHAPTER 15

THE ADMIRAL'S BOTTOM

The knocking on the examination room door had been going on for five minutes before I answered it.

I was doing a physical on a Navy pilot during my Navy reserve weekend in Norfolk. The examinations of pilots are especially thorough. If a pilot is not in perfect health, the plane can crash, killing the pilot and people on the ground. Moreover, I was not a flight surgeon. Flight surgeons have special training in the health of pilots. I was allowed to examine the pilot, because our flight surgeon was sick today. On a later day a flight surgeon would review my patient's record and certify my work as correct. I wanted to do a thorough exam.

"Just a minute!" I shouted at the door. But the knocking persisted. Finally. I finished my exam. "You are fine Lieutenant." I told the muscular young man sitting on my examination table. I opened the door expecting to see a patient, or an enlisted person.

Standing in the doorway angrily glaring at me was my commanding officer, Commander Marcelino, a small Filipino man. Cdr. Marcelino was a bit chubby. He exceeded Navy weight standards. This trait had blocked his promotion to the rank of captain. Standing next to him looking at me sternly was Lieutenant Commander Harrison, his Executive Officer. a tall, gangly, woman who dwarfed her boss. The couple reminded me of the cartoon characters, Mutt and Jeff. I didn't know it at the time, but their presence marked the most serious attack on my competence as a physician that would occur in my naval career.

Cdr. Marcelino was holding a piece of paper. It looked like an official memo. From their demeanor I surmised that I had done something wrong, terribly wrong.

What could I have done? Had I again made a remark that offended someone?

Six months earlier while performing a pelvic exam on an enlisted woman I cracked.

"Is this woman an officer or an enlisted person? We warm up the speculum for officers."

Running the cold. stainless steel speculum in warm water before it was inserted made the exam less uncomfortable. In fact, I warmed up the speculum for everyone. My teasing remark was just meant to add a little humor to the awkward procedure and put the patient at ease. But one patient took me seriously, and I had to answer the question from my commander "What do you mean by warming the speculum for officers, but not enlisted women?"

I explained that I warmed the speculum for all women, regardless of their rank. I was an equal opportunity speculum warmer.

Or had I missed some important physical finding that resulted in harm to a patient? From their posture it seemed that something terrible had happened. Had a patient died!?

Now the commander was again standing in my doorway glaring at me. I stared on the form in his hand, trying to read the upside - down writing.

"What?" was my only response.

Commander Marcelino and Lt. Cdr. Harrison looked at each other as if they were trying to decide who would break the bad news. Finally, the woman spoke.

"The Admiral said your finger was too big to do a rectal exam."

One month earlier on my drill weekend I took care of an admiral. The admiral complained of muscle aches, had a low – grade fever, and had burning when he urinated. He was a tall, handsome man with grey hair. He was resplendent in his dress uniform with gold braids on the sleeves and a chest full of medals. I performed a physical exam and had some blood drawn for testing and ordered a urinalysis. "Please take a seat in the Waiting Room….s sir." I stammered. "When the lab c..comes back we will know more." I found taking care of such a high-ranking officer unnerving.

Thirty minutes later the admiral's aide came back. He was a crewcut young lieutenant with a gold lanyard on his shoulder. "Is the lab work back yet he asked?"

"No." I replied.

The aide retreated back to the Waiting Room.

Twenty minutes passed. The aide returned. "The admiral is getting tired of waiting." the lieutenant said.

The lab results were still not back. The admiral was annoyed.

I was tempted to let the admiral leave. The labs were probably normal. But what if they weren't normal and the admiral had something serious going on? I might have trouble getting him back for treatment.

"I would rather be known as the naval reservist who made the admiral wait, than the reservist who let the admiral leave with a life- threatening problem, and have him die." I thought.

"I am sorry. The labs should be back any minute. I will let you know when they get back." I told the frustrated aide.

Ten minutes later the admiral's labs were reported. His white blood count was slightly elevated, and he had some white blood cells in his urine. I worried that he might have a prostate infection. Prostatitis can be serious, and even fatal. It is treated with several weeks of antibiotics. To make the diagnosis I would need to do a rectal exam.

The admiral was already annoyed, but good medical care dictated that I check his prostate.

As a favor to important people we are tempted to cut corners and not go by the book. There is a litany of medical stories about important people who have died because of this practice, Michael Jackson, to name one, and Prince to name another.

"I'm not going to let the admiral die because I cut corners." I thought resolutely.

I called the admiral back into my office.

"I need to do a rectal exam. I need to check your prostate, sir." I told the angry senior officer. He hesitated for a moment, then sighed and pulled down his trousers and bent over. I inserted my gloved finger and felt for the walnut sized gland at the front of the rectum. The prostate was large and boggy feeling. This could mean that he had a prostate infection.

"Sir, you may have an infection. I will put you on Bactrim. That is an antibiotic that kills organisms that infect the urine and prostate. You can fill the prescription at our pharmacy."

The red- faced admiral stormed out carrying the prescription.

And now my competence was being attacked with a formal complaint that I had caused the admiral pain and suffering by violating his bottom with an overly large index finger.

Ironically, he was a rear admiral.

Recently the quality of medical care rendered in naval hospitals had come under intense scrutiny. This was largely because of the notorious Billig scandal.

Dr Billig was a cardiovascular surgeon hired by Bethesda Naval hospital. It was discovered that Dr Billig was blind in one eye. Normally, this would disqualify him for military service. But the Navy was so anxious to get a cardiovascular surgeon, that this condition was waived, and Billig was allowed into the Navy.

Soon Dr. Billig's competence as a surgeon came into question. The death rate of his patients was high and some of these deaths could be related to his eye problem. Without depth perception his surgery was sloppy. Billig was court martialed and convicted of murder and spent time in prison. Eventually his conviction was overturned. Several high- ranking officers, including admirals, were court martialed and demoted because of their role in Billig's recruitment.

The Billig Case resulted in a revamping of the process of credentialing and determining competence of military physicians. Now the Navy administration was paranoid about complaints of clinical incompetence. The admiral's complaint was taken even more seriously now than it might have been at another time.

I had four weeks to rebut the admiral's charge. I used science in my defense.

The size of the index finger increases with the size of the individual owning the finger. The diameter of the rectum also increases with the size of the individual.

The admiral was six feet one inch tall and I was six feet one half inch tall. We were about the same size.

As part of my research I did a rectal exam on myself. My K Y jelly coated index finger was inserted into my rectum with a minimum of resistance and little pain. Certain conditions increase the diameter of the fingers. Rheumatoid arthritis increases the size of the joints, but I didn't have arthritis, and my fingers were normal.

I searched the medical literature for some formula that correlated the individual's height with the diameter of his index finger and his rectum.

One time I heard an admiral described as a "tight assed bastard." I wondered if this were a physical trait of all admirals. I decided not to use this information in my report.

I performed thousands of rectal exams in my medical career of several decades. I was not aware of a complaint about the size of my right index finger. Certainly, in Navy records, I had never had a prior complaint.

I had seen many more patients, tens of thousands to be exact, at the Veterans Administration hospital where I worked. The quality of patient care is monitored by a department "Quality Management" that keeps records on all complaints.

 I had Quality Management review their files to see if there had ever been a complaint about the size of my index finger and the performance of a rectal exam. An overworked secretary reviewed records for a week. To my relief, I had not had a single complaint, but I wasn't done.

"Has there ever been a complaint that ANY provider had an overly large finger for rectal exams?" I asked, curiously. The secretary sighed, winced, glared at me, and replied. "Well, OK."

 All the thousands of complaints by patients seen in the hospital were reviewed. It took another two weeks. Two secretaries got overtime for this tedious project. The result was "One".

In the history of the Hunter Holmes McGuire Veterans' Administration Medical Center there had been only a single complaint, one, about one provider's performance of a rectal. It was a female nurse practitioner. She was a heavy woman. Maybe her fingers were a bit fat. Soon after that complaint she retired. Probably a coincidence.

Finally, I analyzed my technique of doing a rectal. I used lubricating jelly with every patient. Certainly, I used jelly with the admiral. Although this was not intentional, I tended to use more jelly with important people, such as admirals. This was largely a subconscious trait -.the higher the rank the more jelly.

In the special case of the admiral's rectal exam on the prior drill weekend there was some tension. The admiral was upset over being made to wait. This, combined with his high rank, made me nervous.

It was likely that my finger trembled more than usual when I inserted it into an orifice belonging to a VIP. This high frequency vertical oscillation might have produced discomfort.

With this material I completed my report which was submitted on time with a cover letter typed on Navy letterhead. I illustrated the report with multicolored graphs relating the height of the doctor to the size of his index finger, and the size of the patient to the diameter of his rectum, and then correlating the size of the finger and the size of the rectum. There also was graph plotting the coefficient of friction of a gloved finger against the amount of rectal jelly.

I waited anxiously for an official response.

But I heard nothing more about the admiral's bottom.

CHAPTER 16

GROSS NATIONAL HAPPINESS

"It looks like the Sierra Nevada Mountains with prayer flags!" I shouted into my cell phone. I was talking to my wife Norma who was in the US over 10 thousand miles away. On both sides of me were familiar mountain peaks, like those in the California Sierra Nevada range where I hiked.

But what was different was the line of flags strung on a rope directly above me. They were blue and green and red and yellow and brown and fluttered in the breeze. Each time a flag fluttered it sent a prayer to Heaven.

I was in Bhutan, a Buddhist country north of India, to teach medicine and practice medicine.

I sometime tell people that Bhutan was the most Christian country that I have visited. At this point a puzzled listener counters me. "Wait a minute, isn't Bhutan a Buddhist country?"

Indeed, it is.

I was brought up as a Christian. The Jesus that I knew was a pacifist. "Turn the other cheek." is part of Christ's teaching. Although many Christians are nonviolent, in Bhutan it is national policy. The Buddhist belief is that all life is sacred and not to be violated. Bhutan doesn't even have an army. If it is attacked, it will be defended by India, its big sister to the south.

The king of Bhutan has stated that what is important is "Gross National Happiness", not the "Gross National Product".

Crimes of violence are almost nonexistent. They try to avoid eating animals, and even have the meatless months of January and June. The key element of Buddhism is getting karma. Karma is derived from performing good acts. If one accumulates enough karma, he may be reincarnated at a higher level, or even attain Nirvana (Heaven).

But beyond that, the Buddhism of Bhutan has an eerie resemblance to a major Christian sect, Catholicism.

There are monks and nuns. In the monasteries are statues of holy figures such as Buddha and other religious figures reminiscent of statues of the Virgin Mary and saints seen in Catholic churches. Repetitive chants asking God's blessing are part of both religions. "Hail Mary...." in the Catholic church, and "Om Mani Padme Om" in Bhutanese Buddhism.

Both religions have prayer beads and holy water. Bhutan is a mountainous country with many streams. In many places, prayer wheels are turned by streams. Each time the wheel turns a prayer goes to heaven. The water that passes through a prayer wheel is holy. People are seen by streams filling jars with this precious substance. When a person enters a Bhutanese monastery, he dips his fingers in holy water, just as he does when he goes into a Catholic church.

The Ministry of Health, was located in Thimpu, the capital.

One night the Minister of Health took some of the western health workers out to dinner in the Numgay Heritage Resort, an upscale hotel and restaurant that caters to westerners.

At the table sitting with me were an emergency medicine physician from California, a psychiatrist who had volunteered for two years, an orthopedist from New York, a gynecologist from Idaho, and a physical therapist. The physical therapist had recently achieved notoriety because she had been bitten by one of the many stray dogs in Thimpu.

Sitting at the middle of the long table was the Minister of Health for Bhutan. He was a middle-aged man who looked scholarly in his black-rimmed glasses. He was clad in the traditional "gho", a costume that resembles a bathrobe.

"I want to thank you all for coming to Bhutan. You are not only helping our people, but in addition you are educating our health care workers."

The waiters came in with trays of food. The national dish of Bhutan is the chile. Perhaps this is because the chile grows well in the mountainous climate. Many dishes incorporate the chile.

The minister glanced at the waiters, then continued his speech. "Bhutan does not today have a medical school, but soon we will have a school. And when we do, we hope some of you will come back and teach." He smiled at us.

Then something on the table caught his eye. A fly was fitting around the table. He spoke.

"It can transmit disease by contaminating the food. I want to kill it." He took a breath.

"But the Buddhist part of me says that all life is sacred and should not be killed. I am conflicted. The physician part of my brain tells me that the fly should be killed." He thought for another moment, then, sighed and turned away from the fly.

I spent most of my time seeing patients in the clinic on the first floor of the hospital. The language of Bhutan is called "Dzonka". When a patient or his relative spoke English, I drafted him to be my interpreter until another person who spoke English came along.

Standard medical tests often could not be done because of problems with equipment. Pancreatitis is inflammation of the pancreas that can cause abdominal pain. The diagnosis is usually made by finding elevation of enzyme tests, such as amylase, that measure function of the pancreas. These tests sometimes could not be performed because the lab ran out of chemicals, which were imported from India and other places.

But the ultrasound machine, which studies organs by bouncing sound off them, was still working. The diagnosis was made by studying the pancreas with ultrasound to look for swelling and inflammation.

Ultrasound was used in Bhutan to help diagnose many conditions for which it would not be used in America. You must use whatever is working.

When I walked to work, I noticed red spots on the sidewalk. I wondered if someone was coughing up blood, perhaps somebody with tuberculosis or someone with an ulcer who was vomiting blood. But there were many spots on the sidewalks. There couldn't be that many people with ulcers and tuberculosis. In the hospital I saw signs that said. "Please No Spitting."

What did these signs mean?

One day I saw a patient who solved the mystery. He was a large man with an acne-scared face. He was dressed in a gho.

When he smiled, I recoiled in horror.

His teeth were red, like a vampire who had just fed on a human victim. He reached into the pouch that was hanging from his waist. He pulled out a brown nut which was wrapped in a green leaf. This was betel nut or "doma." The betel nut is commonly used Asia as a stimulant. Chewing the nut gives a high, something like that of cocaine. Its red juice was reputed to cleanse the body of worms, stimulate sexual passion, and do many other things. The downside was that chewing the nut caused cancer of the mouth, larynx, and esophagus.

"I have stomach pain." was another middle-aged man's complaint. He pointed to the middle of his abdomen.

"Does eating make it better?"

"Yes."

I thought he might have a stomach ulcer. I decided to get an upper gastrointestinal X-ray. This involved taking an X-ray after the patient had swallowed barium, to image the gastrointestinal tract. I had to explain to the radiologist what I wanted.

"Oh, you mean a barium meal." He replied

There was no ulcer, but in the intestine, there was an unexpected finding. The column of barium was interrupted by the shape of a roundworm that occupied 6 inches or more of the intestine. The patient's abdominal pain was due to the worm.

"You have a worm. That is causing your stomach pain. i will give you a medication to flush the worm out of your body."

"Will it kill the worm?"

"Yes, probably."

"If I kill a living creature it will take my karma. I don't want to lose karma. All life is sacred."

I thought about the dilemma.

The roundworm was life, just as my patient was. The worm was making the man sick, and it could take his life. This would take away the worm's karma. If the worm was killed, its karma would be preserved, and it would achieve Nirvana or be reincarnated.

I needed to come up with a way of preserving the worm's karma and my patient's karma.

"I will kill the worm, not you. It will take my karma not yours. And by saving you from the worm, the worm will not lose karma." He thought for a moment. He realized the logic of what I said. "I will let **you** kill the worm."

I wrote him a prescription for mebendazole, a medication that kills intestinal worms. When the patient returned from the pharmacy with the pill, I placed it in his mouth. I wanted there to be no doubt that I was the one executing the worm.

All night I heard the constant sound of dogs barking in front of the building. In Buddhist Bhutan stray dogs were not euthanized. They were allowed to run free. They wandered everywhere. I heard that an American physical therapist had been badly bitten by a stray dog.

Timpu is built on mountains. I walked to work down a steep hill. Of to the left, just a few minutes down the hill was the National Chorten. This was a large white building that housed sacred artifacts including the bones of Buddhist saints. A monk sat at the entrance begging. The penitent scattered seeds for the hundreds of pigeons that fluttered about.

An endless line of people walked around the Chorten in a clockwise fashion. Many if the worshipers held prayer wheels which they turned in a clockwise manner. Some chanted "Om Mani Padmi Hom." the sacred chant to the gods. Every cycle of the wheel, every orbit of the Chorten, every chant, increased the karma of the individual, and took him closer to Nirvana.

When you left the Guest House you walked down a dirt road to a large street. Across the street was a brick wall. If you walked around the wall, or got brave and just climbed over it, you found yourself in residential area of small houses. Prayer flags fluttered in front of the houses and children played in front of them. After walking a few hundred feet you came upon a large hotel, the Numgay Heritage Resort. After work, I walked over there and ordered a rum and diet Coke from the bar. The diet Coke, which was imported from India, cost more that the rum, which was fermented in Bhutan.

It was during one of my many visits to the bar that I made an important discovery. While I drank my rum, I watched the TV.

One evening I watched the National Geographic Channel. The episode was about dinosaurs. Just as the waitress brought my drink, a picture of a tyrannosaurus flashed onto the screen. The young woman stopped and stared at the screen. "What is that sir?" For a moment she forgot her job of providing my drink. "It is a dinosaur."

"Where do these animals live?"

"They lived a long time ago. There aren't any now. They are from long ago."

Her curiosity was satisfied. The woman put the drink on the table.

I realized something that I should have known long ago. Regardless of how menial someone's job, she has a need to learn and a fascination with the Universe. I never forgot this.

There was an elevator in the New Hospital, but it didn't work. To get to the Inpatient Medicine Service on the fourth floor you took the stairs.

One morning, as I began the climb from the lobby carrying my laptop, I noticed a Buddhist nun beside me struggling up the stairs. She was about fifty and wearing rimless eyeglasses. She had the short -cropped hair of a monk and the same saffron robes, but the softness of her facial features betrayed the fact that she was a woman. The nun, who was breathing heavily, was carrying a cloth bag that was laden with food and books. "I will take this." I said and grabbed her bag with my right hand. At the top of the stairs I handed her bag back to the smiling woman.

In Buddhist thinking, by helping this holy person, I was increasing my karma, and would receive a reward.

The following Wednesday was a Buddhist holiday.

I decided to spend the day climbing up to the giant statue of Buddha that overlooks Thimpu. An asphalt road wound back and forth up the hill to the Buddha. After an hour of walking I still had not caught sight of the Buddha. It was further away than I thought.

To my right I saw a dirt road. Down the road walked two young woman, wearing the kira, the traditional dress for women. The kira consisted of a rectangular piece of cloth wrapped about the body to make an ankle-length garment..

Behind the women walked three monks.

"Where does this road go?" I asked the women.

"It is a shortcut to the Buddha."

A short cut? That was for me.

I started up the dirt road. Soon it became apparent that it wasn't much of a shortcut. The recent rains had turned the dirt road to mud. The road climbed up to a series of ridges. To make things worse, garbage had been dumped from the ridge down the side of the mountain. I struggled through the mud, holding my "Lonely Planet Guide to Bhutan" in my left hand.

On the ridge above me I could see several women looking down watching my progress.

I felt pain in the middle finger of my right hand. I had cut it on a piece of broken glass, and it was bleeding. The people above me immediately noticed that I was having trouble. My finger was a red flag. Two little boys aged about 8 came running down to me. One of the boys took my book from me and the other took my right hand and helped me up to the ridge. On the ridge were several women and two teenage boys on bikes. One of the women bandaged my bloody finger with a piece of white cloth. The older boys said something to the little boys, and they all left.

I started my climb up the slippery hill to the next ridge. In some places my feet sunk into mud up to my ankles. Up ahead loomed the next ridge, maybe only thirty feet away. A minute later I was nearing the top.

Suddenly a little hand came down from the ridge and took my left hand. It was one of the little boys. Another boy came running down to me. He took my book. On the ridge were their leaders, the boys on bikes, who smiled at me. When I was safely atop the ridge the boys again disappeared.

The lower part of my body was covered in mud. I started up the next ridge. As I neared the top, once again a boy came down and relieved me of my book and took a hand. At the top, another boy grabbed my hand and pulled me on to level ground. When I looked back at the ridge the boys were gone.

Several more times, as I neared the top of a ridge, I was greeted by two small hands.

I began climbing the next hill wondering when I would reach the Buddha. As I neared the top of the hill, I could see rubble and construction equipment. I was almost there. The two little boys scampered down the hill. Each boy took one of my arms and pulled me onto the top of the hill.

The hill was cluttered with piles of bricks, sand, backhoes, dump trucks and a steam roller. Towering above this, sitting on a base was a three- story high golden figure of a Buddha.

But I wasn't there yet. To reach the base you had to negotiate a field of puddles and mud. The boys walked in front of me showing me the safest path to the statue. I reached the base, the final goal of my long trek.

As I stared up at the Buddha, I thought of the boys who had helped me today. I turned and smiled at them.

"Thank you for what you did today." I said. Then I reached into my pocket to get some money to give them. But the boys didn't want a reward. One of them waved the money away.

"Good to meet you sir." he said. Then they all turned and walked away.

I looked down the hill to the city of Thimpu spread out before me. Thimpu is nestled along a river that gradually climbs up a mountain valley. Here and there prayer flags fluttered.

I turned again and looked up at the face of the Buddha smiling placidly at me.

I thought about the events of the day. By undergoing the ordeal of climbing the mountain to reach the Buddha, I was increasing my karma, my virtue. The boys were there to help me accomplish this pilgrimage.

This was my reward for helping the nun climb the stairs in the hospital.

CHAPTER 17
WEST AFRICA TRAINING CRUISE

As looked around the plane I wondered if I had misread my orders.

It was 2004 and I was flying from Paris to Dakar, the capital of Senegal, West Africa.

It was to be my last overseas mission in the United States Navy.

West Africa Training Cruise was a joint exercise between the United States Navy and its allies in West Africa. Out in the Atlantic, the countries were conducting naval exercises. In Senegal combined units of the Senegalese Army and United States Navy would conduct humanitarian medical care

My instructions read. "There are terrorists in Africa, and American military may be a target. Avoid looking military. Dress casually in civilian clothes and don't have a military haircut." I followed the orders. My hair was shaggy, almost unkempt, but almost every other man in the plane had a crewcut. If terrorists used hair style to identify their victims, I would be the only man on the plane to survive.

The next day we were picked up at our hotel and loaded on to a bus and taken to an army base. We were housed in two wooden barracks near an airstrip, one for men and one for women. Each bed was covered with a mosquito net.

That night I took a walk to the air strip. As I neared a hanger, I saw the tip of a cigarette glowing in the dark. "Bon Nuit." I said.

"Bon Nuit" was the reply from the darkness. It was a Senegalese soldier gripping his rifle. The Americans were surrounded by soldiers to protect them from terrorists.

Power was provided to the barracks by a small generator which was guarded 24 hours a day. At night, a guard slept on top of the generator. Early one morning a large snake slithered out from under the generator where it had taken up residence. It was a black mamba, one of the deadliest snakes in Africa. In addition to having deadly venom, the mamba can travel 7 miles an hour, faster than some men can run. When the guard saw the snake, he stood up on top of the generator and began screaming. Another soldier ran up and dispatched the snake with the butt of his rifle.

That night we all gathered in the nearby dining hall to hear a speaker. It was a Navy commander from Force Security to tell us about the terrorist risk. For security reasons I will not give his real name. He reminded me of Colonel Flag, the security officer from the TV series "Mash". I will call him Commander Flagstone.

Commander Flagstone was a short, nervous, man with dark hair and a small, neatly trimmed mustache. His sunglasses showed a distinctive blue tint. He was wearing the Forest Camouflage uniform, which is green to blend in in tropical forests. On his left chest were 4 rows of ribbons. He was standing upright, almost at a brace, like a midshipman at the Naval Academy. Suddenly he relaxed and winked at me. Perhaps this was to put a naval reservist at ease.

"Terrorists are operating in West Africa." he began. "This man has sworn that he will kill you. Study his picture carefully." The commander then distributed a picture of the man who wanted to murder us. It was a black man with short hair, wearing dark glasses. He was wearing a long black robe. Around his neck was the red and white scarf that I had seen worn by members of the Khmer Rouge, the Cambodian communists.

The next morning, dressed in our Forest Camouflage uniforms, we were loaded onto two buses. Behind the buses came two trucks that were loaded with medical equipment. At the head of the caravan was a truck loaded with Senegalese soldiers.

I was in Bus Number 1.

Bus 2 was prone to mechanical problems and frequently broke down. When this happened, the convoy stopped. The Senegalese troops jumped out of their truck holding their rifles and set up a perimeter around the vehicles until the bus was repaired.

Our destination was the village of Pout. Just before we reached the village Commander Flagstone stepped out from behind a tree and motioned us to stop. "We have reconnoitered the village. There are no terrorists around. It is secure!" he shouted, pointing toward the village. We glanced at the village. When we looked back, the commander had disappeared.

Senegal is located in the Sehal, the dry area south of the Sahara Desert. Many crops won't grow in this harsh area. One hardy crop is millet. The millet seed is ground into flower for the baking of bread. Senegal is on the Atlantic Ocean. Villagers who live near the ocean catch fish which can be eaten or sold to the Japanese sushi merchants.

A Fleet Hospital is a movable medical unit. The trucks contained medications, dental chairs, ophthalmology equipment, surgical equipment and a myriad of other things. In the village the trucks were unloaded by a human chain which passed things along into the buildings, most of which seemed to me to be school houses.

Winding from the hospital and through the village, perhaps a quarter mile long was a line of people. They had been waiting all night to see the American doctors.

We quickly set up our practice at the desks in the school. Beside me were a gastroenterologist, a nurse practitioner, a general internist, and several nurses, and there were interpreters. Senegal is part of former French West Africa, so French is spoken commonly. The most common native dialect is Wolof. My interpreter was a Senegalese soldier.

A woman with a baby walked in. The baby was pulling at his ears. The young woman put the baby on her lap while I examined him. His ear drums were red. I diagnosed otitis media, an infection of the inner ear and prescribed an antibiotic and a decongestant. "Va a la pharmacy" I told the woman, proud that I could speak a little French, and pointed to the pharmacy.

The woman leaned forward and balanced her baby on her back, then quickly pulled the back of her dress forward to create a kind of bag to hold the baby. I was amazed at her dexterity. "How often do Senegalese women drop their babies." I asked my interpreter. He said something to the woman, and she smiled and replied in Wolof. "Never" was the answer.

Suddenly, I heard a noise above me. I looked up and saw a large tail hanging from the wooden rafters. It was a huge iguana. "He keeps this place free of vermin, like rats." I thought. "Good for him."

My next patient was a woman dressed in a bright yellow dress. A matching yellow bandana was tied around her head like "Aunt Jemima" on the cereal boxes. She pulled up her dress and pointed to her right leg which was three time the size of the left one. Around the leg was a kind of bracelet consisting of small cloth sacks. These were charms to cure her. In the US I would think about things like a deep vein thrombosis, a blood clot, causing the swelling. But this was Africa. Her leg was large, like the leg of an elephant. She could have a condition called elephantiasis.

A mosquito bites the victim and transmits a tiny worm called a "microfilaria." The worm evolves in the body and localizes to the lymph nodes in the groin and other places. Scar tissue blocks the return of lymph from the legs and the leg swells.

I wasn't certain what the woman had. She could have a clot in her leg. To diagnose this would require an ultrasound test, which wasn't available in this rural area. We had medication which would treat the filarial worm, but nothing to treat a blood clot. I decided to treat the worm, hoping for the best. In the Developing World, you often have to play the odds, and take your chances.

An old man complained of decreased vision in his right eye. When I examined the eye, I was startled. A worm was crawling across the eyeball. This was Loa Loa.

A fly, called the Chrysops fly, bites the victim. The worm is transferred to the human host. The microfilaria worm evolves into a larger worm which crawls around the body, including in the eye.

I put a drop of pontocaine, a topical anesthetic in the man's eye. Then I took a pair of tweezers, and gingerly removed the worm from the grateful patient's eye.

Another microfilaria is transmitted by a large black fly, the Buffalo fly. The organism can destroy the eye and cause a condition called "river blindness."

Many patients came to the clinic complaining of fever, meaning they felt they had a fever. Fever is a sign of many infections, most importantly malaria which infects 500 million Africans annually. Other common symptoms were cough and eye irritation from smoky fires.

The problem was, we had no way of taking a temperature. The organizers of this high profile, expensive, mission, that cost the American taxpayer millions of dollars, had neglected to include a thermometer in the equipment. To correct this oversight, someone was sent to Dakar to buy a thermometer.

Some patients were malnourished, even starving.

 Our own nutritional needs were satisfied by MREs (Meals Ready to Eat), which were plastic covered boxes of food. We were instructed not to give food to the natives for fear that it might start a riot.

 Off in Eye Clinic sun glasses were being dispensed to protect from the tropical sun. In Dental Clinic teeth were being pulled and people were being shown how to brush.

At the end of each day, a report was sent to Washington on how many patients we had seen, how many pairs of glasses were dispensed, and how many teeth were pulled.

When the patients had been seen, we loaded the trucks and filed into our buses for the trip back to our base. As we drove along the road the people cheered us, some of them holding up their recently extracted teeth.

The next day we went to the village of Kayar. As we neared the village, Commander Flagstone again stepped out from behind a tree. "We have reconnoitered the village. It is safe. The ground is flat and sandy, easy to walk on. There are no terrorists." he said as he looked up at the bus windows. And then, as before, he was gone. He was like a phantom.

Kayar is a fishing village. The people prosper selling their fish to the Japanese sushi merchants. In Pout, where people had trouble getting enough to eat, they were thin, and the incidence of hypertension and diabetes were low. But in Kayar, where they people were better fed, diabetes and high blood pressure were significant problems. This was the price they payed, for prosperity.

A young woman complained of abdominal swelling. Her abdomen was distended. Girdling her waist was a ring of small bags. These contained charms to ward off the evil that was attacking her stomach. I lay her down on a table and percussed her abdomen. It made the hollow sound of an air- filled loop of intestine. I rolled her over on her side and percussed her abdomen again. The hollow sound had moved from the middle of her abdomen to the top. Her intestine had floated up. This was a sign that the woman's abdominal cavity was filled with fluid. She had ascites.

 Blood is carried from the intestines to the liver through a large vein, the hepatic portal vein. The blood passes through the liver in a series of channels, then flows into another vein, the hepatic vein which carries it toward the heart. Scarring of the liver, called cirrhosis, blocks the liver channels, and the pressure in the portal vein increases. The higher pressure causes fluid to leak out into the abdomen, causing ascites. Alcoholism can cause cirrhosis, but Senegal was a Muslim country where the people, especially the women, didn't drink alcohol. Viral hepatitis such as Hep B and C can destroy the liver. To diagnose this would require a blood test which we didn't have.

Then I remembered that I was in Africa. "Schistosomiasis can cause ascites." In schistosomiasis, the swimming parasite breaks through the skin of the unsuspecting wader. It makes its way to the liver where it lays eggs. These eggs clog up the liver channels where they block the flow of blood, and the increased pressure causes fluid to leak from the portal veins into the abdomen.

When it boiled down it, here in a village in Sub -Saharan Africa, the only disease that I had a shot at treating was schistosomiasis. "You may have an infection in your liver. I will give you a medication." I told the anxious woman, and my translator spoke to her in Wolof. I wrote a prescription for Biltricide, a medication which kills schistosomes.

"Va a la pharmacy, sil vou plais." I told the woman, who was now smiling.

That afternoon a young woman brought her 8- year old child to the medical clinic. It looked like the boy had a boil on his right shin. When I examined the crater, I saw something wiggling inside. It was part of a worm. The boy had Guinea Worm.

The larva of the Guinea Worm lives in a water flea. When the water is drunk, the larva enters the human host. It evolves into a large worm which crawls around the body. Eventually the worm breaks through the skin.

I used a scalpel to enlarge to wound. Then I took a pencil and slowly wound the white worm up like I was winding up a piece of string. I covered the wound with a bandage and prescribed an anti-parasite medication.

Ten per cent of all the disease in the World is due to impure water.

If you want to provide medical care in a country, you must learn about its culture.

North Africa is largely Muslim, but many of the people also adhere to traditional medical beliefs, such as the belief that disease is caused by evil spirits and charms can ward off disease. One of the most unusual traditional medicine treatments was described to me by a colleague who had worked in Mali, a country to the east of Senegal.

Two children were sick. One had severe birth defects, and the other had whooping cough.

A cow was slaughtered, and its stomach opened. The soup of partially digested grass and intestinal juices was removed and poured on the two sick boys who were lying on the ground.

The boy with whooping cough was cured. The boy with birth defects died.

Mosques rise above the flat, arid, landscape of Senegal. Islam forbids a male physician to examine a woman's genitals, or even discuss sexual behavior.

A young girl presented with a complaint of vaginal discharge. When the western physician asked questions about the girl's sex life, and even raised the question of sexual abuse by her father, the Senegalese interpreter refused to translate.

Another Muslim tradition is that of "alms giving." It is perfectly fine to ask for someone else's possession.

On the weekend our group went on a game safari.

Senegal has attempted to restore its game herds for tourists. We drove across the savannah in several trucks. We saw a herd of cape buffalo cooling off under a shade tree. In another place we saw an oryx, a horned antelope.

Our guide was a young woman who noticed that I was carrying my rain coat.

"I need that rain coat. I really need that coat. I need it." She asked

"I need the coat too."

"But I really need it." she persisted

"See that woman over there." I pointed to the red- haired woman in the next truck. It was Master Chief Cafoncelli, a "no nonsense" woman who was the senior enlisted person on the trip. "If I give you my raincoat, she will beat the Hell out of me!" Realizing that she had reached an impasse, the guide finally gave up.

The horizon was dominated by baobab trees. The branches of these strange trees look like roots reaching for the sky. The baobab is therefore sometimes known as the "upside down tree."

Our safari stopped at one of these trees. Scattered among the roots were human bones. These were the bones of the singers and the story tellers, known as "griotes".

The story was, that for many years it was the tradition to put the bones of the griotes among the roots if the baobab tree. A law was passed forbidding this practice, and Senegal was stricken by a severe drought. This was regarded as a sign from Heaven that the law was wrong. The law was rescinded, and the drought came to an end.

On Monday we went to another village. A young woman carrying a baby on her back sat down and talked to my interpreter. "She says she has no milk."

For milk to be produced, a woman must have a normal pituitary gland. If after the baby is born there is no milk, it can mean that the pituitary gland has been damaged at the time of delivery. As an endocrinologist, my interest was piqued.

When the woman picked up the baby and handed it to me, I recognized the real problem. The baby seemed to weigh nothing. The skin of its face was wrinkled like the face of a very old man. Its head and eyes seemed oversized compared to its tiny body. It looked like a tiny gargoyle. The baby was dying of starvation.

"This child needs to be hospitalized!" I shouted at the nearby Senegalese Army physician. Another soldier took the baby from me. I was reassured that the infant would be cared for.

Two young American women occasionally worked with us as translators. They were Born- Again Christian missionaries.

"How can you proselytize in a Muslim country?" I asked Miss Watson, a trim woman with long curly blond hair. "Trying to convert a Muslim to another faith is a crime punishable by death." She gave a calm smile and replied. "Dr. Schmitt, we don't proselytize, we just tell them that God loves them."

I heard a story about the two Christian women.

They lived in a Senegalese village. One night, men broke into their house to rob it. They injured one of the women.

The villagers were outraged at this violation of their hospitality law. They hunted the criminals down and carried them out in the Atlantic in the fishing boats. Then weights were tied to the men and they were thrown overboard to drown.

When Miss Watson was asked about the story, she didn't deny it, nor did she express any Christian sympathy for the criminals.

"God is watching over us." she said with sincerity.

I was slated to retire from the Navy on July 29. I needed to do something special for my colleagues. I wanted to provide something precious, something that was hard to come by in this hot desert, something that was unbelievably pleasurable. I decided to get them ice cream.

Senegalese men were allowed onto our compound to sell things, like masks and other works of art. "Could you get me ice cream enough for 40 people?" I asked one of the men. "Money is no object."

"No problem."

I gave the man a hundred American dollars. I was exhausted from two weeks of intense work in a harsh environment. I went into my barracks and lay down under my mosquito net and slept. I dreamed of root beer floats and banana splits. Sometime later I felt someone shaking my shoulder. It was one of the optometrists. "Thanks for the ice cream. Why don't you have some with us?"

Anything is possible anywhere, even getting ice cream in the desert, if you have enough money.

The following day was my last day in the Navy. At the afternoon Retreat ceremony, when the American flag was taken down, I was called up and it was handed to me.

My interpreter gave me a patch from his uniform, and I gave him the flashlight from my medical bag.

The flag, with the patch on top of, it, resides in my curio cabinet in a place of honor

CHAPTER 18

THINGS WRITTEN ON THE WALL OF A CALL ROOM

On the fourth floor of the McGuire Veterans Hospital is the Inpatient Medical Service. In addition to patient rooms and nurses' stations there are rooms where physicians sit and discuss patients. Posted on the walls are a variety of messages, including the ubiquitous takeout menu of Yen Ching, the nearby Chinese restaurant. On a whiteboard in the Team 4 room, over the years, different anonymous writers have recorded the words of patients and staff. Some are recorded here.

"Everyone has to go through DTS (delirium tremens) some time in his life." (from a patient)

"By the look of his stool he is constipated." (from a nurse)

"If I don't leave the hospital today, I will divorce my wife." (from a patient)

"I'm not here to raise hell. I'm here to get well." (patient)

"Can't I stay here one more night? I'm having my bankcard overnighted here." (patient)

"That prison -chiseled body and hair that can't be tamed." (doctor describing a patient)

"I listened to him pee and by the sound of it he peed 200-300cc." (nurse commenting on a patient)

"Patient may benefit from rectal stimulation." (from a surgeon)

"There is no link between diabetes and diet. That is a white myth like, Larry Bird and Colorado." (from a patient)

160

The following story was told to me by a colleague.

A young woman was being seen for her first clinic visit after leaving the Army.

"Thank you for your service." my friend began. "What can I do for you?"

The young woman thought for a moment, then began talking.

"I want get on birth control pills."

"Fine."

"I want to get my thyroid tested. My mother has thyroid problems."

"Fine, I can do that."

"And I want to get and EGD."

"What? "

"An EGD. I want to get an EGD."

EGD' stands for 'Esophagogastroduodenoscopy. It is an invasive procedure in which a tube in inserted through the mouth into the stomach. My colleague was perplexed by this unusual request from a young woman.

"Do you have any problem with your stomach?"

"No."

"Have you ever vomited up blood?"

"No."

"Have you ever passed tarry black stool. Sometimes that means that your stomach is bleeding. Blood turns black in the intestinal tract."

"No, my stool is fine."

"Well, have you ever had an EGD before?"

"No, never."

"Well, an EGD is a procedure used to diagnose problems in the upper intestinal tract. They start an IV, and give you a sedative. They will spray the back of your throat to make it numb. Then they insert this long black tube. They run it down into your esophagus, the swallowing tube." He paused for a second to see if she was understanding what he said. She nodded.
"And" he continued "it goes into your stomach, and they look for bleeding ulcers and cancer. Then they push it into the first part of the small intestine, the duodenum. Sometimes they see ulcers there. If they see something suspicious, they may do a biopsy.

But you tell me you have never had an ulcer. Sometimes there are complications from an EGD. The stomach can be perforated by the tube. This can cause a serious, even life- threatening infection. But you tell me you have never had any problems with your stomach. Why do you want and EGD?"

The young woman cleared her throat and spoke.

"I just want a High School Diploma!"   (She meant GED, a Graduation Equivalence Degree.)

Mr. Delbert Castle was one of the nicest patients that I ever had. Every Christmas he sent me a card thanking me for being his doctor. At Easter he set me another card. He volunteered in the hospital, bringing stray wheelchairs from the parking lot and other places back to the hospital.

When I saw him pushing a wheelchair, I thanked him for his service. He looked up and said "This hospital has been good to me. You have been good to me. I want to give back."

He was forty years old, of medium height and slightly stocky. His brown hair was graying at the temples. He always wore slacks, a white dress shirt, and a blue cap with the words "Operation Desert Storm" embossed on it.

Mr. Castle's medical problems were relatively minor. He had mild hypertension, and elevated cholesterol. Both of these problems had, at one time, been controlled with diet and exercise, but, when he gained weight, they required medication.

Whenever I made a change in his treatment he smiled sweetly and said. "Yes doctor. Whatever you say." He was the perfect patient.

His profession was listed as "student", but he seemed a bit old for a student and he never discussed any courses that he was taking. During an office visit I brought up subject of his occupation.

"And you are a student? What are you studying?" The innocent smile on his face turned to a frown for a second then it reappeared.

"I don't go to school anymore. That was years ago."

"What do you do for a living now?"

"I got some money from my mother before she died. I am getting some interest on that."

"Yes?"

"And I rob stores."

He seemed perfectly comfortable with this last revelation. In fact, he was eager to tell me about the shady part of his life. "Dr. Schmitt, you're not mad at me for telling you that are you?"

"No, not mad. Just a little disappointed."

"I never hurt anybody. I just take what the stores can afford to lose. They have insurance. On a rainy day I walk in in my raincoat. Then it is easy. I just slip an item like a dress shirt or a fishing reel under my trench coat. Fishing reels are worth a lot of money. I like sporting goods stores. Doc, you aren't mad at me are you.?"

I shook my head, amazed at my patient's story.

"And when I am in the store, I case it. I can look at the doors and the alarms and decide if it is worth breaking into at night. Then I go back at night with my friend Alvin and we break in and clean house.

Alvin owns a wrecking yard. People go there for car parts. But he likes to rob stores. It excites him, or so he says. Then, I make a lot of money. I never hurt anybody. I don't bring a gun. And Doc, I contribute to causes like homeless children and dogs. I am a sentimental slob at heart." He laughed for a minute. "Doc, I am a kind of Robin Hood. Really."

The principles of patient confidentiality forbade me from revealing my patient's criminal behavior. He wasn't endangering the life of anyone. He was just confiding in me because he trusted me.

"You are committing a crime. You will wind up in jail. I like you. I don't want you to go to jail. You don't carry a gun, but security guards do. Some night you might be caught and get shot, and I will read about you in the papers."

"I am OK, Doc. Thank you. But I am pretty cagy. I case the store pretty carefully. I take a lot of time. If the caper isn't right, I don't do it. I read a lot about crime. Thank you for being my doctor. By the way I am out of my cholesterol medicine." He shook my hand and left the room. I was moved by his trust.

 Delbert Castle missed his next four appointments with me. I wondered if he had moved away.

But one day he returned to my office. He was eager to tell me what had happened.

"Doc, you were right. I finally got caught. I am out on bail. My brother put up the money."

"What happened?"

"I robbed a sporting goods store with Alvin. It was at 2AM. The store was empty. We took lots of fishing reels and poles. And we took some hunting rifles and shells. Normally I would never steal weapons. I like animals. It was Alvin's idea. He said rifles could be fenced for a lot of money. When we left the store, it was pitch black. We packed everything into the back of Alvin's truck and drove away. It looked like the perfect crime."

"But what happened?'

"Well a cop who was checking out a drunk who was lying on the sidewalk happened to notice Alvin's pickup truck driving by. It was late at night and the cop had OCD (obsessive compulsive disorder). He also had a good memory. The next morning, when they found that the sporting goods store had been robbed, the cop remembered Alvin's truck, and damn it, he even remembered the license."

"Yes, a smart cop."

"But Alvin had taken something like that into account. He had planned for everything. He knew he might be spotted. So, he switched his license plate with a license from another car, one of the pieces of junk in his wrecking yard. Alvin had read that that was the way to fool the cops."

"Go on. But you still got caught?"

"Yes. Well, Alvin switched the license plate with one from another car that he owned!"

I am an expert on capsaicin. This is partly because my wife, Norma, is a bird nut.

The bane of the bird lover's existence is the squirrel. Squirrels are forever breaking into bird feeders to get the seeds. They find ingenious ways to get to the seeds. They shimmy up poles. the skinniest poles, to bird feeders. They make impossible leaps from trees to the tops of feeders that hold their prize, birdseed.

I imagine bevies of scientists in laboratories writing on chalkboards their strategies for eliminating the squirrel threat.

Capsaicin is found in chili peppers. It interacts with Substance P in the tissues. Substance P transmits pain in mammals, but not birds. When birds eat birdseed laced with capsaicin, they are fine. But the mouths of squirrels burn, and they avoid the seeds.

Capsaicin is used to treat pain in humans. It initially stimulates Substance P release, causing acute pain. Then Substance P in nerves is used up, and pain relief occurs. The net effect is that capsaicin relieves pain.

The rash of deaths from narcotics has spurred use of alternate pain relievers such as capsaicin. But there can be complications.

A 50- year old man had chronic low back pain. His physician prescribed capsaicin cream which the patient applied twice a day to his lower back.

The man was driving on the freeway on a hot day in a convertible with the top down, and he began sweating. The sweat ran down his back and mixed with capsaicin cream. The goopy mixture then continued down to his buttocks and ran between the cheeks to the rectum. The rectum is well-supplied with nerve endings that are loaded with Substance P.

The man noted excruciating pain in his rectal area. His car began swerving back and forth.

A highway patrolman noted the erratic driving, and pursued the vehicle with his siren blaring.

The patient was in so much pain that he ignored the siren. Then he remembered that he had a bottle of water in his car. He pulled over and poured the water onto his buttocks. The patrolman called for backup and warily approached the vehicle with his gun drawn.

"Get out of the car!" he demanded.

"It's OK. I am having a problem. My butt is on fire!" screamed the patient.

When the patrolman looked inside and saw what was happening, he holstered his gun. "I will help you!" he shouted, and went back to his patrol car to fetch his own water bottle. He ran back to the patient's vehicle and poured the water onto the patient's bottom.

The backup cop arrived. He too cautiously approached the car with his gun drawn.

When he realized the situation, he too fetched his water bottle and began pouring his water on the hapless rear end.

Eventually the fire was quenched, and the grateful patient thanked the cops and drove away.

CHAPTER 19

THE GRAND MOSQUE AT MANAMA

"Move slowly. Hold your hands out in front of you, sir."

The voice came from a soldier standing behind a wall of sandbags forty feet in front of me. Standing behind him were 3 other soldiers wearing camouflage uniforms. They held rifles which, while not pointed directly at me, were pointed in my direction. In the sand fort I noticed a machine gun.

 It was February of 2004. I was beginning an assignment in the Navy Clinic in Manama, the capital of Bahrain.

 I was in civilian clothes. We were ordered not to be seen in public in uniform in this Arab country. I carried my uniform in a clothing bag in my right hand

I walked across the "No Man's Land" and stepped through a metal detector. A soldier inspected my bag. Another checked my ID. Suddenly, he snapped to attention. "Welcome aboard sir." The other soldiers behind the barricade followed his example and saluted me.

Once inside the small one -story clinic I put on my uniform and began seeing patients. Why we were ordered not to wear the uniform in public is uncertain. Perhaps it was to avoid the impression that Bahrain was occupied by American invaders.

Every morning I walked several blocks from my hotel to the clinic. On a hanger I carried my uniform. As I passed curious Arabs, I believed they all know that I was an American serviceman.

Bahrain is a liberal Arab country. Some women wore traditional burkas, which covered their entire bodies, including their heads.

Others were bare headed. Likewise, some men wore western clothing such as slacks and tee shirts. Others wore traditional robes.

One day I saw an ominous figure crossing the street in front of me. It was a bearded man. His head was covered with a cape and his body was covered with a white robe which went down to his knees. His legs were protected by white leggings. This was a Wahabi, a member of the sect to which Osama Bin Ladin belonged. Wahabis believe that Westerners should be driven from their land, using violence if necessary.

An alternative way of dealing with the uniform problem was to leave it in the clinic and put it on each morning when you got to work. One flight surgeon gradually deleted articles of clothing over time. First, he omitted the blouse and wore a tee shirt. After several weeks he omitted the khaki pants and wore his jeans. After another few weeks he excluded his black Florsheim shoes from his uniform, and walked around in his jogging shoes. No one seemed to care about this breech of uniform policy. Perhaps it was because the flight surgeon was "getting short", which meant that he would be leaving the Navy soon.

Manama is located on the north end of the island of Bahrain. On a clear day, when you look north, you see a dark shape above the horizon. It can't be a cloud because it never moves. It is the land mass of the largest peninsula in the world, Arabia. Arabia is the home of Muhammed.

Muslims believe that in the Seventh Century the angel Gabriel appeared to Muhammed and revealed the word of Allah, or God. Thus, was founded Islam, which within a century took over much of the known world. Islam dictated strict rules of behavior, including abstinence from alcohol and sexual purity.

Running from the island to Arabia is a causeway. Arabian men use this artery to get from Arabia to Bahrain where then can drink alcohol and hire prostitutes.

In 1990 Saddam Hussein, a brutal dictator, occupied Kuwait and threatened to attack Saudi Arabia. This would have given him control a major portion of the World's oil. The Coalition responded with Operation Desert Storm which expelled Iraq from Kuwait.

The attacks on 9/11 on the World Trade Center and Pentagon, were orchestrated by Al Kaida, Al Kaida had taken up residence in Afghanistan under the protection of the Taliban, another fundamentalist Muslim cult. Between Iraq and Afghanistan lay Iran, a hard- line Muslim country linked to terrorism. Reports that the totalitarian regime of Iraq had weapons of mass destruction resulted in Operation Iraqi Freedom, or the Second Gulf War, which led to the occupation of Iraq and the overthrow of Saddam Hussein.

The US Central Command, headquartered in Bahrain, coordinated military activities in Iraq and Afghanistan.

The Medical Clinic, was one of a complex of buildings. The sides of the buildings formed a wall. The only entrance into the compound was through the Command Post. Sophisticated electronic gear projected from the roofs of several of the buildings. Entrance to these buildings required a high level of security clearance. These were the areas where the top- secret planning of the Second Gulf War and the war in Afghanistan occurred.

The clinic was used by servicemen coming from and going to the combat zone. They were extremely concerned about what was placed in their records, especially things that related to mental stability.

One of my first patients was an Army sergeant who had returned from the Gulf. He was a compact little man of about 30. He wore the light- colored desert camouflage uniform and a broad brimmed campaign hat. He was accompanied by his wife, a tiny woman in a red dress.

"I want to find out what is wrong with me." the nervous man said. "I am having trouble sleeping sometimes. And sometimes my right leg tingles, and sometimes my left arm tingles. Once I dropped a cup that I was holding. My vision got blurry a few weeks ago. Sometimes I feel my heart pounding." His attentive wife rubbed his arm in sympathy as he spoke, the she looked at me. "And he breaks out into sweating." she added.

"Did you get blurry vision in one eye or both eyes?"

"Both of them." I knew that most serious disorders that affect the vision would not affect both eyes at the same time. Transient blurring of vision in both eyes could mean something less ominous, like a migraine.

I performed a physical exam, paying attention to the nervous system. I carefully examined he neck to see if the thyroid gland was enlarged. An overactive thyroid could produce a rapid heartbeat and agitation. His thyroid was normal.

"Your exam is totally normal." I told the sergeant. His wife smiled in relief.

"But what could it be?" asked the sergeant.

His symptoms were transient and could not be related to any one anatomical area or body system. Multiple sclerosis is a disease which attacks separate parts of the nervous system, causing symptoms that cannot be related to damage any single part of the nervous system. MS can cause inflammation of the optic nerve. But this would cause blurriness in only one eye, not both eyes as the sergeant described.

 The sergeant was stressed. He had seen Iraqi soldiers burned to death in their vehicles.   There was one diagnosis that best fit the symptoms, post- traumatic stress disorder, or PTSD. In 2004 there was considerably more stigma to this diagnosis than there is now. I searched my brain for another word.

"Anxiety." I replied. The sergeant grimaced.

"You are saying that it is all in my mind?"

"No, that is not what I said."

"You are saying that I am crazy?"

"No that is not what I am saying." The diagnosis of anxiety ran against the sergeant's idea of toughness, of being macho, of being a fighter. If I wrote this in his record, it might impact on his career.

"Shit! I want to see another doctor."

I quickly obliged the sergeant.

 It was unnerving to see soldiers who were carrying weapons, especially when they were angry.

"I hate Muslims. I just want to kill Muslims." said a patient. He was a chunky man in a camouflage uniform. His crewcut hair was so short that he seemed to almost be bald. He was about twenty-five and he wore brown rimmed glasses. Attached to his belt were several hand grenades. "I want to kill Arabs. I hate Muslims!" he repeated. as his voice increased to a shout. "My friend worked in the Pentagon and they killed him on 9/11." The young man paused, took a breath, then continued.

"I'm a Christian. Christianity is the true religion. My minister in church said Islam is an evil religion. Muslims are fake. I want to kill Arabs. I am a Christian." As he spoke, he fingered his belt near one of the grenades. His eyes were open wide, and his lips formed something between a grimace and a smile.

As part of his training he was taught that the Iraqi soldier was his enemy. He needed to be able to kill the enemy without hesitating. Shades of grey in making the split- second decision who you should shoot are eliminated. Thoughts that his enemy might not be totally evil and deserve killing would make him hesitate and spoil his aim and allow his enemy to kill him. This young man had, in a sense, been brain-washed. In addition, his Christian roots were feeding into his hatred of the Muslim.

 Beyond that, I wondered if he had a psychiatric problem, such as paranoia.

I fretted with how to deal with this young man. The rules of medical confidentiality dictated against my violating his trust and informing his commanding officer of his problems. And I didn't think that he was acutely homicidal. But I could be wrong.

"I think you need a rest." I told the young man. "I will put you SIQ, sick in quarters, for a month."

 "Sick in quarters" was convalescent leave. The soldier just didn't have to report for duty. There was no stigma associated with it.

"OK."

 Realizing that I wasn't going to write anything bad on his record or contact his commanding officer, his tense muscles relaxed.

174

"And one more thing. I would like to have you see a psychiatrist. There is no shame to this, he will help you. My wife is a psychiatrist. Is that OK?"

I wondered if putting the psychiatrist in the picture would be the deal breaker. But the young man just nodded weakly. There wasn't a psychiatrist on the base.

"I will send you to a psychiatrist out in the town. He is an Arab, probably a Muslim. Do you have any problem with that?" To my surprise he shook his head.

I wondered if hooking this man, who hated Muslims, up with a Muslim physician was a good idea. Maybe when he met a caring physician his loathing of Muslims would soften. But on the other hand, if his words about killing Muslims were real, he might kill the man with one of his grenades. To my relief the young man bonded with the Arab psychiatrist and improved and was sent back to duty.

Bahrain is an island in the Persian Gulf. At one time the major source it its wealth was the pearls that came from the oysters in its surrounding waters. Just when the market for pearls was going south, oil was discovered. Bahrain is the first island in the Persian Gulf where oil was found.

I was housed in the Gulf Hotel, a few blocks from the Central Command Headquarters. The hotel had nine restaurants. Each morning, at breakfast, I watched wealthy Arab sheiks in their finery sitting at the surrounding tables. This was probably the plushest hotel where I ever had stayed, but because Bahrain was only five hundred miles from Iraq, I was deemed to be in a combat zone and was receiving Combat Pay.

The birth of my first grandchild was imminent.

On February 18, I called Virginia. Bahrain was covered by a sandstorm that was blowing in from Arabia. The sand blocked out the sun. At 400 PM in the afternoon it looked like night. "We are in a sandstorm." I told my wife who answered the phone. "It is my first sandstorm."

"And we are having a snowstorm." Norma remarked. "And you are a grandfather. His name is Caleb. It's from the Bible."

Very near to my hotel was the Grand Mosque of Manama. It is the largest building in Bahrain. At the center is a huge white dome topped by a spire. Below the dome are three levels of arches. The entrance is a high arch. To the sides are two high minarets. At the top if each minaret is a room.

In previous days an imam climbed to the top of the minaret and called to prayer. Five times a day, at dawn, near midday, in late afternoon, at sunset, and at bedtime, the faithful were called to prayer from the highest point of the mosque.

"Allahu Akbar" (God is most great) "Allahu Akbar."   "Come to prayer. Come to success." .. Allah Akbar.......Allahu Akbar.......There is no god but Allah."

I used the dawn call to prayer as my "wakeup call."

As I studied the magnificent building, I wondered how the call to prayer was accomplished. Was this a recording from a radio that was placed on the top of the building, or did someone climb up there on a narrow stairwell and deliver the prayer?

One day, to satisfy my curiosity, I walked into the mosque. Before I went in, I removed my shoes. Women entered the mosque through a separate entrance with their heads covered.

Nearby I saw a library where several women sat.

I was met near the entrance by a bearded young man dressed in white. This was an imam, or Muslim priest.

"I have a question. When the call to prayer comes, do you climb all the way up to the top of the mosque and speak through a microphone, or do you just use a recording.

The young man smiled at my question. He was incredibly handsome. His eyes were blue, not brown and his facial features, highlighted by his beard, reminded me of the late actor Jeffry Hunter who played Jesus in the movie "The King of Kings." Yes, the imam reminded me of Jesus Christ. He touched my shoulder and motioned me toward the center of the huge room. He pointed to a microphone, suspended at the level of my shoulders.

"Look up."

A wire ran from the microphone up to the top of the dome "When I call to prayer I speak in here. And it comes out up there. It is in real time. And I don't have to climb up there." The young priest, happy to be able to answer my question, smiled, showing perfect white teeth. They looked like the pearls that Bahrain was famous for exporting.

"I have been in a mosque before, in Turkey, but I have never met an imam."

"Yes, Istanbul has many mosques. Are you a Christian?"

"Yes, I was raised as a Christian. But I am interested in all religions. Since 9/11 many people in America are afraid of Muslims."

"Did you know that Islam means 'peace', and "submission to the will of God."

"Yes."

"In the Qur'an all of the prophets of the Bible, Abraham, and Isaac, and Moses, and Jesus, are recognized as messengers of God. Mohammed is a messenger of God. The Qur'an is, in part, based on the Bible. Many of the traditions of Islam are mentioned in the Bible. For example, you took off your shoes before you walked into the mosque. In Exodus, God commands Moses 'Remove the sandals on your feet, for the place where you are standing is holy ground.'

Muslims are forbidden to eat pork. But the Bible forbids the eating of pork. Have you read the Old Testament?"

"Yes."

"In Leviticus it is forbidden to touch the carcass of a pig." At this point the young man grinned playfully. "Do you think this means that it is a sin to play football? A football is called a 'pigskin'."

I smiled at his whimsy.

"Our women cover their heads. But did you know in the New Testament it is said that it is disgraceful for a woman not to cover her head in places of public worship." I was amazed at his knowledge of the Bible.

"Christianity comes from Judaism, and Islam is derived from both of them. All three religions tell us to love each other and to love God. Some interpret the Bible and the Koran differently than others, and even corrupt their religions. In Christianity, the Catholics and Protestants killed each other over difference in their belief. In Islam, the Shiites broke off from the Sunnis after Mohammed died. They are both Muslims, but they kill each other for difference in their faith.

Do you believe that the God of Islam, the God of Judaism, the God of Christianity, which is the same God, the God of the

Universe, approves of killing for differences in interpretation of his teachings?"

"No. I don't." The young man's sonorous voice, his sparking eyes and his wisdom had practically hypnotized me. I was nearly in a trance.

"We live in a huge universe. The Earth is but a speck of dust. God is everywhere. On the Earth one tends to adopt the religion of where he is born." The imam paused and smiled at me. Then he resumed speaking.

"If you are born in India, you become a Hindu. If you are born in Israel, you become a Jew. If you are born in Brazil, you become a Christian. If you are born in Arabia, you become a Muslim. That is the way it goes. Do you think that the God of the billions of stars in the Universe, the God who loves you and me, holds it against you where you are born?" I shook my head. The young man continued.

"Islam and Christianity teach us the same thing, to love God and to love Man. Yes, people will misinterpret or intentionally corrupt religion to serve their own needs. And they will kill, such as occurred on 9/11. That will always happen. But what counts today is that I am a Muslim and you are a Christian and we are the same and we come from God and I love you."

I felt my eyes watering at the young man's speech. I couldn't think of what to say. I was nearly paralyzed. I wondered if there was some law against touching an imam.

"Thank you." These were the only words that I could manage.

I hugged the young man and he smiled and embraced me.

CHAPTER 20

TWO LETTERS

I could have gone to jail.

During my medical career I have received many letters. Often, they were first sent to my supervisors, such as the Hospital Director, then forwarded to me. Most of the letters have thanked me for my good care of the patient. I have been especially glad that these letters were seen by my boss. But, on rare occasions, I have gotten a negative letter that was critical of me.

The best and worst letters that have come to me were from the same patient.

In 2002 I became the primary care physician of Mr. James Bedford. His previous physician had retired from the VA.

Mr. Bedford was an African American man of about 50. He was tall and handsome and articulate. His thick glasses gave him an intellectual look. He reminded me of a college professor.

Mr. Bedford was being treated for endocarditis, an infection of the heart valve. The infection had spread from the heart to the bones of his spine. Each day a visiting nurse came to his home and administered antibiotics through a catheter that had been tunneled under his skin into a large vein. Mr. Bedford's arm veins had been destroyed by frequent use. When he needed blood work, I drew it from a vein in his groin. He tolerated this painful procedure stoically. When it was done, he smiled and thanked me.

"I am grateful for what you do for me. You are a great doctor." he said with a smile.

Mr. Bedford had two sources of pain. He had the back pain, and he also had painful ulcers of his legs. His pain was being treated with Percocet, a pain pill that was a combination of oxycodone, a narcotic, and acetaminophen (Tylenol).

In 2007 I received a manila envelope from the Hospital Director's office. It contained a letter from Mr. Bedford.

"Dr. James Schmitt is the best doctor in your hospital, the best doctor in Virginia. Patients sit in the waiting room talking about how wonderful he is. He is certified in four different boards, more than any doctor in your hospital. And he even makes house calls. He goes to poor countries like Honduras to save the lives of poor people. This man is a saint! We pray for him in my church every Sunday. It is a great privilege to have Dr. James Schmitt as my doctor."

Mr. Bedford's letter was accompanied by a note from the Hospital Director. "Thank you for all you do for our veterans." I was taken aback to receive such a glowing letter, a testament of confidence that had been relayed through my bosses. I put it aside, thinking that I might frame it and hang it in my office.

A few months later Mr. Bedford told me he needed to speak to me.

"My daughter was murdered by her boyfriend." said the anguished man. I gave him a hug of support and asked him if he needed any medication to help him with his stress. He declined.

I heard another rumor about the murder of a patient's daughter. I thought I was hearing about Bedford's daughter again, but, in fact, the daughters of two my patients had been murdered by their boyfriends. In both cases, the murderer was a convicted felon who had a gun.

At one clinic visit Mr. Bedford politely told me that his back and leg pain were worse. He grimaced as he spoke to me. "I will increase your pain meds." I said.

In order to monitor patients on controlled substances, including narcotics, amphetamines, and benzodiazepines, such as valium, periodic urine drug screens are performed as frequently as every month.

These tests serve two purposes.

First, they look for illegal substances such as cocaine and marijuana. Second, they look for the drug that the patient is taking. A patient taking large amounts of oxycodone, such as Mr. Bedford, would have oxycodone in his urine. Fentanyl, the most powerful narcotic, is not detectable in the urine.

A relatively common finding of drug abuse is a urine that is negative for oxycodone but positive for cocaine. This tells the physician that his patient is selling oxycodone or trading it for cocaine, and it is time to stop the narcotic.

But at this time, 2011, the oxycodone test was felt to be unreliable. It could be negative when the patient was taking his oxycodone. A story circulated around the hospital about a policeman who was wrongly accused of selling his oxycodone when his drug screen falsely indicated that he was not taking his oxycodone.

Sometimes, when I reviewed a patient's record, I found that he had no recent urine testing. Before I could renew his narcotic, I was mandated to screen his urine. Often, he had run out of his medication before he had the test.

Mr. Bedford never had illegal drugs in his urine, but sometimes his urine was negative for oxycodone. This was dismissed by me as being due to the uncertainties of the test and because I trusted him. What was important to me was that his urine was clean, there was no marijuana or cocaine in it.

In 2011 I went on a medical mission in Bhutan, a Buddhist country north of India. When Mr. Bedford came to get his monthly narcotic refill, he saw my colleague, Dr. Vinnekova. She ordered a urine drug screen. By this time the oxycodone screen was more reliable.

The test came back negative for any drugs including oxycodone. Dr. Vinnekova, a matter of fact Russian woman, was a more cautious, less trusting individual than I was. She immediately discontinued Mr. Bedford's oxycodone. He angrily protested.

"I was driving from New York to Richmond. I didn't want to be impaired. I did what Dr. Schmitt told me. I didn't take Percocet because I didn't want it to affect my driving."

When I returned from Bhutan, he reiterated his excuse. I wanted to help my old friend.

"Mr. Bedford, when did you get back from New York?" I asked

He thought for moment.

"June 27"

"And you hadn't taken Percocet when you were driving?"

"That's right."

"When you got home did you start taking Percocet again?"

"Yes, I did."

"Well you had a urine drug screen on July 2. If you had resumed Percocet on June 27 it would show up in your urine. And your urine was negative. The test suggests that you weren't taking your Percocet. That is why Dr. Vinnekova stopped your Percocet."

I noticed that Mr. Bedford was perspiring. He gave a nervous smile, then spoke.

"You see what was really going on was that my daughter was stealing the Percocet and trading it for cocaine. That was what was happening. But now I am going to lock it up. She won't get it anymore."

I was stunned. He had changed his story. The man that I had trusted, who had been my friend, had lied to me. Percocet was being diverted to a use other than control of his pain

"We will have to try other ways of controlling your pain. I have no choice but to stop the Percocet."

Percocet sells on the street for up to $80 a pill. By stopping his Percocet, I was wrecking a business that netted him thousands of dollars a month.

My patient frowned.

At about this time Mr. Bedford was admitted to the hospital with congestive heart failure. The Attending physician told him that she would give him Percocet only when he was in the hospital, but not when he was discharged. At this point the patient became angry and signed out "against medical advice." This proved that he did not want Percocet for his own personal pain relief, but to carry with him to sell.

My mental image of Mr. Bedford taking narcotics that I prescribed to relieve his leg and back pain disappeared. It was replaced by the picture of the medication that I prescribed for Bedford being sold to a college student. Then, in my mind's eye, the student died of a drug overdose.

I remembered Mrs. Evers, a woman who Army doctors placed on morphine and Percocet her chronic foot pain. Sometimes she brought her grandchild to the office with her. I blew up examination gloves to make a balloon for the cute little boy. Many years later Mrs. Evers informed me. "My grandson died of a narcotic overdose." Then she quickly added without a trace of emotion, "But I never abused narcotics."

I was no longer a reliever of pain, but a dispenser of death. I was determined to fix this problem.

On Thanksgiving I received a card from Mr. Bedford and his family.

"Thanksgiving is a time to be joyful for all that we have and thank God for his many blessings." read the card. When Christmas came around, I felt sorry for Mr. Bedford, who might not be able to buy presents for his family, because I had taken away his income from selling oxycodone.

Several months later I received a page at home. It was the Chief of Vascular Surgery.

"We are having a problem with Mr. Bedford, your patient. We have him on Percocet for the pain in his leg ulcer, but he keeps asking for higher doses. And we think he is intentionally making the ulcer worse, so he can get more narcotics. What should we do?" The vascular surgeons had restarted the Percocet despite my notation in Bedford's record that he was abusing the drug.

"We think he is selling it. Stop it right away!" was my terse reply.

A moment later my phone rang. It was Mr. Bedford. "What am I going to do about my pain!?" he demanded.

"You don't need narcotics for that little ulcer on your leg."

"But what about my back pain!?"

"If you have more pain go to the Emergency Room."

For a moment the line went quiet. Then Bedford spoke in a low voice.

"Doctor Schmitt I know where you live. Is this your address?" He read off my home address. "My lawyer wants to send you something. Is that your address?" I hung up the phone.

I never received a letter from his lawyer.

The next morning while, I was at work, something told me to google the name of James L. Bedford. Here it was.

"James L. Bedford is an inmate at Bland Correction Institute." the report began. "He has been sending an excessive number of legal briefs to the courts. These documents are felt to be frivolous. A judge has instructed Mr. Bedford that he can henceforth submit only one brief a month."

I calculated the time that Bedford had been incarcerated. It was a least 13 years. Then I recalled that he had once asked me to write a letter to a judge stating that he was free of illicit drugs. I assumed that this for some traffic violation. It was for something more serious. James Bedford had just been released from prison and he was on probation when he began coming to the VA hospital.

He was a convicted felon and he had bragged that he knew where I lived.

I called Norma at home. "This man is angry at me for stopping his narcotics. He is a convicted felon. He knows where we live. Be careful."

That evening when I arrived home the house was dark. The doors were locked with the dead bolts. I knocked several times.

186

There was no answer. I wondered what had happened to my wife.

"Is that you Jim?" a voice came from inside the house. When Norma had established who I was she opened the back door. She was hiding in the dark from Mr. Bedford.

For weeks after this episode, when I came in the front door of my house Norma asked, half seriously, "Is that you Mr. Bedford?"

I reviewed Mr. James Bedford's medical record carefully. He entered the VA medical system in 2002 with a diagnosis of "leg ulcers due to injecting drugs into the leg skin." This process is known as skin popping. A year after this he developed an infection of his heart valve called endocarditis. The organism in this infection was staphylococcus aureus, a common skin organism which had traveled to his heart and to his backbone.

Bedford began coming into the Emergency Room in the wee hours of the morning. He complained of back pain, and the exhausted Emergency Room physician usually gave him Percocet.

I made a point of telling every Emergency Room physician not to prescribe him Percocet. I documented it in his electronic medical record that he had a history of abusing and diverting narcotics. I was angry that Bedford had fooled me. I resolved that he was not going to get a single Percocet to sell.

One evening my home phone rang. It was Bedford. "I have read my medical record. You are the one who has stopped my Percocet!" he shouted. Then he hung up.

I was the only one blocking the flow of narcotics to this convicted felon. Drug related murders were common in Richmond. Sometimes gunshots were heard near the hospital. A patient had been murdered in the parking lot.

Would he try to eliminate me? As I walked in the dark to my car in the huge staff parking lot, I worried that Bedford was crouched behind a car with me in his rifle sight.

I wondered what else he might do.

A month later I received a certified letter. It was from the Virginia State Medical Board. They were investigating me.

James Bedford had filed a complaint. In the envelope was a letter that was neatly hand printed by Mr. Bedford. This second letter from him was quite different from his first one.

"Dr. James Schmitt is my doctor. Sometimes my urine drug screen is negative for Percocet. When my urine drug screen is negative for narcotics, Dr. Schmitt says this is OK. 'Just give me $150 and I will give you 180 Percocet.' I take the money out to his house and he orders the pills. Sometimes when I call his house he is not there, but his wife tells me just to bring the money over. That is not right. I am a veteran and I am not supposed to pay for my medications."

Bedford had reviewed his electronic medical record. He found that sometimes I prescribed Percocet when his urine was negative for oxycodone. He was now using this against me.

I almost admired his cleverness

"I would like to speak to you directly about the details of the matter." the letter from the State Board read. Please note that a report will be forwarded to the Board without benefit of your information if no response is received from you, and you may be the subject of disciplinary action."

Some physicians turn to the dark side of prescribing and give narcotics to patients without an exam. The drugs can be sold with a huge profit, so the patient is only too happy to pay the physician whatever he asks. Prescribing, with no questions asked sometimes results in death from overdoses. Physicians involved in this activity can lose their license, be imprisoned, and even have been convicted of murder.

Bedford's charges, if substantiated, would mean the end of my medical career, and I could be sentenced to prison. His path to narcotics would again be clear. He was angry that I ruined his lucrative business, but perhaps the main reason for his complaint was getting me out of the way.

What angered me the most was that he implicated my wife in this crime.

I called the nurse investigator and asked her to come to my office immediately. Two hours later a middle-aged, grey haired woman, wearing a lab coat, arrived.

I handed her a statement that I had written about James Bedford several months previously.

"This guy was out to ruin me. I ruined his business of selling narcotics. He was making thousands of dollars a month."

The woman thought for a moment. "Well I guess we don't have to suspend your medical license immediately. Is there any evidence in his record that he abused narcotics?"

"Yes," I showed her the note from years earlier that discussed his skin popping of drugs.

I explained why I had given Bedford Percocet when his urine drug screen was clear.

"You were just looking for dirty urine." the nurse replied sympathetically, beginning to understand what had occurred.

She interviewed our pharmacist about my drug prescribing habits. Then she sat down with me. She believed my story.

"Narcotic abuse Is an epidemic. More people die from drugs than from traffic accidents. The State Medical Board is overwhelmed by this problem. You need to protect your reputation and your family from people like this." She made some notes, then left.

I received a letter from the Board stating that no disciplinary action would occur. I could keep my medical license.

I was furious with Bedford. Then I thought about his life.

He was born into the ghetto that surrounds the VA hospital. He had become addicted to drugs. He was a convicted felon. One daughter was murdered by her boyfriend, leaving her child without a parent. Another daughter was a drug addict. Cocaine had wiped out half of his heart, and he had congestive heart failure.

Mr. Bedford's life had been set on this course at the time of birth. I began to pity him.

I had risked my career and my family's safety to prevent narcotics from hurting innocent people.

In 2013 James Bedford turned sixty-five and he was eligible for Medicare. He began seeing a vascular surgeon for his leg ulcer.

The surgeon resumed prescribing Percocet.

CHAPTER 21

THREE RED HERRINGS

Webster's dictionary defines a "red herring" as "something that draws attention from the central issue."

The term may have been derived from a practice of training hunting dogs by dragging a kippered herring to lead them on a false trail.

Red herrings sometimes happen in the practice of medicine. When they occur, they may distract the physician and the patient from the correct diagnosis and delay treatment.

Regina Cartridge was a 45-year old African American woman. Her beautiful tan face was framed by carefully braided hair that was now beginning to show a trace of gray.

 Mrs. Cartridge thought that her neck pain was just due leaning over her computer for eight hours every day. Despite her bipolar disorder, she had been able to hold down a job as an accountant. When she began getting shooting pains down her left arm she worried and went to her family practitioner.

 "You might have a pinched nerve in your neck." her primary care physician, a heavy-set grandmother, remarked. "To be safe we will get a neck X-ray."

The neck X-ray showed mild arthritis in the neck, not unusual for a 45- year old woman such as Ms. Cartridge.   What caught the attention of the radiologist was not in the neck, but above the neck. The neck film takes in the lower part of the skull. At the base of the skull is a bony semicircle, called the "sella turcica" or "Turkish saddle", so named because it resembles the saddle of the ancient Turks who conquered much of Europe. The sella contains the pituitary gland, the master gland that controls several other glands including the thyroid, adrenal, and sex glands. It also makes prolactin, a hormone necessary for lactation. Ms. Cartridge's pituitary was slightly enlarged. This could mean that there was a tumor of the pituitary gland.

An MRI (magnetic resonance imaging) of the pituitary gland was performed. An MRI shows the smallest details of the body. Ms. Cartridge's pituitary gland contained a small tumor. She was referred to an endocrinologist.

It was determined that her pituitary function was normal. The tumor was thought to be just an incidental finding or "incidentaloma". It was possible that the tumor could grow, and eventually affect the optic nerves that run next to the pituitary gland. To follow the course of the tumor the endocrinologist recommended that a prolactin level be obtained every year and an MRI be done every year.

The family physician's plan was to do the MRI annually. If the brain MRI showed that the tumor was growing into the visual tract, the next step would be to refer Ms. Cartridge to an ophthalmologist for formal visual testing

Within a few months Ms. Cartridge began getting headaches and transient loss of vision.

She reported these alarming symptoms to her family physician. Worried that the pituitary tumor was enlarging, an MRI of the brain was ordered. Her family doctor was following the algorithm of the endocrinologist. An MRI was scheduled for the following week. However, Ms. Cartridge forgot the appointment and missed the MRI. Her vision improved, and she decided that she did not need the MRI.

A few weeks later her headaches and decreased vision returned. She visited an emergency room. "I have a pituitary tumor. I want an MRI." she demanded. However, the wait was over an hour and she left without being seen. Her bipolar disorder made her impatient.

She noticed that her night vision was impaired. She stopped driving at night. She returned to her family physician. "We need to get an MRI we need to check that pituitary tumor." the physician said. Her plan was to get the MRI first, then get Ms. Cartridge's vision tested. An MRI was scheduled for two days later. Ms. Cartridge promised to keep the appointment, but again she missed her appointment. "I forgot the appointment. I have trouble concentrating. I just forgot. I will be OK. I think I have migraine."

She failed to keep another appointment for a brain MRI. Her mental disorder made it difficult for her to keep appointments, especially where a wait was required. Several months later, while visiting her invalid mother, Ms. Cartridge noticed an alarming phenomenon. She could no longer read newsprint, and could barely read the headlines.

She went to a local ophthalmologist who checked her visual acuity. Her vision was only 20/200 in both eyes. This meant that what normal people could see from 200 feet away, she could see only when she was 20 feet away.

Ms. Cartridge was legally blind. When he looked at the back of her eye through an ophthalmoscope, the physician was alarmed. The optic nerve, a white disc on a pink background, was dying.

Based on his patient's history of a pituitary tumor, he believed that the tumor was growing outward and destroying the nerves that ran next to it. He sent her to a nearby emergency room with a quickly scribbled note. "She is going blind. This is probably due to her pituitary tumor. She needs a brain MRI."

"I demand a brain MRI!" the agitated woman screamed at the Emergency Room physician. I have a pituitary tumor." The frightened Emergency Room physician scheduled a brain MRI which was performed few days later.

The MRI was normal. There was no pituitary tumor growing into her optic nerves and causing blindness. What was making Regina Cartridge blind?

Another cause of optic atrophy and blindness, especially in obese women who have hypertension is a condition called 'pseudotumor cerebri". In this condition, increase in the pressure in the brain occurs. It can cause headaches and gradually destroy the optic nerves. To diagnose this condition, you measure the spinal fluid pressure.

A spinal tap was performed on Ms. Cartridge. A needle was inserted between the vertebrae at the level of the top of the hips. Clear spinal fluid ran into the needle and into a plastic manometer. The level of the fluid climbed and climbed to the level of 60 cm of water. A normal pressure is below 20 cm. Her cerebrospinal fluid pressure was elevated, destroying her optic nerves and causing her blindness.

To lower the pressure additional fluid was removed. This was repeated several days in a row. Then a shunt was placed in Leanna Cartridge's brain to carry the extra fluid out of her brain, and tunneled under her skin to a vein in her neck. But it was too late. Her spinal fluid pressure had been elevated too long. The best she could do was count fingers held in front of her face.

Her blindness could have been prevented if the cause had been recognized earlier.

The diagnosis of a pituitary tumor directed Ms. Cartridge and her physician that a critical test was the brain MRI, the best test to monitor the tumor. The pituitary tumor was a red herring that diverted attention from other causes and delayed making the correct diagnosis.

As soon as my pager went off, I knew it was the Emergency Room calling me about an admission. I was doing a two- week stint as Attending Physician on the Inpatient Medical Wards.

"We have a patient down here with hypophosphatemic paralysis." the resident physician related. "The patient, Mr. Robert Hammond, is a 28 -year old man who woke up with paralysis of both arms. He can't move his arms and his serum phosphate level is 0.8 mg/ dL. "

Hypophosphatemia means that the serum level of phosphate is low. Phosphate is a substance in the body which is necessary for production of energy. A normal serum phosphate is 2.5-4.5 mg/ dL." Mr. Hammond's phosphate level was critically low. A phosphate of this level can lead to muscle weakness and breakdown which can impair ability to breathe, and fatal cardiac rhythm problems.

The resident was Dr. Shariff, a dark young woman who had grown up in Pakistan. She and I scurried down to the Emergency Room.

Lying in bed 9 was a black-haired young man in a hospital gown.

"I am Dr. Schmitt, and this is Dr. Shariff." I began. "I have heard that you can't move your arms."

"Yes, I woke up this morning and I couldn't move them."

"Did you injure them. Did you have a fall?" asked Dr. Shariff.

"No."

"Have you been eating regularly?" she continued. "Starvation will lower our phosphate."

"I have been on a diet. Some days I fast."

"Do you drink alcohol?"

"I drank a six pack yesterday." We knew that alcoholism can lead to low phosphate.

"Can you raise your arms?"

He made the attempt. His shoulders moved a bit, but otherwise he was paralyzed. We completed the exam. Then I spoke to the young man.

"Well your phosphate is low. That is a salt in your blood. Yours is very low. We will need to replace it. We are giving you some in your IV. Do you have any questions?"

Mr. Hammond shook his head. We debated whether to admit him to the Intensive Care unit to monitor his breathing. We knew that low phosphate can paralyze breathing. We decided that with exception of his paralyzed arms, he was stable and could be admitted to a regular medical ward with close observation.

As I drove home that night I reflected on the case of Mr. Hammond. Both of his arms were paralyzed by low phosphate. This had to be unusual. This was a unique ca-se. I could write it up and gain some notoriety in the medical literature.

Then I had another thought. Maybe the low phosphate was a red herring. Maybe there was another cause of the paralysis. I called the hospital and talked to the resident on call. "Maybe the low phosphate is a red herring. Get a Neurology consult."

A few hours later a neurologist examined Mr. Hammond.

"I think he has bilateral brachial plexitis." read the neurologist's note. The brachial plexus is a bunch of nerves that runs from the spinal cord to the arms. It controls movement of the hands and arms. Brachial plexitis is an injury to these nerve bundles. I had never before heard of this condition.

I googled it.

Yes, here it was. It is called the Parsonage- Turner syndrome. It was initially described by Doctors Parsonage and Turner. It had to be vanishingly rare, especially when both arms were involved. Maybe I could still write a paper.

The following morning, we examined Mr. Hammond again. His weakness was unchanged. "I am having chest pain." he remarked.

Dr. Shariff and I scratched our heads wondering if we had missed something. Our patient had chest pain and weakness in his arms. "Could he have a dissecting aneurism?" asked Dr. Shariff.

A dissecting aneurism is a weakness in the wall of the aorta that can spread to the arteries nourishing the brain and heart and causes strokes and heart attacks. This is what killed the actor, John Ritter. It might even involve the nerves that control the arms. To look for an aneurism we order a CAT scan of the chest.

An hour later the radiologist paged us with his report. "Your patient doesn't have a dissecting aneurism, but..." The radiologist paused, perhaps for sarcastic effect, then he continued "both of his shoulders are dislocated."

Both of his shoulders were dislocated? How could this have been missed?

Our patient had a chest X-ray. This had been read as normal. We looked at the chest X-ray. The lungs and heart were normal.

At the very edge of the X-ray field were the shoulders. Both shoulders were out of their sockets. This was missed by the radiologist. The X-ray was read electronically by a radiologist in California. We joked that the man was distracted because he was in a hot tub with a pretty girl.

When we went back and examined Mr. Hammond again, it was obvious that both of his shoulders were dislocated. And now he remembered that this had happened before. He evidently had been born with some laxity of the ligaments that made his shoulder joint unstable.

We called the orthopedic surgeons who came and popped the shoulders back into place.

We were chagrined that we had missed the true cause of our patient's weakness.

The emergency physician's report that the patient was suffering from paralysis due to low phosphate had led us down a path of medical error. The low phosphate was a **red herring.** The failure of the radiologist in California to see the dislocated shoulders compounded the problem.

Mr. Hammond made a full recovery.

"Mr. Oliver Keesee is a 60 year- old salesman who noted that he has been more unsteady for the last few days. He has fallen twice." Dr. Laura Webster, the Emergency Room Resident, began her presentation. "He carries the diagnosis of multiple sclerosis. He has had falls before, but not this frequently. He was scheduled to have a spinal tap to check the fluid for multiple sclerosis, but he failed to keep his appointment."

I was Attending Physician in our Emergency Room and the resident was required to consult with the attending physician on every case.

I knew the multiple sclerosis was a disease in which the myelin that coats the nerves was damaged. Nerves are the wires that carry information from the body to the brain and from the brain to the body. Damage to the wiring can cause weakness and numbness in widely scattered areas in no definite anatomic distribution. A patient could have blindness in his left eye, tingling in his left arm, and weakness in his right leg. The most common form of multiple sclerosis was the relapsing- remitting form in which the patient has an exacerbation, then gets better for a while.

I walked over to the patient who was in bed 4. Mr. Keesee was of medium build. His full head of hair was white as snow, as were his bushy eyebrows.

"Did you hit your head when you fell?" I asked.

'No." This was an important question. A head injury would mandate an emergency CAT scan of the head to look for blood on the brain. But there was no history of this. I examined Mr. Keesee. Both of his legs were weak. I moved his big toes up and down. "Is this up or is it down?" I asked. He grimaced.

"I can't tell."

I knew that sensation from the body traveled up the spinal cord to the brain through pathways at the back of the spinal cord, called the posterior columns. The fact that my patient could not tell the position of his toes suggested that the posterior columns were damaged.

"You have been having these spells of weakness that come and go for years?"

"Yes, they think I have multiple sclerosis. I was supposed to get a spinal tap to check my protein in the fluid. But I chickened out. I should get it now."

"Let us get a Neurology consult." I asked the resident.

Within 20 minutes the chief of Neurology, an athletic appearing man with a totally bald head appeared with his entourage of interns, residents and students. The group went into Mr. Keesee's cubicle and closed the curtain.

A half hour the team emerged from behind the curtain. The Chief walked up to me and touched my shoulder. He spoke with an air of authority. "Tertiary syphilis. We will take him on our service".

His pronouncement surprised me.

Syphilis is a venereal disease caused by an organism called a spirochete. It has four stages. In primary syphilis there is an ulcer or chancre on the penis or labia. Then the spirochete can disseminate through the blood and cause fever and a rash. Then it becomes dormant, a condition called latent syphilis.

Months to years later the spirochete can take up residence in the heart, destroying valves, and in the nervous system, causing dementia and spinal cord damage. This is called tertiary syphilis. The organism tends to attack the posterior part of the spinal cord. This could cause unsteadiness and falling, such as happened to Mr. Keesee. The treatment of syphilis in any form is penicillin. The more advanced the disease is, the more penicillin you give.

Mr. Keesee was admitted to the Neurology Service where, I assumed, he would be given penicillin.

Three weeks later I found a brown paper envelope in my mailbox. The word "Confidential" was stamped in red ink. This always meant bad news. It was a letter from the Peer Review Committee.

The Peer Review Committee reviews patient records for quality of medical care. The letter concerned Mr. Keesee. The day after admission he had undergone an MRI of his brain. The MRI showed a large subdural hematoma on the right side of his brain. A subdural hematoma is a collection of blood on top of the brain. It can cause pressure on the brain, and even death. It is regarded as a neurosurgical emergency. The next day the patient was taken to surgery where the clot was removed. He did well and was discharged.

What triggered the review was the fact that Mr. Keesee was transferred to a surgical service within three days of hospitalization. Both I and the Chief of Neurology were criticized for missing a blood clot on the brain. "You should have obtained a CAT scan of the head in the Emergency Room." the reviewer said.

The patient's report that he had multiple sclerosis was a red herring that made us stray from the correct diagnosis. Fortunately, he did well.

I took the rebuke from the peer reviewer seriously. I began doing more CAT scans in the Emergency Room.

One day I saw a young man who had abdominal pain. I was pretty sure that this was just gastroenteritis. But, to be certain, I ordered a CAT scan. A CAT scan of the abdomen subjects the patient to the same amount of radiation as 200 chest x-rays.

If I missed an abdominal emergency in the ER today, I could be sued, or at a minimum be criticized by the peer reviewer. But, if 20 years from now, the patient got cancer from unnecessary exposure to radiation, I would, most likely, not get into trouble.

The CT was, as I expected, normal.

That night, when I told my wife, Norma about this young man, she scolded me.

 "You exposed that guy to all of that radiation to prevent criticism. What if he gets leukemia? Treat the patient, not the peer reviewer!"

CHAPTER 22

THE GIRL IN THE RED DRESS

The birds were the giveaway.

 The fourth- floor window just reached the tops of the trees. Birds stood in the branches feeding their chicks that occupied large nests, but the birds weren't sparrows, or pigeons, or even seagulls such as you would see in the US. They were large birds, feeding huge chicks, in giant piles of sticks.   They were marabou storks.

This couldn't be America.

I was in Africa. I was staring out the window on the fourth floor of Mulago Hospital in Kampala, Uganda. The hospital had no air conditioning, and the window was open to let in a breeze.

 When I turned around the contrast between American hospitals and those of Uganda became even more stark. Patients lay in beds lined up against walls. But other patients lay on mats on the floors. And here and there, a man lay on a bed that was next to that of a woman. Sitting next to some beds were the families of patients who had brought food for their loved ones. In Mulago hospital there was no kitchen that prepared dietician- designed meals. If a patient at Mulago was to eat, the food had to be provided by his family.

Some of the patients were covered with blankets. The blankets had been brought by the families. The blanket signified that the patient's family was supporting him. Patients who had blankets tended to live longer.

On a wall were two posters.

One of them discussed prevention of Ebola, a viral disease that is very contagious and has a high mortality rate. Health care providers are especially at risk for Ebola. They come into contact with the patient when they think he just has the flu. In one rural clinic 80 per cent of the health care workers died because they failed to realize that the patient had Ebola. The poster even discussed the proper method of disposing of bodies.

The other poster read "Support Acid Victims." In Uganda, a common practice is to throw acid on the face of someone you don't like. Often the victim of an acid attack is the husband's mistress, and the attacker is the wronged wife. Acid scars disfigure and stigmatize the victim. The poster had two messages. "Don't throw acid on people" and "Be supportive of acid victims".

In one corner of the room a partition had been created to separate a patient from the other patients. A glance revealed the reason. Lying in the bed was a horrible sight. The man's face was covered with ulcers. Much of the skin was gone, revealing fat, and even exposed muscles and bone. The eyes were sunken, and the lips were twisted in a kind of sardonic grin. This might have been in part due to the agonizing pain that was being felt. It was if the patient had been the model for one of the native masks that had been made to terrify evil spirits.

The unfortunate man had tetanus.

Tetanus is caused by a bacterium that lives in the soil. When the bug gets in a wound it makes a toxin that affects nerves and prevents muscles from relaxing. In some patients the jaw can be prevented from opening, resulting in the term "lockjaw". The patient can't eat or drink. Many patients with tetanus die.

Fortunately, in the US and other advanced countries patients are routinely immunized against tetanus. These shots cause the body to make antibodies which neutralize the toxin. The tetanus shots, plus good wound care have made tetanus extremely rare in the US. Until I came to Uganda, I never saw a case of tetanus.

The patient had never been immunized. And he had AIDs, which weakened his response to infection. He had a skin infection which covered his body. Open sores had become dirty, letting in the tetanus bug. Now he had a florid case of tetanus. The patient was given antibiotics and a specific antibody to the tetanus toxin. But it was hopeless, and he died two days later.

It was 2009 and I was working as a volunteer in Mulago Hospital. AIDs, malaria, and malnutrition were the triad of killers that afflicted the population. They worked together. If you had malaria you were more likely to die of AIDs. If you had AIDS, you were more likely to die of malaria.

Mulago Hospital was regarded as a center of medical excellence, a place where patients could go when their situation seemed hopeless. The hospital has even been called. "The Harvard of East Africa." Regardless of this, two thirds of the patients died in the hospital, or were dead within a few months of being discharged.

"Of what use is working in the Developing World to the practice of medicine in the United States.?" I am asked.

One reason is that you see things in the Developing World that are less common in the US.

HIV impairs the ability to fight many infections. In the 1980s when the AIDS epidemic appeared in the US, I saw many of these infections, including pneumonia from the pneumocystis organism, and blindness from cytomegalovirus. With the advent of chemotherapy that attacks the AIDS virus, these infections decreased in the US, but they are still common in Africa.

A health care provider needs to know what these infections look like. To see them he goes to Africa.

In America there is the concern that, in our aging population, the tetanus immunizations will wear off and we may see an epidemic of tetanus. My experience with the tragic patient lying in the corner of Mulago hospital prepared me to care for tetanus cases in America.

The hospital was full of death. Young people in their 20s and 30s commonly died. Often the deaths came from neurological problems such as strokes or brain hemorrhages. The AIDS virus predisposes to these conditions for reasons that are not totally clear.

In an American hospital the frequent deaths of such young people would be the subject of angst and regret. In Mulago Hospital I became desensitized to the human tragedies. If every time a young person died, I cried and it ruined my day, I would be spending most of my time crying.

Contributing to the atmosphere of tragedy was the inability to obtain tests that are easily available in the US.

One of my friends at the hospital was a 70- year old cancer specialist from North Carolina. He told me the story of an 18-year old girl being treated for leukemia. He wanted to check the count of platelets in her blood. Platelets are little particles that help clot blood. If her platelets were too low, she could bleed. If he knew about this, he could give her a platelet transfusion to prevent the bleeding.

Unfortunately, the hospital could not do the test, and the specimen had to be sent to another hospital. Meanwhile, the young woman bled into her brain and died. Several days late the platelet test returned. The young woman had essentially no platelets in her blood. A platelet transfusion could have saved her, but it was too late. As the old physician told me what had happened, his voice cracked, and he sobbed.

A 50 year- old woman was admitted to the hospital after falling on her back. Her legs were weak, and she could not control her bowels or bladder. This pointed to pressure on the lower spinal cord. Relief of the pressure could reverse the injury and prevent further damage to the spinal cord. This needed to be done as soon as possible, even within hours. The neurosurgeons could do the procedure. Before they would touch the woman, they required a radiographic image of the area. The test was a CT myelogram. This was a CAT scan obtained when dye was injected into the spinal fluid that surrounded the cord. This would show exactly where the bone was pressing on the cord and tell the surgeons where to operate.

This test cost 350,000 shillings (the currency of Uganda) or about 120 dollars.

The problem was that the woman couldn't afford the test. Without payment the test would not be performed. It was as simple as that. In the US there would be some fund that would pay for the test, some insurance policy, or the test would just be done, and the hospital would suck up the loss. You never would dream that a woman would go untreated and be permanently paralyzed for lack of funds for a test.

But America is a rich country with a huge budget, and the country can absorb a loss. In Uganda that is not the case. It is cash and carry.   The woman got weaker and weaker as the days went by and the chance of saving her spinal cord was lost.

Finally, a week later, her church came up with the money for her X-ray. It showed compression of her spinal cord. The neurosurgeons operated, but it was too late. The woman would be paralyzed for the remainder of her life.

A 65 year- old man presented with shortness of breath. He had heart failure. In addition, there was a block in the conducting system of his heart that prevented it from beating more than 30 beats a minute. He needed a pacemaker. The pacemaker would help his heart pump better. The pacemaker cost several hundred dollars. He didn't have the money. He lay in the hospital for weeks struggling for breath. Finally, friends got together and pooled their funds. The old man got his pacemaker and he walked out of the hospital.

In Uganda **money** is **life.**

In these cases, only a small amount of money was needed to ensure good medical care.   I, and any other doctor in the hospital, could have provided the money. But we didn't.

In America it is practically considered unethical for a physician to give a patient money.

In a place like Uganda, if a physician opens his wallet to fix financial problems, he will very soon become a poor physician. If he tries to pay for tests and medications for needy patients, the doctor will very soon be calling his wife. "Honey, we need to take out a mortgage on the house. I am going to give the money to the people of Uganda."

I developed the philosophy that as needy as someone seemed, I would not give him money, whether he was a patient in the hospital, or someone begging in the street.

208

A short walk from the hospital and up a small hill is the Makerere
School of Medicine. The students from here come to the hospital
to be taught by the physicians. Near the school is the Institute for
HIV Research. If you walk between these buildings, you come to
a fence. On the other side of the fence is a dirt road. A short
distance from this road is a one-story building. This is the Guest
House for visitors to the hospital. It was my temporary home.

This month a kind of "reality show" was going on in the Guest
House. A team of anesthesiologists had arrived from America.
We were all sitting in the dining room.

One of the men, a physician, was hitting on one of the women, a
nurse anesthetist.

He was a stocky man of about 40 years. "My wife doesn't
understand me." He said to the young woman sitting near him.
Her long black hair was done up in a bun. She was clad in a
scrub suit. She had recently been in the Operating Room. He
reached over to touch her shoulder and she shied away from
him. She seemed not to know what to say. Perhaps this was
because the man was her supervisor and she didn't want to
offend him. "Come on. You like me. I know you do." Then he
reached for her again. He grabbed her shoulder and pulled her
toward him. The young woman looked around the room for help.

I, like the other people in the room, was embarrassed to witness
such behavior. I stood and moved toward the couple. But before
I reached them, a man who had been sitting in the corner
shouted.

"Anthony, leave Crystal alone! Have you been drinking?"

The other man was about 40 years old. He was a compact,
athletic individual. He too was wearing a green scrub suit. He
grabbed the hand and removed it from the woman's shoulder.

Anthony glanced around the room looking from face to face. He suddenly realized that he was behaving badly in front of witnesses. He walked into his bedroom and slammed the door.

Sitting quietly observing this drama was a young woman. Her head was covered with a ball of curly blond hair. On her hooked nose, held together by a thick brown frame, was a pair of thick lenses. I don't remember her name. I will call her Ida.

Ida was an Infectious Disease specialist who had come to Uganda to do research on AIDS. She worked in the AIDS Research Institute.

"I hope I don't get AIDS myself." she said. "I work with bodily fluids from AIDS patients. I need to be careful with them. If I got AIDS people might think I got it from sex. I don't have sex. That would be embarrassing. I am careful with the fluids, but you can't be too careful. I heard of a doctor who got stuck by a needle from an AIDS patient and he died of AIDS. He wasn't careful. I am careful. I wear gloves. I wash my hands."

She paused and stared off. She remembered something.

"Excuse me." she said. She got up and went into a bathroom. I heard a faucet running. When she returned, she was rubbing her hands.

"I am going to climb Mt. Kilimanjaro." she said, changing the subject. "My girlfriend climbed Mt. Kilimanjaro. Near the top the weather got bad. At night the temperature got below freezing. Those porters don't have special clothing. Some of them just walk around in old tennis shoes and tee shirts. Several of them died of exposure that night. My girlfriend let her porters in her tent, and they didn't die. If the weather gets bad when I climb Mt. Kilimanjaro, I will let my porters in my tent too. I won't let them die."

Halloween had just occurred. I called home to see how my grandchildren had done. "Mikey was a robot and Debbie was a kangaroo." my wife said. Mikey was five and Debbie was just two, and this was the first time she had gone "trick or treating". I smiled at the image of the sweet little girl standing on someone's front porch holding out her bag begging for candy. Then I teared up a bit. I was getting homesick.

The next day was a Saturday, and Ida and I decided to walk to the tombs of the ancient kings of Uganda.

Kampala, like San Francisco, is built on hills. It is a busy, chaotic, African metropolis. The favorite mode of transportation is motor scooters and motor cycles. Small shops and restaurants are crammed together. The sidewalks were taken up by vendors selling their wares. Here a woman had her stash of pens and pencils spread out on a cloth. There a man had a box full of used books. Another man was selling guide books to Uganda. And there was every form of food. Ears of corn were roasted over open fires. In another spot, fish caught in nearby Lake Victoria are being cooked.

We avoided the food. This was in part because of the cholera epidemic that was occurring. Cholera is a bacterial disease that causes profuse diarrhea. If not aggressively treated the patient can die of dehydration. Thirty people had already died of cholera. The source of cholera was thought to be contaminated water used by the food vendors in the preparation of their wares. We avoided all contact with food merchants.

Here and there disfigured men sat on the sidewalk hawking pencils, books, trinkets, anything they could sell. Some of the men had missing legs, others missing arms. Still others had mutilated faces. They had been soldiers in the Ugandan army under the brutal dictator Idi Amin. In 1978 Amin's army invaded

Tanzania. Tanzania retaliated by invading Uganda, and Amin was driven out to exile in Arabia.

When people reached their hands out to me to beg, I waved them away.

Ida and I soon found ourselves climbing a hill. This was Kasubi Hill. At the top of the hill was a large thatched dome. This was the palace of the former king, Muteesa, who greeted European explorers in the late 1800s.

Huge poles supported the ceiling. Ida and I were told to remove our shoes before we entered the building. She was upset at having to remove our shoes. "The floor is dirty. You don't know who has been walking here. There are resistant bacteria and fungi in Uganda."

Inside the building we saw a large curtain of bark cloth. Behind the curtain were the tombs of four Ugandan kings. These were closed to visitors. Ida was anxious to leave the building. Being forced to remove her shoes seemed to have ruined her day.

"Do you know how many millions of feet have been on the floor?" she whined. "There could be anything there, antibiotic resistant bacteria, rare fungi that will eat your heart out. You could get something that wasn't curable."

She reached down and removed her socks and threw them into a nearby dumpster. Then she replaced her shoes. "I have to go home and wash my feet." she said anxiously. I am going back to the Guest House." She walked rapidly away and disappeared down the hill.

I went home on my own. I decided to walk down to the center of the city, then go up Kampala Road to the medical school. I soon found myself on a side street heading down the hill. The street was lined with small houses and stores and vendors. Suddenly, I noticed something blocking my way. It was a small red shape.

Standing in front on me on the sidewalk was a little girl, aged about two. She was wearing a red dress. She was a little black Debby, my granddaughter. She extended her right hand to ask for money. I glanced to my left. Up the hill, half way hidden behind a tree, was a man watching the little girl. This was probably her father.

"This is a scam." I thought. "She is begging to get money for her father." I looked down at the innocent face. She was without guile. She was just doing what her father told her to do. If I gave her money her father would get it, but she would benefit from it. Besides, she reminded me of Debbie, my granddaughter.

My barriers to giving money collapsed. I reached in my pockets and took out every shilling that I had. I put them in the little cherub's outstretched hands.

Then I walked away to allow her father to retrieve her and the money.

CHAPTER 23

AN INCIDENT IN PENSACOLA

As I drove across the Monitor-Merrimac Bridge I glanced at the Norfolk Naval Base on my right. In the early morning light, I tried to count the number of aircraft carriers. Sometimes there were as many as four. Sometimes there were none. The fewer carriers there were, the more unstable the world was. Or so I surmised.

If there were a lot of hot spots in the world, all or most of the carriers were deployed. If the world was safe, the carriers wouldn't be needed, and they would be in port. As I strained see the ships, among the destroyers and battleships and smaller screening vessels, I counted three carriers.

I was on my way to Sewell's Point Branch Clinic for monthly drill with the Navy Reserve. I was looking forward to my morning. I would see patients, but before that would come the most interesting part of the day, my medical mystery story with Commander Farouk Presswalla. Dr. Presswalla was a medical examiner for the state of Virginia, and a Navy reservist.

Each morning, while the patients were being checked in, he discussed cases in one of the treatment rooms. Doctors and nurses and corpsmen crammed the small treatment room to listen to the lecture on forensic pathology. Patricia Cornwall, the crime writer, had, for a while, worked in his office to learn about forensic medicine.

But Dr. Presswalla was a spellbinder too.

"The body of a pretty young woman was found in an alley". The dark- complexioned man began, as he pushed his black-rimmed glasses up on his nose. He was pudgy, but his shoulders were muscular from the many pushups he did every day. This helped him rack up a huge total at the time of physical fitness testing.

As a child he emigrated to America from India. He spoke with a refined accent.

"We considered sexual assault, but her pants hadn't been removed. We did an autopsy and there was blood at the base of her brain. But there was no skull fracture, no evidence of trauma to explain the blood. So, I dissected further. There was a massive hemorrhage at the base of the brain from a ruptured aneurism. There was no assault. This young woman just was unlucky. She had an aneurism which had burst. There was no crime."

We sighed and glanced at each other at the resolution of the mystery. CDR. Presswalla started on another case.

"A 45 year- old man was found in a motel room. He had been dead for several days. There was a puncture wound in his chest. It went right through to the heart. That was the cause of death. What do you think the murder weapon was?" He looked around the room.

"A knife?" piped up a corpsman.

"No."

"A gun?" asked a nurse

"No." Dr. Presswalla looked around the room. "Any more guesses?" The audience was silent.

"Well the murder weapon was a shoe." The audience gasped in surprise.

"A shoe?" asked a physician. Presswalla smiled. He was a professor talking to his class.

"Yes, a shoe. But a specific kind of shoe, a woman's stiletto-healed shoe. He went into a room with a prostitute and she decided to kill him for his money and credit cards. He was drunk, and he fell down. She just stood on his chest on one foot. That killed him." The audience seemed skeptical.

"The point of stiletto heel is only a sixteenth of a square inch in area. The prostitute weighed 150 pounds. So, doing the math, pressure on the victim's chest was 2400 pounds per square inch. The heel went right through his chest like a knife through butter and killed him."

We gasped at this revelation. We had almost forgotten the patients that are waiting for us.

On another morning the commander discussed a case that is dear to his heart.

"Carl Coppolino was an anesthesiologist who was accused of murdering his wife by injecting succinylcholine into her." We knew that succinylcholine was a paralyzing agent. The victim would stop breathing and die.

"Her body, which had been in the ground for months was exhumed. At the autopsy, traces of succinylcholine were found in the brain. A needle track was found in the left buttock and along the track were traces of succinylcholine. But the breakdown products of succinylcholine, succinic acid and choline, are found naturally in the body.

At the Coppolino trial, the medical examiner was cross examined by F. Lee Bailey, the famous defense attorney, who years later defended O.J. Simpson. Mr. Simpson was accused of murdering two people.

'Doctor. You found succinylcholine in the deceased's left buttock.'

'Yes.'

'Isn't it true that the components of succinylcholine can be found naturally in the body?'

'Yes.'

'Well, doctor. How do you know that these findings wouldn't normally be found in a body that has been in the ground for the same length of time?'

'I did a control.'

F. Lee Bailey was amazed.

'Doctor, do you mean that you checked the succinylcholine level in a body of the same age as the deceased, of the same sex, that had been dead for the same length of time, and had been in the ground for exactly the same period of time?'

'Yes, I did.'

The defense attorney grimaced in amazement.

'Well Doctor, would you be so kind as to inform me and the distinguished members of the jury how you accomplished this amazing feat.'

'I checked the level in the other buttock.'

Dr. Presswalla smiled broadly as his story about a smart medical examiner concluded.

It was time to see patients. Sitting in chairs outside of the wall in front of my office were naval reservists of all ranks. Scattered among them were members of other services, mostly Marines, but also some Air Force and Army.

"If I don't finish your physical by noon, I will buy you lunch." I announce to the group. I never had to buy anyone lunch.

Healthy young servicemen may require just a "Short Form" physical, which requires completion of a questionnaire and pulse, blood pressure and weight. Every five years a complete physical is done.

One year a young lieutenant completed a short form physical. His private doctor had found protein in his urine. A note from a kidney specialist stated that the condition was benign, and that the lieutenant's military career should be affected. So, I passed him.

Five years later I saw the lieutenant for another physical.

"Please take off your blouse." I asked the young man. He warily undressed. I was shocked by what I saw. There was a hole in his abdomen. Out of this hole was running a plastic tube that had been taped to his chest.

"What is this?" I asked.

"I have end- stage kidney disease. I have been getting peritoneal dialysis for two years. I have been drilling as usual. I have been passing my physical fitness requirements. I have been fine. They want to give me a kidney transplant. I hope I can stay in the Reserves."

I was startled by what the young man told me. His kidney disease had rapidly progressed to where he needed to go on dialysis.

With peritoneal dialysis, the patient runs special fluid through a catheter into the peritoneal cavity, the cavity of the abdomen. Impurities from the blood move into the fluid. After an indwelling time of hours, the fluid is allowed to run out of the abdomen, carrying the impurities with it. This needs to be done every day. The young man was staying alive by doing peritoneal dialysis at home. Despite this, he passed his physical fitness testing, running and doing sit-ups and pushups, with the catheter in place under his jogging suit.

I was impressed at the young man's determination. His kidney problem certainly would disqualify him for military service. There was something know as a "waiver" which would allow someone to serve despite a medical condition. In this case, I couldn't get a waiver, and the young lieutenant was discharged from the Navy.

During drills urine drug screens were obtained. It was important that servicemen are free of illegal drugs. A number from 0 to 9 was drawn out of a hat. If the number was the last number of your social security number, you were tested.

The downfall of some sailors was marijuana. Marijuana stays in the system for a long time, sometimes for a month or more.

Some reservists reported for duty confident that their number would not come up. Even if it did (or so they thought), the cannabis that they smoked a month ago would be out of their system. When their number was drawn, they learned, to their horror, that pot was still in their urine, and they were discharged from the Navy

A strict chain of custody was maintained with urine drug screens. A label with the name was placed on a bottle. Then the serviceman was escorted to the restroom where he or she was observed to pee in a bottle. At one time there was a rule that sailor could not be observed to urinate by someone of a lower rank.

With the exception of admiral, captain was the highest rank. You couldn't go wrong if you had a captain available to watch someone pee. The problem with this was that some captains had to spend much of their time in the restroom watching people pee. This rule was changed, and it became acceptable for a person of any rank to accompany you to the restroom.

Some people's reserve duty was extremely important to them, even the major thing in their lives. For one Navy chief, the Reserves was his only source of income. He lived in his car. He kept his uniform in his car. He used the rest rooms of service stations. At night he put the front seat back and slept. On the morning of a drill he came early and showered and shaved in the restroom. He always looked sharp in his uniform. You would never have guessed that he lived in a car.

To stay in the Reserves, you had to be physically fit.

Twice a year we had PRT or "Physical Readiness Testing." Our weight was measured. Then we had to do as many pushups and as many sit-ups as we could in two minutes. After that we ran a mile and a half for time.

Physical fitness testing sometimes resulted in tragedies. The Pulmonary Clinic at Portsmouth Naval Hospital is known as the Boyle Memorial Clinic.

Commander Boyle, who was a pulmonary specialist, was swimming in a pool to pass his physical fitness requirement. Suddenly, he collapsed and went into cardiac arrest. The doctor who was swimming next to him pulled him out of the water. CPR was performed, but Dr. Boyle did not survive.

Some servicemen with unrecognized, or even hidden medical conditions, exercise to keep their military careers.

A smoker stops smoking on the day of physical fitness testing. His body, which has been exerting heavily, has an oxygen debt. After his run, he lights up a cigarette. He inhales carbon monoxide, which blocks oxygen delivery to his heart. His heart fibrillates, and he drops dead. Sudden death among servicemen at the time of physical fitness testing is a common phenomenon.

An Air Force physician recounted this story to me when I was in the Air Force.

A nineteen- year old enlisted woman, Airman Jefferson, was standing in her dormitory talking to her roommate. Suddenly the young woman stopped speaking and began seizing. She collapsed in a ball on the floor. An ambulance was called and the EMTs began CPR. The airman was taken to the Emergency Room at the nearby Air Force base.

In the Emergency Room Airman Jefferson was found to be in ventricular fibrillation, a lethal heart rhythm. Shocks were delivered to her chest in attempt to restore her heart rhythm, but she remained in ventricular fibrillation. CPR continued, and several drugs were administered to try to restore her heart rhythm. Labs were drawn.

Her labs returned. A single abnormality stood out. Her serum potassium level was critically low, only 1.5 milliequivalents per liter. Normal is above 3.5 meq/L .

 Potassium is a salt necessary for normal electrical activity of the heart. The low potassium level triggered the chaotic rhythm. Massive amounts of potassium were administered, but it was too late, and the young woman died.

Why was the potassium so low? At first her roommate declined to say anything, but finally she revealed what happened.

Airman Jefferson had upcoming physical fitness testing in two weeks. This included a weigh in. The young woman went on a crash diet. To get off more weight she began taking diuretics.

And, to get every possible ounce of weight off of her body, she began taking laxatives.

Crash dieting decreases the salt intake of the body. Low sodium intake triggers secretion of a hormone, aldosterone, which causes the kidneys to hold on to sodium in exchange for potassium, which is lost in the urine. The diuretics caused more potassium wasting by the kidney. The laxatives added to these losses.

The net result of Airman Jefferson's crash diet was that her potassium dropped to the lethal level, and her heart stopped.

The carrier the USS Enterprise came into drydock in Newport News for refurbishing. At Newport News, near Norfolk, was a shipyard. The huge carrier was being painted with lead-containing paint. A concern was that the crew could be exposed to high levels of lead which can cause damage to the nervous system, bone marrow, and other areas of the body. I was assigned to the Enterprise to monitor lead levels in the crew.

The huge vessel was totally out of the water. I walked up the gangway and into the ship. I quickly found the Medical Department.

An overhead speaker blared. "Who was that officer who walked on the ship without saluting the Bridge!?"

An important truth was made apparent to me. Whether or not a Navy ship is in the water or in dry dock, it is still a ship, and the formalities must be observed. By barging onto the ship unannounced, I committed a horrible breach of etiquette.

I ran out of the ship and down the gangway. Then I retraced my steps. I saluted the Bridge to my left, then looked at the officer on the deck.

"Permission to come aboard sir?" I asked.

"That's better sir." He said. "Welcome aboard!"

In about 1990 Portsmouth Naval hospital went to a paper-free, fully computerized medical record. This was a boon to medical care. It did away with thick charts filled with yellowing pages, covered with sometimes illegible writing. But the computerized record had its down side.

If the physician didn't log off the computer, someone could get into the medical records of patients, and use them to get personal data, such as social security numbers. Physicians who failed to log off their computer were counseled and reprimanded because of this dangerous breach in security. However, some physicians continued to walk away from an open computer terminal.

One day a busy intern went home without logging off his terminal. The following day he was summoned to the Admiral's office. He wondered what the matter could be. He was ushered into the office where the Admiral sat. The red- faced admiral eyed the nervous intern and spoke. "What do you mean by sending me this Email calling me a flatulent idiot!?"

In 1999 my naval reserve unit made a trip to the naval base at Pensacola, Florida. The rooms at the Bachelor Officers Quarters were not ready. To kill time, we went to Maguire's, a local watering hole to eat and get drinks. When we checked in, we were told there was a few minutes wait. "I want to call me wife. Do you have a phone?" I asked the hostess.

"It's in the Men's Room." the young woman said, pointing toward the back of the restaurant.

Thirty feet away was a wooden door with writing on it. "**MEN**" it read.

I walked through the swinging door. Near the door was a pay phone. I put some quarters in and dialed my home number.

As the phone rang, I casually glanced at the machine next to the phone. What did it dispense? Combs? Candy? Cigarettes? Condoms?

It dispensed Tampons.

"What is a tampon machine doing in the Men's Restroom!?"

A sense of dread overtook me as I searched for an explanation for this conundrum. Just as the obvious answer entered my brain, the door open and two women sauntered in.

"I am in the Women's Restroom!"

I ran out the door. I looked more carefully at the door. "MEN" was written in large letters. But, close inspection showed a tiny arrow pointing from the words to the opposite door. Below the word "MEN", written in tiny letters, was the word "women".

Careful reading of the door revealed that it was the door of the Women's Restroom, and the opposite room was the Men's Restroom. I felt like a pervert. I had gone into the women's restroom.

I studied the writing on the other door. "WOMEN" read the lettering. But extruding from the word was another tiny arrow pointing to the opposite door. Below this, written almost as an afterthought was the small word "men."

Reassured that this was truly the entrance to the Men's restroom, I pushed through the second door. There was a pay phone, but no tampon machine.

For a second, I relaxed. Then I looked at the urinals.

Standing at the urinal with his back to me was an individual that I hoped and assumed was a man. But running from his head to below his waist, more beautiful, and lush than in any woman that I had known, was a cascade of shiny black hair.

Seeing this lush feminine figure in the Men's room, right after my misadventure in the Women's bathroom was more than I could handle.

"Oh no!" I shouted and ran out the door.

I gave up on my phone call to my wife. Now I realized that I had a full bladder. But I didn't dare use the restrooms at McGuire's Pub.

I walked past my group that was still waiting for a table and out the door. Nearby was a Shell station. The door of the Men's Room was clearly marked with no sneaky arrows. I walked in, and sighed as I emptied my bladder.

Back at McGuire's Restaurant we were taken to our tables. In our room were shelves that were occupied by oak wine barrels. We had a clear vantage of the rest rooms. Men and women walked past us wanting to relieve themselves, and then screamed as they realized that they were in the wrong bathroom.

It was a running joke in McGuire's that people strayed into the wrong restroom. It was entertainment for the customers.

I wasn't amused. I felt violated. I might have PTSD from the trauma. I thought about suing. I could say that I could never again feel comfortable entering a public restroom. I might get millions.

But in the end, I didn't sue

CHAPTER 24
A STORY WITHIN A STORY

The aroma of Vietnamese cooking wafted from the kitchen. Diners in the surrounding tables chatted and smiled and laughed. But when I looked at the faces at my table all I saw was gloom.

I was at the Mekong Restaurant, a Vietnamese restaurant, a few miles down Broad Street from the Medical School, with my second -year medical students. They had just taken a difficult exam and they seemed to think that they hadn't done well.

Medical students come from near the top of their college classes. They are used to doing well. In medical school, their classmates are also the cream of the crop. In my class in medical school half of the class had made Phi Beta Kappa in college. Medical students find the transition from being an honors student to just being "average" as distressing.

As I looked out at the students who now are digging into their Vietnamese food, I marveled at the diversity.

When I was a medical student in the late 60s less than 10 per cent of the class were female. Now, in 2013, over half of the Virginia Commonwealth Class is female. And there is tremendous racial diversity. The most common surname in the class is Kim. I can often match my list of names with people by just looking at them. Alice Chang has got to be the Asian female in the group. Robert O'Malley, the red- haired boy, must be the only Caucasian male in the group.

My wife Norma thinks that all medical students are starving. She approves of me taking them out for dinner. Tonight, I would feed them, but I also wanted to boost their morale.

This evening we were discussing the case of an old man in a nursing home. This was a lead in to the subject of Geriatrics.

"If you want to specialize in Geriatrics you can do one of two things." I began. They looked up from their plates. "You can take a three-year Geriatrics fellowship where you do hands-on care of the elderly.... or you can remember just one thing."

"What?" asked the African American woman sitting in front of me.

"Everything gets worse after age 40.

To be precise everything gets 1 per cent worse per year after 40. Your kidney function drops off. Your lung function too.

Your cardiac function declines. That is why so many old people die of heart failure. Your liver doesn't breakdown poisons as well. Everything gets worse after age 40......except one thing." The group looked around the table at each other to see if anyone knew the answer.

"Your knowledge stores, your memory. That is why healthy young people like you, in the prime of life, have to sit at a table and listen to a decrepit old man like me. You may be able to run a marathon faster than me, but I know more than you."

The faces betrayed almost no emotion.

"I have hundreds of old people who adore me. They are my ace in the hole, my protection. If they ever try to fire me, the hospital will be attacked from four sides by an army of old men driving motorized wheelchairs and scooters. The men will be screaming hideous war cries through edentulous mouths and swinging urinals over their heads. That is why they won't fire me."

I glanced at my audience for a trace of amusement. But they were glumly silent.

"My memory stores have millions of bites of data that I have accumulated over the years. They create the record of my medical adventure. You are beginning your medical adventure. Practicing medicine provides great material for writing, for example a murder mystery. Arthur Conan Doyle, the author of the Sherlock Holmes Mysteries, was a physician.

Here is story someone could write." The class stared at me. They were depressed, and I wanted to cheer them up.

"Sometimes an old person dies at home. The family calls the Rescue Squad or the police. When they get there, they see no evidence of foul play. There is no knife sticking out of the chest. You can't do an autopsy on everyone. If someone is old and sick, you are not surprised that he has died. The Rescue Squad, or the Police, call the patient's physician.

'Doctor, would you be willing to sign a death certificate on your patient?' they ask. The doctor knows that his patient has medical problems such as heart disease or cancer and consents to sign the death certificate. That is the end of it. The doctor has tremendous power. He can cover up a murder if he wants.

Suppose a patient's young wife, Mrs. Timmons, and I have been making eyes at each other. And the patient has a lot of money. The wife and I decide to kill the man and run off to Brazil with his money. 'He is old and will die soon anyway' the handsome 40year- old woman says.

What will the murder weapon be?"

Without waiting for the students to answer, I continued.

"Medications, drugs. Drugs can help patients, but if improperly used, they may kill the patient. Every year many thousands of patients die from medication errors. The doctor has a tremendous amount of power. He can prescribe a poison and he can dispose of the body. He can literally get away with murder!"

At my use of the word "murder" two of the students stopped eating and looked up from their Vietnamese food. I was relieved to be getting their attention. I continued my story.

"Mr. Timmons has congestive heart failure and atrial fibrillation. Mr. Timmons is taking several medications, including digoxin. Digoxin helps his heart by increasing the power of muscle contractions. By slowing the rate, it also allows more time for the ventricle to fill with blood, so more blood is ejected with each contraction.

But digoxin has a down side. Excess amounts of digoxin may cause lethal changes in the heart rhythm, such as ventricular fibrillation. Digoxin comes from the foxglove plant that may grow in your back yard. During the middle ages one way of bumping off a king's rival was poisoning him with the foxglove. This the reason we monitor digoxin therapy with a blood level.

One day I call my patient. 'Mr. Timmons let us see how you do without digoxin. I want you to stop it for a while.' The old man stops the medication.

Three months later I call Mr. Timmons.

'Mr. Timmons. I am checking on you. How are you doing?' He tells me he is doing about the same, or perhaps a little worse, or even better. It doesn't make any difference. I continue with my lethal plan.

'Mr. Timmons, I want to get you back on digoxin. I want to load up your body to get the level back. First start taking four of those pills per day. I will call you in two weeks.' The patient agrees to do what I have instructed him to do without question. He trusts his physician.

Fifteen days later I call Mr. Timmons. He is noticing some nausea. This is because his digoxin level has climbed into the toxic level. 'Don't worry about the nausea.' I reassure him. 'That will go away. Once your body gets used to the medicine again you will feel better. Now I want you to increase the number of pills to 8 pills per day. Pretty soon you will be feeling better'.

"What I tell him is medical nonsense. But he believes me. I have it planned that the pill count will be correct. No one will know that I changed the way he took his pills. The old man again acquiesces. Four days later the toxicity to his heart reaches the lethal level and he collapses in his living room."

Four of the students had now stopped eating. A piece of tofu fell from a student's fork onto his lap.

"Great!" I thought. "I am a spellbinder."

"Mr. Timmons' wife calls the Rescue Squad. She sits on the couch looking at her husband's inert body. When she hears the ambulance siren, she begins doing CPR.

Two heavy set men dressed in black uniforms rush in through the unlocked front door. Close behind them is a dark young woman. Her facial features betray that her ancestors came from India.

'How long has he been down?' asks the older man. 'Did you see him collapse?'

'I found him like this.' says the tearful Mrs. Timmons. 'He could have been like this for two hours. I came home from the store and found him like this. I have been doing CPR for an hour. I took a Red Cross course."

The older man, Mr. Craft, feels for a pulse. Finding none, he touches his patient's skin and moves the arm.

'He is already cold. He is going into rigor mortis. I am sorry ma'am, but your husband has passed away.' Mrs. Timmons begins sobbing.

'He had a bad heart. I knew this would happen someday, but not today.'

The plan is for the EMTs to call me and ask if I would sign a death certificate. The old man seemed to have died of natural causes and this should be no problem. Then Mrs. Timmons would have her husband cremated. This would destroy any evidence of foul play".

All the students had put their forks down and were staring at me.

I continued my story.

"During this time, the young woman who accompanied the men from the Squad has been wandering around the room. She studies the paintings on the wall.

Miss Sybil Dhar was a college student who had majored in art history. But in her junior year she decided that she wanted to be a doctor. In addition to taking premed courses, she was accompanying EMT groups to get firsthand experience with patients".

'You are going from Art History to Medicine? That makes sense.' says Mr. Craft sarcastically'.

The young woman speaks.

'Mrs. Timmons I am sorry for your loss. I was looking at these paintings. Who did them?'

'Why my husband did. After he retired as a stock broker, he took up painting.'

'He is very good. I noticed this painting on the easel, the painting of the men fishing on the river at night.'

'Yes, he was working on it when he died.' the wife sobs.

'I notice a difference between this painting and his earlier paintings. For example, there is a yellow ring around the stars. The skin of the men looks more yellow. You don't see this in his earlier work. Did he take digoxin?'

The wife is stunned by this question. Her hands tremble. 'Yes. He did. Why do you ask?'

'Digoxin, especially when taken in toxic doses, can cause painters to use more yellow. Digoxin is derived from digitalis. The Dutch painter, Vincent van Gogh, was said to take digitalis, to prevent seizures. One of his paintings "The Starry Night" shows a yellow ring around the stars. Many of his other paintings use a lot of yellow color. Mr. Timmons' last painting shows this effect, something not seen in his other paintings. I wonder if he could have digoxin toxicity. Could I count his pills?'

Mrs. Timmons brings in her husband's bottles of pills. Ms. Dhar counts them. The number of digitalis tabs is correct. There is no evidence that Mr. Timmons had taken too much medication. I planned it that way.

Miss Dhar seems disappointed. She turns to Mr. Craft. 'We should still get a digitalis level.'

Mrs. Timmons winces. 'Do we need to do that? My husband has been through so much.'

'They can just get some blood and measure the level. They don't have to do an autopsy.' The young woman looks at Mr. Craft and speaks. 'For completeness we should definitely do that.'

Craft frowns. This was an open and shut case of an old man dying of a heart attack. He had done this hundreds of times. He wanted to leave and go to lunch.

'This is the last time I am going to take a pre-med on runs with me.' he angrily thinks.

He mutters under his breath 'An art history major!'

'We really need to check a digoxin level.' Ms. Dhar persists.

Craft sighs and calls the State Medical Examiner.

The body of Mr. Timmons is loaded into the ambulance and taken to the office of the Medical Examiner where a complete autopsy is performed. Mr. Timmons has significant heart disease but did not die of a heart attack. The blood digoxin level is 9 times the therapeutic limit. The patient died of digitalis toxicity.

The art history student's instincts were correct.

The police become involved with the case. Mr. Timmons' phone messages have been erased, but my phone record shows that I had called him three days before he died.

It is common for a patient to call his physician when his health is deteriorating, but it is much less common for the physician to call the patient." The students gave a knowing nod.

"The police question Mrs. Timmons and search the house. A firearm is found. Mrs. Timmons finally confesses to the plot to kill her husband. The backup plan was, if the digoxin failed to kill her husband, for her to shoot him and claim it was an intruder.

234

Mrs. Timmons testifies against me in return for a reduced sentence.

I am convicted of first- degree murder and sentenced to 75 years in prison. "Your patient trusted you. You violated the Hippocratic Oath!" the angry judge shouts.

Mr. Craft, the head of the Rescue Squad, writes Sybil Dhar a glowing letter of recommendation and she gets into medical school."

Having finished my tale, I looked at the students sitting at the table and grinned. I hoped that I had cheered them up.

"So, class. If you get tired of being a physician, you can write murder mysteries." The students still looked miserable. My story was lost on them, it hadn't cheered them up. My time had been wasted.

The session finished, they got to leave. As they were walking out, I gave my final inspirational message. "Ladies and gentlemen, the World is your oyster." They didn't seem to be convinced. They shuffled toward the exit.

Suddenly, one of the students, an Asian woman in a green blouse, turned around and walked back to me. She was grinning.

"Thank you, Dr. Schmitt. I do feel better. I didn't want to say this in front of the other students, but I **Was** an art history major in college.

CHAPTER 25

ESCAPE AND EVASION

"There has to be an easier way to get a course for free." I thought as I looked at the blazing sun and rubbed the sweat from my neck.

I was walking across country with thirty other servicemen. The Texas terrain was arid and barren. There were dry gullies, evidence that in other times there had been heavy rains and floods, but now the ground was parched. Here and there was a patch of brush. Now and then a scorpion, or some large insect, was seen scurrying along the ground.

We wore camouflage uniforms. Attached to our belts were two canteens. This was required for walking in the hot desert.

"Walking" is a euphemism. Actually. we were being herded. At either side of us was a stern-faced Army sergeant. The sergeants made sure that we stayed together and didn't stray off the trail.

Two hours earlier a bus had stopped on a deserted road and let us out.

We were taking the Combat Casualty Course, a course that teaches servicemen how to care for the casualties of war. A section of the course is a two-day course called Advanced Trauma Life Support. This course I needed to pass in order to work in the Emergency Room in my hospital. By taking it as part of the Combat Casualty Course I saved over a hundred dollars. Now as I sweltered in the heavy uniform, I was beginning to regret my decision.

We were using Land Navigation to get from the bus to our new home. We were given a map and a compass. The map showed the site of our camp, roughly five miles to the east. By using the compass to determine our direction, we would eventually arrive at our camp. To make sure there were no mistakes, the sergeants hovered over us.

In three hours, we came to a clearing. Six or eight metal tent poles lay on the ground. Nearby was a pile of canvas. These were our tents. We inserted the poles into a canvas and pulled and within a few minutes we had put up our tent.

In my tent was a group of ten servicemen. There was an Air Force major, two Navy chiefs, two Army nurses, two Army physicians, two Army podiatrists and me. One of the podiatrists and one the Army physicians were woman.

Our cots ran in a line the length of the tent. My cot was next to that of the female physician.

Two years earlier the Navy had endured the infamous "Tailhook" scandal.

In 1991 over 4000 Navy and Marine Corps aviators met in Las Vegas for the annual Tailhook Convention at the Las Vegas Hilton. The event deteriorated into a drunken orgy in which many women were subjected to groping, disrobing, and assault. An investigation resulted in disciplinary action, court martial and demotion of several naval officers. Several senior officers resigned in the backlash of this event.

In the early 1960s I took Air Force ROTC at the University of California, Berkeley. At that time ROTC was a requirement. Even in those days there was a tendency to denigrate women in the military service.

One of the instructors, an Air Force major would stand in front of the class and poke fun at women in the military. "They are considered "crack" troops." he smirked, in a veiled reference to the vagina. His audience, which consisted of horny young men, laughed at his remarks.

There has been the belief by some that manliness, i.e. testosterone, equates to bravery and military prowess. The other side of this belief is that estrogen, e.g. femaleness, represents weakness and a woman is the antithesis of the ideal military officer. Moreover, the female is the natural reward that the military man receives for his bravery. So, when alcohol was added to the mix, it was not surprising that the Tailhook scandal occurred.

During the night in our tent, an attractive woman lay in the bed next to me. Regardless of our mix of hormones, she was my colleague and fellow officer. When she dressed and undressed in the next bed, I just turned away until she was done. It was as simple as that.

We were mustered out of our tents at 4 AM. It was important that before you put your boots on you checked them for a scorpion that took up residence during the night. We stood in the dark at elevated wooden counters eating our hot food. Despite the early hour and morning cold, I looked forward to the upcoming entertainment.

We moved to a large tent where lectures were given. The director of the course and major speaker was Colonel Mullins, an army orthopedic surgeon.

Colonel Mullins was a tall, thin man of about 45 years. He wore eyeglasses with black frames. He was as much an entertainer as a lecturer.

Among the services, the Air Force was regarded as the least macho, the least hands on, the most intellectual. This was because the Air Force was the most technology- driven service.

As opposed to the Navy, and especially the Army, there was no direct contact with the enemy. A running joke was that the Air Force consisted of softies, refined gentlemen who didn't get their hands dirty. They spent their day in front of computer screens.

One morning the subject was chemical warfare. During Operation Desert Storm, which had occurred a few years earlier, there had been the concern that the army of Iraq would use the nerve gas, sarin. Exposure to sarin could cause paralysis and death.

Special suits, called NBC (nuclear, biological, and chemical suits), were designed to protect the servicemen from the weapons of terrorism, including nuclear radiation, biological agents, such as anthrax, and chemicals, such as Sarin.

We were instructed to carry our gas masks with us at all times, even when going to the shower. To keep us on our toes we were sometimes attacked with tear gas. The goal was to don the gas mask within 9 seconds.

Colonel Mullins flashed slides of an NBC suit on a screen at the front of the tent. It covered the entire body. When fully dressed, the person wearing it looked like a Martian from a grade B science fiction movie. (I will not give the real names of the suits).

"In the Army this is called a G70 antichemical, biological and radiation suit." the colonel began. He spoke slowly and deliberately, with a slight drawl.

"In the Navy it is known as the RF60 NBC Survival uniform."

"The Marines call it the PF50 All Purpose Survival Suit."

The colonel paused and stared out at the audience for a moment. Then he resumed speaking

"And in the Air Force it is called an **ENSEMBLE!**"

On another day we were giving the assignment of designing a perimeter in the time of war. For this purpose, a large board with movable pieces had been placed on a table.

"Here is the hospital." began an Army physician pointing to the board. "And here is the ammunition dump. Here is the radiation decontamination area. And here is the command post."

"Very good." said the instructor.

Now it was an Air Force officer's turn to set up the camp. He pointed to the board. "Now let us get this out of the way. Here is the Officer's Club, and here is the Golf Course!"

At one time, we were told, animals, such as goats were shot to provide realistic experience in treating bullet wounds, but this practice was felt to be inhumane. Now we cared for goats that had been anesthetized.

In a large room at another part of the base unconscious goats lay on tables. We practiced treating various conditions. For example, fluid was injected into the pericardium, the sac around the heart. This condition, called pericardial tamponade, prevents the heart from pumping normally and can be fatal. The emergency treatment of this condition was to put a needle into the sac to remove the fluid, a procedure known as pericardiocentesis.

After the exercise the goats were sacrificed. They were stained with green dye. This was to prevent the meat from being eaten after we were done with them.

No effort was spared to create a realistic combat environment. We crawled out on a mock battlefield under simulated gunfire to treat casualties. Some of the casualties were dragged across the battlefield on stretchers. Watching everything that we did were the ubiquitous sergeants. If someone looked overheated or exhausted, they would pull him out of the group and ask him how he felt.

Toward the end of the course was an Escape and Evasion exercise.

The scenario was that the servicemen were marching at night. Suddenly they were attacked by the enemy and they scattered in the dark. The goal was to make it back to the base camp without the enemy capturing you.

The role of the "Enemy" was played by the sergeants.

One night we sat in a room while the sergeants went over the plan.

The sergeants were all dressed as plants. They wore skintight rubber suits that sprouted branches and leaves. I wondered if when they weren't babysitting for students, the sergeants wore the wonderful camouflage on commando raids.

One of the men, who looked like a magnolia bush with a head, spoke. "When we capture you, we will take away your ID card and draw a red line across your neck. You are dead, kaput" To make his point he moved his finger across his neck in a cutting gesture. "Almost nobody ever escapes. We are good at catching you, real good. We are practically invisible." He smiled and nodded at the other trees and bushes in the room and they gave knowing grins.

"And one more thing. You will see that the area is marked off by yellow tape. It is important that you stay within the tape." He glanced at the other sergeants and smiled. Then he continued his speech.

"Several years ago, when we did this exercise, we had an Army doctor. He, well, …he got a little carried away. When we attacked his group, he ran and kept running. He hid in the trees and we never got him. After several hours we wandered around the area calling for him. But he was gone. We looked for him all night, but we couldn't find him. We had to call his wife to tell her he was missing.

We thought he might have had a heart attack and died in the bushes. We had hundreds of people looking for the doctor. The Texas State troopers were called, and they brought in bloodhounds. We used a pair of his undershorts for the scent. Two days later the bloodhounds tracked him to an abandoned building. At first, he wouldn't come out. He had lost track of reality. But one of his friends went in and told him it was all a game and he should turn himself in. Finally, he did.

So, Ladies and Gentlemen, for Heaven's sake, please stay within the yellow ribbon!"

The sergeant paused. Then he remembered something.

"And one more thing, if you go behind a bush in the dark to take a leak, make sure that that bush is not me!"

We each had a partner. My partner was Kathy Wilms, the female podiatrist who shared my tent. She was a timid little woman who seemed a bit out of place in this rough and tumble combat course. Even in her camouflage uniform, she reminded me of a blonde Barbie Doll.

We marched out in the darkness two by two in a long line.

When we were in a gully between two hills there was an explosion and the sound of gunfire. "We are under attack!" came a shout. We all scattered. I took Kathy's sweaty left hand in my right hand. I am not sure why I did this. Perhaps I did it to calm her fears. I had already formulated a plan to foil the sergeants. I needed her to stay close to me. Maybe this was the reason.

In order to win the game, you had to make it back to the base before the sergeants got you. The base was the small building where the briefing had occurred. I guessed that the sergeants would be waiting in the trees between the point of attack and the base. Most people would take that route and be picked off. But I would fool them. I would move away from them. My competitive nature was aroused.

Holding Kathy's hand tightly in mine I led her into the brush away from the building. She did not seem to resent my holding her hand. Her relaxed, warm, fingers willingly curled around mine as I led her in the darkness. I enjoyed protecting this soft, feminine person. It was the nearest that I had come to committing adultery since I had been married.

We moved to the darkest, furthest corner of the perimeter, away from the nefarious sergeants. But we weren't going to get lost. I had a plan.

In the sky, about thirty degrees above the base, was a bright yellow object. It didn't twinkle like a star. It had a steady, dull, yellow light. It was a planet, the planet Saturn. This was a beacon for the location of our base. As far afield as we got, we couldn't get lost.

"That is Saturn, the planet with rings." I told Kathy. "We just head toward that, and we will be home." I felt like a frontiersman guiding a damsel in distress. She squeezed my hand as a sign of her confidence in me.

We looped around toward the base building. In the dark we saw lines of prisoners being led off to captivity. They all had the shameful line of red on their necks.

Kathy and I stepped into the back of a line of prisoners. The sergeants just thought we were prisoners. When the line got within thirty feet of the base, we broke away and ran. Still holding hands, we crossed the finish line. We hadn't been captured. Kathy and I hugged.

We got to play hide and seek in the dark with men dressed as trees, and we won. What could be cooler than that?

A few days later the course came to an end. "I am sad that I will never see you again." Kathy said.

"I will write you." I replied.

I cherished the sweet moments in the dark during the Escape and Evasion Exercise. It was one of the best parts of the man-woman relationship, a man and a woman working together, and the man protecting the woman.

Kathy did not know that I was married, and for all I knew she had a significant other too. To write her a letter that, by the way, mentioned that I was married, would destroy the magic. It was a brief, romantic, special, moment, with no strings attached. It would reside in our memories for ever.

I never wrote her a letter.

CHAPTER 26

THE BROWN PAPER PACKAGE

The mysterious package arrived in the clinic on a Monday. It was a rectangular box, wrapped in brown paper, which was tied with a string. It was addressed to "Dr. James Smith." They misspelled my name. I wondered if it was a bomb. I listened carefully. It wasn't ticking. Finally, I picked it up and cautiously shook it. There was a rattling sound. I cut the string and tore open the paper. Inside was a letter and a smaller box. I read the letter.

"Dr Smith, Daniel Peterson is faking! He is not disabled. He is ripping the American taxpayer off. I am a taxpayer. He is ripping me off! I took this tape at a party." The letter was unsigned.

Mr. Peterson was my patient. He was a World War II veteran who fought in the battle of Iwo Jima. While attacking a Japanese machine gun placement, he was shot in both thighs. This prevented him from walking. He was given ninety per cent service -connected disability. This meant that he would receive ninety per cent of his base pay in disability.

Every four months I saw Mr. Peterson in my office. He was an overweight man with grey hair. He was always in a wheelchair. In each of his thighs was the entry wound from a Japanese bullet. When I asked him to lift his legs, he could barely move them. He almost never spoke, only occasionally uttering a "yes" or "no" or just grunting. He seemed apathetic, possibly even depressed. Perhaps he was thinking about his experiences on Iwo Jima.

His young wife did all the talking   She was a heavy, buxom, woman who was twenty years younger than her spouse. She had a pretty face. With her ample breasts, she seemed almost voluptuous.   She reminded me of the Venus of Willendorf, a prehistoric stone figurine of a huge breasted woman, thought to be a fertility symbol.

 At one clinic visit I noticed that Mrs. Peterson was heavier, and her breasts were even larger.   "I am going to have a baby." she said, giving a faint, awkward smile.   Looking at Mr. Peterson slumped down in his wheelchair, staring blankly at the Examination Room wall I couldn't help wondering how the reproductive act had taken place.   At age 60 Mr. Peterson became a father.

Three years later the mysterious package arrived.

I inserted the tape into my machine.   On the television screen was the living room of a large house. Music was playing. It was a party.   Sitting in chairs were people happily chatting, laughing, and drinking beer. A few people were dancing to the music.

At the front of the room, closest to the camera was a familiar figure. He moved his legs high in the air with the musical beat. His wheelchair was gone, and the masked expression was replaced by a delighted grin. It was Mr. Peterson. I was stunned by the miraculous recovery of my patient.

Then I remembered the letter.   The anonymous writer was calling my attention to disability fraud.   Mr. Peterson was not disabled. He was getting monthly checks from the Government under false pretenses.

I was conflicted as to what to do about the tape.

Mr. Peterson's disability was determined by a board in Washington, not me.   Should I send the tape to the board? Should I confront Mr. Peterson with the tape?

I discussed that matter with Tom Reed, our patient advocate. "Do nothing." was his terse reply.

Over the next seventeen years Mr. Peterson's health deteriorated. He developed diabetes mellitus. First, it was treated with pills, then with insulin. At 75 he developed congestive heart failure. At 80 he had a stroke which paralyzed his right side. Another stroke two years later affected his left side. He became increasingly demented. He missed several clinic appointments. One day I received a phone call from his wife. "My husband died last week." she said. "Thank you for all of your good care." Then her voice got low and almost seductive. "Come over some time and have a cup of coffee." I declined.

I heard nothing more of Mr. Peterson for three years. Then I received a phone call from the local American Legion post.

"I have Mrs. Peterson here in the office." the man on the phone said. "If you would be willing to state that Mr. Peterson was 100 per cent disabled for the last ten years his life, she can get a widow's pension." I thought back to the VCR tape from years earlier. It showed that Mr. Peterson was faking his disability. I described the tape to the American Legion representative.

"Oh" was his reply. "But you can speak to Mrs. Peterson." He put her on the line.

"Dr. Schmitt. If you will write a statement that Daniel was 100 per cent disabled for the last 10 years of his life from his service-connected leg paralysis, I can get a widow's pension. Can you do that for me?"

I brought up the tape. This seemed not to phase her. "Can I come and see you tomorrow?"

The following morning Mrs. Peterson came into the clinic. She had gained even more weight and her hair was becoming grey.

"If you will say that my husband was 100 percent disabled for the last 10 years of his life from his service- related condition, I can get a widow's pension. I deserve it. I took care of him when he was sick. I deserve it." She seemed to be ignoring what I told her on the phone.

"I received this tape that showed him dancing at a party. He was not disabled. He wasn't even 90 per cent disabled. And now you want me to say that he was 100 per cent disabled from his leg problem for ten years. The tape showed him dancing. He was faking. I would be lying."

"Danny had to do some things to get what he needed." She was admitting the fraud. "But I deserve that pension. I took care of him when he was sick and frail. I deserve it." Her mouth opened an inch and the slits of her eyes narrowed as she pleaded with me. She touched my wrist with her hand.

Still looking into Mrs. Peterson's eyes, I thought of all that I owed to disabled veterans, like those who fought for us after 9/11.

I was in Azerbaijan, a Muslim country not too far from Afghanistan, when the World Trade Center was attacked.

Waking up from my nap in my hotel, I I turned on the TV and saw the World Trade Center on fire. I numbly listened as the newsmen described the plot against our country. I felt violated and scared. I wondered if it was part of a larger plot to kill Americans.

When I walked down the street, I braced myself to be killed every time someone came up behind me. I was grateful to the brave young men who went to Afghanistan to protect me.

Several years later I saw one of these soldiers in a wheelchair at our VA hospital. There was a huge defect in the left side of his head, the result of a brain injury from combat in Afghanistan. Half of his brain was gone. The wheelchair was being pushed by the tragic young man's smiling mother, happy that her boy was alive, and she was going to be able to care for him for the rest of his life. This young hero deserved the gratitude of me and his entire country, and everything that the country could do for him.

But every time a benefit is established, there are those who will abuse it.

Getting disability money is a major theme at Veterans' Hospitals. I am told that, at the time of their discharge, servicemen are taken into a room for a meeting with the disability counselor. "List at least one condition." they are told. They search their bodies for any abnormality.

Peyronie's disease, a condition where the erect penis bends to one side, and tinea versicolor, a fungal condition that discolors the skin are commonly cited conditions. Any joint pain is also listed. Significant medical conditions that occurred during service, such as diabetes or COPD are listed. They don't have to be related to combat. They just are noticed during military service.

Forty- five percent of servicemen leaving the Service are applying for disability for an average of 11 conditions. The irony is that these conditions were not disabling for military service but are declared as disabilities at the time of discharge.

Years later when the veteran's health deteriorates as a result of aging, and he develops heart disease, or has a stroke, he may try to connect these problems to military service. He will cajole his physician into writing a "Nexus Letter". In this letter the physician tries to connect the patient's current health problems to his military service.

One of my patients was diagnosed with sleep apnea at age 60. He wanted me to try to connect his sleep apnea to his military service 40 years earlier because he noticed that, in the Army, he "fell asleep a lot."

Patients sit in waiting rooms discussing how to increase their service- connected disability.

"I want to get 100 percent. I am going to say I have PTSD." I heard a veteran say.

This false disability takes money away from veterans such as the young man in the wheelchair who gave his all for his country. Veteran's groups such as the American Legion lobby for veterans to get benefits.

"Mr. Lacy how are things going?" I once asked one of my patients. He was a 37 year- old man with bipolar disorder.

"Not good. I am getting a $500 a month for being housebound. That means I can't leave the house, or I will lose the money. So, I can't leave home. I would like to take some college courses, but my psychiatrist says that would mean that I am not bipolar, and I could lose my disability."

If Mr. Lacy had any potential to work for a living, it was being lost by his absence from the work force. His disability check disabled him as much as his bipolar disorder and doomed him to a useless, boring life. Eventually he will have been out of work so long that he is incapable of getting a job. His only option for increasing his income will be trying to get more disability. The incentives for disability are often perverse.

I looked back at Mrs. Peterson.

She would get some money from Social Security, but not a lot. Her son would be in his 20s. Could she pay for his college? Her son had a difficult life. His father was already an old man when he was born, and then his father died.

Mr. Peterson became frail and sick, but this was because of his age, not his gunshot wounds. I empathized with Mrs. Peterson who took care of him in his declining years.   All I had to do to help them was to tell a little lie. I glanced at Mrs. Peterson who was looking hopefully at me.

"I will think about it. I will let you know tomorrow."

The following morning Mrs. Peterson phoned me. "Dr. Schmitt. Have you made up your mind? Will you write that letter for me?"

"No, I will not."

CHAPTER 27

WHY ARE THE COTTON FARMERS SUICIDAL?

The truck was dwarfed by the huge white ball that it carried in its back. It reminded me of a muscular ant scurrying away from a picnic with an oversized morsel of cake.

It was 2007. I was in Bangalore, India, as a medical volunteer at Bangalore Baptist Hospital. As my driver took me to the hospital, I saw another truck, and another. It was like a line of ants taking bits of food to their hill. Towering above the trucks were huge balls of cotton. Hanging on to the sides of the bales, like tiny aphids accompanying the ants, were men and women getting a ride. These were cotton farmers taking their crop to market.

In 1990 I was mobilized in the naval reserve for the First Gulf War, Desert Storm. Saddam Husain had used nerve gas on the Kurds and there was concern that he would use it against Coalition troops.

Nerve impulses are transmitted through acetyl choline, a chemical. Acetyl choline is broken down -by another chemical, cholinesterase. Nerve gas, such as Sarin, binds cholinesterase. Acetyl choline is not broken down, and abnormally high levels develop. The result is muscle paralysis and death.

In 2003, I was again mobilized for the second Gulf War, Iraqi Freedom. Again, there was the concern for nerve gas exposure, but there were no definite cases of nerve gas poisoning.

I began to think that nerve gas poisoning was a mythical concept, but that was about to   change.

Bangalore Baptist hospital is a relatively new hospital. The Director of the Hospital proudly took me to the new wing which was clean, white, and high tech. I could have been in an American hospital.

It was only when I walked outside and saw poor women in saris, holding children, lined up to get into the hospital, and sacred cows wandering around the grounds, that I remembered that I was in India.

The Director was especially proud of the modern Intensive Care Unit. Almost every bed was occupied. In each of two of the beds a male patient was on a ventilator.

"What is this man's problem?" I asked the Director. A tube was in his trachea and as the machine cycled his chest moved.

"This man is a cotton farmer. He attempted suicide with insecticide."

I remembered that some insecticides contained a chemical called organophosphate, which works like nerve gas to paralyze the nervous system.

"And this man?" I asked about the ventilator patient in the next bed.

"Also, a cotton farmer. He also attempted suicide with pesticide."

Sitting up in the next bed smiling at us was a man of about 40 years. Fluid ran from a small bottle into the intravenous line in his wrist. On the bottle was written the word "atropine."

"This man is recovering from his suicide attempt. He also ingested insecticide."

I remembered that atropine was an antidote for nerve gas poisoning.

In the next bed was yet another farmer who was recovering from a suicide attempt.

"Why are the cotton farmers committing suicide?" I asked the Director after we had left the ICU.

The grey-haired man in the lab coat smiled as if he welcomed the question. He began speaking like a professor beginning a lecture.

"India is an agrarian country. Sixty per cent of the people are farmers. Farming is a risky business. You have droughts, insects, crop failures, and other causes. Certain crops, such as coffee and cotton are volatile. The price goes up and down. When the price goes down the farmer's family suffers. The farmer can go bankrupt. And there is a readily available poison, the insecticide. So, the farmer sometimes kills himself. Most of the people in India are Hindus. In Hinduism you are reincarnated, you come back again, maybe to a better life."

"So, does the cotton farmer commit suicide so that he can come back to a better life?" I asked. "He just reboots?" I smiled at my use of a computer term in referring to reincarnation.

"Yes, that is probably a part of it. The government of India is aware of the problem. And measures are now being taken to relieve the farmer's financial burdens and prevent suicide."

The treatment of nerve gas exposure is atropine, which blocks the acute affects. Later a drug called L- PAM is given to further reverse the effects of the poison. If the patient is sick enough, he is placed on a ventilator to help him breathe. As I glanced back toward the Intensive Care Unit, I realized that I had gained firsthand knowledge of the treatment of this poison, from a surprising source.

When I left Bangalore Baptist hospital I was not finished with India.

For many years I have sponsored foreign medical graduates. They work with me for several months. Then I write them letters of recommendation which they use in their quest for jobs and residencies in America.

Dr. Park was a gynecologist in South Korea. Performing abortions generates a major portion of the work of a gynecologist in South Korea. When Dr. Park converted to Catholicism, he would no longer perform abortions. He couldn't make a living as a gynecologist. So, he moved to the US to retrain as an internist.

Dr. Muhammed was an Iraqi physician. During the Coalition bombing of Baghdad in 2003 Dr. Muhammed worked in an emergency room. The emergency room was hit by bombs and several patients were killed. When the war ended, Iraq was in such chaos, that Dr. Mohammed moved to America where he worked with me before he began new job.

Dr. Kadian was a young woman who went to medical school in India. When we worked together, we talked about Hinduism. I told her that I was going to India.

"My father will be waiting to greet you in New Delhi." Dr. Kadian told me.

At the Delhi Airport two men were waiting for me. A white- haired man was holding a sign "Dr. James Schmitt." This was Dr. Kadian's father, Professor Kadian. Next to him was a younger man, his driver.

We drove to Kurukshetra, a city in Haryana State, to the west of New Delhi. I was given a room in the Guest House at the University.

That night there was a knock on my door. It was Dr. Kadian's driver. He was accompanied by an older man. Both men had the last name of Singh. The driver was a muscular man that I guessed could be no older than forty. He wore a white dress shirt and his hair was recently trimmed. His appearance was appropriate for the driver of a university professor.

The older man was thin. His hair was white, and he wore thick glasses. He was dressed in a white uniform. He was a cook. He carried a bottle of Jim Beam Whiskey. "This is for you." he said. "A gift from Doctor Kadian."

They apparently thought that all Americans drank whiskey. The cook opened the bottle and handed me a glass. "Just a little." I said. "I still have jet lag." Then he poured a large glass for himself and the driver. The two men sunk into soft chairs and relaxed.

"I would like to come to America sometime." said the driver, a boyish looking man. He poured himself another drink.

"Yes. My cousin went to America for a visit. Disney World is very good." said the mellow cook with a smile. His speech was beginning to slur.

The driver took a package of cigarettes from his breast pocket and proffered it to me.

"No." I declined. He put a cigarette in his mouth and lit it.

The two Mr. Singhs, now totally intoxicated from Jim Beam, sat across from each other chatting in Hindi and sipping whiskey. Then they stopped talking, and the cook began snoring. Both men were asleep.

After a half hour the driver woke up. He glanced at me, then at the cook. He shook the cook awake and said something to him in Hindi. The men got up to leave.

They smiled broadly as they handed the now half empty whiskey bottle to me.

The following morning Mr. Singh, the driver, drove me to a famous religious site, the site of the battle of the Bhagavad-Gita.

The younger Dr. Kadian had told her father that I was interested in religion. Professor Kadian had designed a VIP tour of religious sites.

Hinduism is thousands of years old. It teaches that the soul never dies. It is reincarnated into a new body. Living a good life gives one karma, or merit, which results in reincarnation into a higher state. With bad karma, one may be reincarnated into a lower status, even into the body of an animal.

Hinduism has many gods, as many as thirty million. The most important gods are Brahma, the creator of the Universe, Vishnu, its preserver, and Shiva its destroyer. Vishnu sometimes comes to earth as a human, called Krishna. I always wondered if the similarities between the words "Krishna" and "Christ", the son of God, who also came to Earth as a human, indicated some connection between the two beliefs.

Hinduism has many sacred writings. One of them is the Bhagavad -Gita which is a discussion between Krishna and Arjuna, a warrior, during a great battle, about the meaning of existence. The site of this battle is one of the most sacred sites of Hinduism. The Bhagavad-Gita is sometimes called the Bible of Hinduism.

Afterward Mr. Singh drove me to a Hindu temple. The temple reminded me of a museum. In glassed- in areas were manikins of Hindu gods. A priest put a red dot on my forehead, and wrapped a red band around my wrist. The red dot and the band increased my karma.

Then I was taken to Professor Kadian's house for lunch. In the entry was a statue of the God Shiva. Next to it, on a shelf, was a smaller statue of the elephant- headed god, Ganesha.

The legend was that in a moment of anger, Shiva beheaded his son. This distraught god replaced the head of his son with that of the next creature that he saw, an elephant. Ganesha is the god of good luck.

At lunch I met a young physician and his wife, a beautiful young woman whose porcelain features were framed by a purple silk sari. "I understand that you are interested in religion." the young woman said.

"Yes, I was raised as a Christian, but I believe that there are many ways to God. Hinduism is one of those ways."

"Even with thirty million gods?" Hinduism has millions of gods. The young woman seemed to be questioning her own religion.

I remembered what the Imam at the Grand Mosque in Bahrain said to me three years earlier. "Does God punish you for where you were born?"

People adopt the religions of the area where they were born. The young woman was a Hindu because she was born in India.

"Does God punish you for where you were born?" I repeated the Imam. "You are a Hindu because you were born in India. Hinduism teaches you to be good to your fellow man, like Christianity. Krishna comes to earth in human form to help man, just like Christ. The names are even similar."

The young woman, seemingly comforted by my remarks, smiled.

The driver and the cook drove me back to the Guest House. On the way we stopped at a two- story building and went inside. Men sat at tables drinking tea and beer and talking.

I gathered that this was just a break in the work day for the two Mr. Singhs. I walked outside to take a picture. Five minutes later the cook came running out the door. He was gasping for air. When he saw me, he clutched his chest as if he was having a heart attack. He bent over to catch his breath. Then he motioned me back inside.

This episode told me that Professor Kadian had given the men explicit instructions not to let anything happen to me, perhaps at forfeiture of their jobs. Realizing this, I sometimes played a cat and mouse game with them. I walked fast, forcing them to keep up with me. This was especially hard on the driver, who smoked. After I stopped, I waited for the young man, who eventually caught up with me. When he stopped, he bent over gasping.

 I reveled in the fact that I was more fit than a man who was at least 20 years my junior.

The next morning the two Mr. Singhs, and the elder Mr. Singh's wife and daughter and I drove north to the city of Haridwar.

The Ganges river is the holiest river in India. The holiest part is at Varanasi, one of the holiest sites in India.

People come from all over India to bathe at Varanasi and wash away their sins. Bodies are cremated on the shores of the river and the ashes kicked into the water. Sometimes the bodies are incompletely burned, and the remains are seen floating in the water. The sewage from one of the most populous parts of India flows into the river. The E. coli bacteria concentration at Varanasi is 10 million per cubic centimeter. This, technically, makes the river a sewer.

 At Haridwar the river is closer to its source, the Himalayas, and much cleaner. I picked Haridwar as the site of my pilgrimage to the sacred river.

The way to the river from our parking place was downhill through a series of switchbacks. I began running down the hill. I delighted in playing "hide and seek" with the men who had been tasked with watching over me. When I reached the edge of the river I turned to see if I had outdistanced my pursuers.

A minute later the driver came running up. He was terrified that he might have lost me. When he saw me, he bent over and began gasping for air.

For an instant I was thrilled at having bested the young man. But when I noticed the pained look on his face and that he was still gasping for air, I felt guilty. My chasing game was cruel.

"You should stop smoking. There is some gum you can chew that will help you stop." I said to the poor young man as I patted him on the shoulder.

The shore of the river was covered with people. Some were clothed. Others were naked. In the water pilgrims waded to receive their purification.

Standing very close to me was a stark-naked man. His hair was long and white. In his hand was a trident. This was a holy man. The trident was a sign that he was a disciple of Shiva.

The wife and daughter of the cook, still wearing their saris waded into the water. Once in the water they pulled their saris up to let the water run over their bodies.

I undressed and quickly waded into the river. The water was fast moving and cold. The cook and the driver grabbed each of my arms and helped me to a cable that hung down into the water. I grabbed the cable, but they still held tightly on to me. If I were swept away, they never would able to explain it to their boss, Professor Kadian.

I was immersed in the most sacred river of the Hindus. My entire body was covered with holiness. I needed to find something to be healed from.

I noticed that I occasionally had skipped heart beats. They were probably premature atrial contractions. I closed my eyes and said a prayer. Then I checked my pulse. The annoying heart beats were gone. I was cured. It was a miracle, perhaps.

We exited the river, dried off, and began the long drive home. It was growing dark.

One of the women said something in Hindi and the driver stopped the car by the side of the road. The women hiked up their saris and squatted to urinate. The cook did likewise. The driver stared at me. I didn't move. "It is OK Sir, Indian tradition." He assumed that I was too embarrassed to urinate on the side of the road. I wasn't. I just didn't have to pee.

The following morning, Mr. Singh, my driver, drove me to Agra, the site of the Taj Mahal. In Agra we stopped at a restaurant where I ordered curried lamb. The owner, a Muslim man of about 50 wearing a white dress shirt, sat down at my table.

"My Uncle has told me to be good to you." he said. "Anything you want I will give you." I assumed that his uncle was Professor Kadian. Was Professor Kadian really the man's uncle, or was he a figure like "The Godfather" who had power over him?

My meal was free.

A teenager came into the restaurant. The driver began talking to him in Hindi. Their tones escalated, and they seemed to be arguing. The argument was about the boy's fee for guiding me into the Taj Mahal.

Finally, they agreed on a price and we walked to the Taj Mahal. The boy led us through an entrance that I was told was secret, reserved for special personages, like Presidents of the United States, or so I was told.

In the Sixteenth Century, the Mughals, who were Muslims, came from what is now Afghanistan into northern India. The monotheistic Muslims who ate beef, but thought the pig was unclean, came into conflict with the polytheistic pork- eating Hindus, for whom the cow was sacred.

One of the Mughal emperors was Shah Jahan. When his second wife, Mumtaz Mahal died, the mourning emperor built a mausoleum for his beloved, the Taj Mahal.

I have seen many great monuments in the world. Machu Picchu, a hidden city in the Andes that looked like it has just been abandoned, the giant Pyramids of Egypt, the Great Wall of China that goes on for two thousand miles, and Angkor Wat, the largest religious structure in the world, but none them prepared me for my first view of the Taj.

Through an arch at the end of a long moat, I saw a white mosque. It was built on a marble platform which raised the building above the ground so that the background was blue sky. On either side of the huge dome were smaller domes. Further out were minarets for the calling to prayer. Entry into the mosque was through a high white arch. The total effect was of jaw dropping beauty and symmetry.

We took off our shoes before we entered the mosque. At the center of a huge room was an opening. Tourists stared through the opening down at the tombs of Shah Jahan and his wife.

Being in such a magnificent temple of Allah, I decided to pray for better health. I have an astigmatism of my left eye. I prayed for my vision to get better. I removed my glasses and looked around at the magnificent walls that were inlayed with precious stones. I did seem to see more clearly. Maybe it was another miracle.

One of the lenses fell out of the frame, making a tinkling sound on the floor. This signaled the driver to leap in to action. "No!" He shouted to warn off anyone who might want to get my lens. Then he got down on the floor and crawled around until he retrieved the lens.

The next day we headed into the Punjab to the Golden Temple, the most sacred shrine of the Sikhs.

Sikhism, which was started in the 16th century by a man named Guru Nanak, combines elements of Hinduism and Islam. Like Islam, Sikhism believes in only one god and forbids the worship of religious images, but like Hinduism, Sikhism believes in karma and reincarnation.

My driver brought his son, a boy of about ten with him. On the way we stopped to pick up an elderly Sikh man.

The old man was a feast of white. He had a long white beard and was dressed in a white robe and turban. As I sat in his living room, he took lychee nuts from a bowel and removed he shells one by one. Then he handed each nut to me. This was a sign of hospitality and respect.

Then we all headed to the east to Amritsar, the site of the Golden Temple. As we neared Amritsar we stopped at a small house where the old Sikh's mother lived. The tiny woman, who was dressed in a white sari must have been close to a hundred years old. After a short visit, she hugged her son, and waved to us, and we drove to the Golden Temple.

To enter the temple, we had to cover our heads with a kind of cap and remove our shoes and cover our feet with a cloth shoe.

The temple was in the middle of a huge reflecting pool. To get to it we walked along a stone causeway. The huge golden building was topped with domes. On the top of each dome was a spire. The structure seemed to be a combination of Muslim and Hindu architecture.

In 1984, this peaceful scene was disrupted by violence. An extremist Sikh sect took up residence in the temple. India's Prime Minister, Indira Gandhi ordered her military to attack the sacred temple. In response to this sacrilege, Mrs. Gandhi's Sikh body guards assassinated her.

Inside the building men in long beards wearing turbans looked at sacred texts and chanted. We were at the heart and soul of a great religion. My back was aching from prolonged standing. I prayed for relief, and miraculously, the pain seemed to be better.

A parishioner had the choice of lingering in the temple and praying or walking through. We decided to just walk through the temple.

When we were outside, we removed our caps and foot coverings and walked toward our car.

A woman approached us. She was about 40 years of age, and her clothes were tattered. She extended her hand to beg. Having just left the center of Sikhism I was imbued with religious zeal and charity. I wanted to help the woman.

I looked in my wallet and found a 3000 rupee note, worth about 45 American dollars. Gripping the bill, I extended my hand to the woman. She smiled with delight, and took the bill in her hand.

In the blink of an eye, the hand of the driver grabbed the bill and took it from us.

"No, No, No!" the angry driver shouted. "In India good jobs, government jobs. No have to beg. No, No!" The woman, seeing her treasure fly away, began sobbing.

One day we drove to a small village. As we walked down the narrow street, I heard people shout. "U.S. M.D! U.S. M.D! (United States Medical Doctor)". People stretched out their hands to touch me. It was as if I had magical properties. I felt like Jesus walking through the multitudes.

I was taken into a small house. On a small bed lay an old woman. She was very frail. "US MD" someone said. The old lady stretched out her hands and touched my face. She smiled. I wondered if she thought that just touching me would cure her. Or maybe she was blind and wanted to see what I looked like.

I was then driven to a huge house. It was in the middle of a flat plain. The house was surrounded by a concrete wall. I noticed young men driving cattle in from the fields. Next to the house was a row of cattle. They were being milked by hand.

There was a huge drawing room on the first floor of the house. Sitting on couches against the walls were ten or twelve men. They were drinking tea and conversing in Hindi. A bowel in the middle of the room was filled with lychee nuts.

I had no idea what this group was. A political meeting perhaps, or a gathering of local farmers. I wondered if they had come to honor their American guest. They didn't see to pay much notice to me.

I wanted to say something. I wanted attention. I decided to tell a story, the story of the dog and the dead rabbit. One of my wife's coworkers told her this story. She initially thought it was true, then realized it was a joke.

"Two couples lived a across the street from each other." I began. The Indian men turned toward me and listened. "The Smiths had a rabbit that they kept in a cage. The Jones who lived a across the street had a dog, a Labrador Retriever."

A tall man with a bald head began translating in Hindi.

"One day Mrs. Jones heard a scratching on her back door. When she opened the door. she saw her dog. He had something in his mouth. It was covered with mud. When she cleaned the mud off, she was horrified. It was the body of the rabbit from across the street. She called her husband. 'Our dog has done something terrible. He has killed the rabbit from across the street.'

The husband studied the body of the dead rabbit. He glanced out the window and saw that the car of the owners of the rabbit was gone. They were out.

'The rabbit was old. We can wash off his body and dry it. Then we can put it back in the cage. When they get home, they will just think that he died of old age.'

Mr. and Mrs. Jones washed he body of the bunny and then Mr. Jones carried the body across the street and put it back in its cage." I stopped to allow my interpreter to translate, then resumed my story. Some of the men nodded to show they were listening.

"Several days passed. Then one day, Mrs. Jones saw Mrs. Smith coming toward her house."

She invited Mrs. Smith in to have some tea. After a while Mrs. Smith began talking. 'You know, the other day something strange happened. Our rabbit died. He was old. We buried him in the backyard. Then we went to the store. When we got home, we found his body back in the cage!"

The humorous catch in this story was that the dog had not killed the rabbit, but just dug up the body that its owners had buried.

The bald man translated.

Having delivered the punchline for the joke, I looked around the room for laughter. There was no laughter. There was dead silence. I glanced at the faces. There was not a single smile. The men seemed to be in deep thought as they mulled over the story. They glanced at each other awkwardly. Finally, one of the men spoke.

"Did they kill the dog?"

Something had been lost in translation, or perhaps, Indian men were not familiar with the behavior of Labrador Retrievers.

The time for me to return to the US arrived. I was driven to the airport by Mr. Singh. I looked through my wallet for Indian money. It was of no use to me in America. I discovered the 3,000 Rupee note that Mr. Singh stopped me from giving to the poor woman at the Golden Temple.

I handed the bill to my driver. His eyes lit up as he saw the money. "For the driver?"

"Yes, for my driver." He was moved at my gift. His eyelids crinkled in a smile and tears formed.

I reached into my pocket and retrieved a pack of nicotine gum. As I handed it to the driver, I gave him a hug.

"Try to stop smoking."

CHAPTER 28

THE RED FIRE ENGINE

"Give us your wallet or we will kill you!"

The speaker was a young African American man who was brandishing a large knife. Behind him stood another man.

I began working in the Veterans Administration Hospital in Richmond, Virginia on October 1, 1983. It was to be several months before my family came to join me. I lived in an upstairs room in one of the hospital buildings.

It was a lonely time for me. I often walked to a fast food restaurant a few blocks away.

One Saturday evening my walk was interrupted by two young black man who stood blocking my way. One of them was holding a knife. "OK. Give me your wallet." In my wallet was a five-dollar bill which was to pay for my dinner.

"That's it?" the man asked incredulously. "You have to have more than that. OK empty out your pockets!" I turned my pockets inside out. There was nothing in them but lint.

I was a bit embarrassed by the lint. Had I known that I was going to be robbed I would have had cleaner pockets.

"That's it?" the other man asked unbelievingly. He turned to his friend and asked. "What is this guy, a truck driver?" Then he looked back at me. "If you tell anyone about this, we will find you and kill you."

"Don't worry. I won't tell anyone." The men turned and ran away toward a nearby mall. I went back to my room and called the police.

It quickly became known that Dr. Schmitt was robbed while going to dinner. Patients and staff vied to have me over to dinner to protect me from the criminal element.

 One of my patients was Edward Landrigan, a Navy veteran of about 65 years of age.   His friends just called him "EL".

Mr. Landrigan was a WWII vet who had served on a submarine. He wrote a book about the Submarine Service which was in the process of publication.

EL was a big man, with a large frame that supported a weight of 280 lbs. He looked like a wrestler who had gone to seed. His bulbous nose and coarse facial features were topped by a shock of white hair. He had a deep booming voice that projected like that of an opera singer. When I told him that I had just left the Navy, we bonded.   Somehow, he learned that I had been mugged while walking to dinner. "You should come over to my house for dinner." he said. I do believe that he meant that I could come over every night, but occasionally I took him up on his offer.

 He lived in a small house in Chester, about 15 miles from Richmond. He proudly showed me his vegetable garden, a 20 - foot by 30- foot plot that grew all of the vegetables that he could use, with plenty left over to supply to his friends and neighbors.

 He was married to his second wife, Emily. Emily was an English woman whose first husband was an American soldier who survived the D Day invasion. Emily and her husband had been good friends of EL and his wife Nancy. After their spouses died EL and Emily married. Emily, with her trim figure, calm demeanor and soft speech with its refined British accent, contrasted with her husband's great size and his loud rustic speech. Despite their external differences, they seemed to adore each other.

We had a dinner of steak, and vegetables from their garden, and a bottle of inexpensive wine.   On the walls and on cabinets surrounding the small table were pictures of EL in his Navy uniform, pictures of him with a woman that I assumed was his first wife, and pictures of Emily with her first husband. All the photos were black and white, attesting to their age.

"That's my first wife Nancy." my host said, pointing to a picture of a dark-haired woman in a blouse and skirt standing next to a young man in a sailor's uniform. This was EL in his 20s.

"I had a nice sheet metal business. I had two men working for me. Then Nancy got sick. She got weak and short of breath. It was her heart. She needed a new valve. We didn't have insurance. I took all the money from my business to get her a new heart valve. I had to sell everything. Laid the men off. And Nancy died anyway." he said regretfully.

"Now I live on my Veterans' pension. And, oh yes, I have my book. 'Submarine Sailor'. It is being published and I might make some money out of that." He smiled at Emily who was placing large slices of cherry pie on the table. "Emily and I do fine. Don't we?" Emily nodded.

EL had a keen mind and he loved to talk. He made insightful comments about every subject under the Sun. He had surprisingly liberal views for an old white man who grew up in the South. He was against racial discrimination in any form.

"Some of the finest people that I have met were black people." he remarked.

"Two houses down from me is Fred Garth. He landed on Utah Beach on D Day. His arm was nearly taken off by a cannon shell. The boy next to him was a black man. The black man took off his boot and used his sock to make a tourniquet and stopped the bleeding. Then he got Fred to the medics. He saved old Garth's life.

Garth grew up in North Carolina. He believed in the separation of the races. But not anymore! The black man and Fred kept in touch. And do you know what happened? When the black man went back to his home in Alabama, he had to ride at the back of the bus. He couldn't even drink out of a water fountain. He risked his life for those people, and they treated him like that." EL shook his head in disgust.

I admired EL tremendously. With his pale white face, heavy build and ubiquitous tee shirt he looked like a "red neck." but out of his big mouth, spoken in his soft Virginia drawl, came words of insight, tolerance, and wisdom. His tiny house in Chester became an intellectual oasis for me to escape to from the stresses of working in a Veteran's Administration hospital.

Despite Mr. Landrigan's obesity, he had none of the complications of obesity. Even though he loved bacon, his cholesterol was ideal. Despite his stoutness he didn't have diabetes. He carried his large body around without developing chest pain and his electrocardiogram was normal. He loved potato chips. As his physician I counseled him to watch his diet and lose weight. "I will do it." he answered, but he never did.

EL's book became a success. He invited me to accompany him to book signings. He knew that I liked to write. This was his way of honoring my writing aspirations. Maybe he thought that I would meet a publisher at the store.

The huge bear of a man sat in the stores booming out anecdotes about his WWII service as he signed books. His life was so interesting that people came to hear about it. He was thrilled at being the center of attention. His whole life came down to this.

Sometime in 2000 EL bought a red scooter. This was the return of the red fire engine of his childhood.

There are two times in a man's life when he wants a little red fire engine. The first is when he is very young, maybe even before he can walk, when he sees a real hook and ladder truck speeding down the street with is siren blaring and firemen in their helmets hanging on for their lives. He points at the engine and chortles and says something that his proud parents are sure means "fire engine". They may decide to wait for a few months until he can sit up and his back muscles are stronger before they buy him a toy engine that he can sit on and push around.

The second fire engine comes much later.

The boy has become a man.

He may have significant medical problems, such as emphysema or heart failure, making it difficult to walk without becoming short of breath. He might be a diabetic with ulcers on his feet that make it difficult to walk. Poor circulation may have even caused gangrene necessitating the amputation of a leg. He could have had a stroke paralyzing part of his body. He may even have had a spinal cord injury that paralyzes him from the waist down, and he has become a paraplegic.

These conditions create the need for mobility aids. The paraplegic may do fine with a wheelchair. Having use of his arms allows him to push its wheels for propulsion. The patient with heart or lung problems may do best with a scooter, a small car that he drives, requiring no physical exertion.

But the patient may have none of these problems. He just wants a scooter.

The owner of a scooter can zip around hospitals and malls with ease. He can go faster than someone who is walking. He can do something that no one else can. He can drive a car inside of a building. It reminds its owner of the toy fire engine that he had as a child. The fact that it is often orange, not red, is not a problem.

Some of the happiest smiles that I have seen on patients are those in their little cars gleefully zipping past those who must walk.

Mr. Landrigan's weight began to increase after he got his scooter. My most vivid image of EL was of him sitting in his scooter smiling, with a bag of potato chips in his hand.

I was shocked at his weight gain.

Landrigan was a writer with a great sense of humor. I wanted to use some humor in my discussion of his obesity.

WC Fields was a comedian in the early part of the twentieth century. He had a skin condition called rosacea which over time caused a bulbous nose called a rhinophyma. This condition is often due to heavy alcohol use. His big nose added to his comic image. WC Fields was also known for his wit.

I discussed WC Fields with my patient.

"'Everything worth doing is either illegal, immoral, or fattening' was one WC Fields' quips."

EL grew up watching WC Fields on the screen and was familiar with his sayings.

"But let's look at that sentence a little more closely." I said.

My patient smiled and nodded. I continued my analysis.

"If you do something illegal, you eventually go to jail. Everybody knows that jail food is full of fat and carbohydrate and will make you fat. So, you can just simplify that phrase to "Everything worth doing is immoral or fattening.""

EL chuckled.

"But let's go even further." I continued. "People who do immoral things, eventually commit a crime, and they wind up in jail eating fattening prison food. So, you can shorten WC Fields' saying to.

"Everything worth doing is Fattening!"

EL laughed uproariously. I was proud to tickle the sense humor of such a creative man with my own whimsy.

But he didn't stop eating potato chips.

By January of 2002 Ed Landrigan weighed over 400 pounds, the maximum weight that the scales in our clinic can measure.

In 2003 Operation Iraqi Freedom began and I was called to active duty in the Navy Reserve in Norfolk.

Very early one Saturday morning I stopped by the VA hospital on my way to Norfolk. There at the entrance to the Emergency Room was EL and Emily.

"He feels terrible. He has a fever." Emily said. She usually was unflappable, but today she was worried. In contrast to his usual jovial nature, EL sat silently in his wheelchair and stared into space. "They will take care of you." I said and patted him on the shoulder. Then I drove to Norfolk.

The next day I called the VA hospital. EL was being treated for a urinary tract infection and was doing better.

When I came home on the weekend my mother in law was visiting. Suddenly she looked up from the newspaper that she was reading. "Wasn't that man you knew named Landrigan?" she asked

"Yes, Ed Landrigan." I replied.

"He died."

I was stunned. I looked at the obituary. There was a picture of EL as a young man in the Navy. Somehow, I thought that EL with his wisdom and decency would never die, just as a young man I believed that my father would never die.

EL had a long obituary, as befitted a war hero and a writer.

Months later, when the war ended, I returned to the VA hospital. I reviewed EL's medical record.

He was given antibiotics to treat a blood infection that spread from the urinary tract. He was doing better, but then he aspirated some food. His ability to oxygenate his blood declined and a tube was placed in his trachea and he was placed on a respirator. He was moved to the Intensive Care Unit. In the ICU his lung function continued to decline, and he passed away. His family consented to an autopsy.

The autopsy report described a man that was so heavy that he couldn't be weighed.

"The subject is a man who weighs in excess of 500 lbs. The lungs are engorged with fluid. There is bilateral pneumonia. There is no pulmonary embolism. The heart is enlarged and weighs 1.2 kilograms. There is no myocardial infarction. The liver is engorged with fluid. The brain is normal." read the report.

The final cause of death was given as "Respiratory Failure Due to Aspiration."

The death was not a complication of obesity such as diabetes or coronary artery disease, but obesity itself.

EL had choked on his food. His abdomen was so large that he couldn't generate a good cough to keep it out of his lungs. The food caused pneumonia which impaired his ability to oxygenate his blood. His huge abdomen restricted the movement of his lungs and he died from lack of oxygen.

I shuddered at the mental image of the huge shape of my once brilliant friend lying naked on a cold metal table in the morgue.

I have no doubt that the scooter shortened my mentor, Edward Landrigan's, life.

Using a scooter reduces the amount of energy expended by a patient. He no longer walks, but just moves with the pressure on a pedal and the turn of a steering wheel.

I doubt that many patients drive their scooters to the gym where they work out.

Scooter owners burn fewer calories during the day than their friends who walk. Every 3500 calories gained results in a pound of fat. This increases risk of diabetes and heart disease.

When my patients ask for a scooter, I emphasize the importance of exercise in maintaining good health. There is evidence that walking decreases risk of heart failure, and that using a scooter increases risk of diabetes. Walking prolongs life.

I tell my patients the story of Edward Landrigan.

Sometimes they give up their pursuit of the red fire engine and begin walking more.

Ed Landrigan, the story teller, would like that.

CHAPTER 29

DON'T NAME YOUR FISH!

In both of our houses in Richmond we had fish ponds that we stocked with goldfish. They kept the mosquito population down by eating the larvae. We even had a white koi that we named Roger. We bought Roger when he was small, … and cheap. Soon Roger grew into a beautiful, white, foot long koi. We congratulated ourselves for buying him so cheap when he was small, but over time he had become a valuable mature koi.

One morning, the pond was muddy, and some of the buckets that contained the water plants were overturned…and Roger was gone. Ten feet from the pond, in the shrubs, we found Roger's body. Some creature, probably a raccoon, had caught Roger and carried him off where he died. For some inexplicable reason, the koi's body was not eaten.

We were saddened by Roger's demise and decided never again to give a fish, at least an outdoor fish, a name. From now on Norma stocked our ponds with feeder fish-tiny gold fish that were used to feed other fish in fish tanks. They only cost 12 cents apiece and within months became grown goldfish.

In the winter the pond froze almost to the bottom, leaving a small space near the bottom for the fish to live. In the spring, when the pond thawed, we looked anxiously to see if any of the fish had survived the winter.

One year we were thrilled to learn that five of the fish had survived the winter. One of them was pure white, another was red in color, and another had beautiful white markings on top of the gold. We began to think of these survivors if not quite "pets", at least "fish of significance" that lived with us.

That spring and summer the fish tripled in size. Again, we congratulated ourselves at having gotten such great fish from cheap feeder fish.

We went away on our summer vacation.

When, a week later, we drove back into our driveway, and looked at the pond, we witnessed a crime being committed.

A large snake was swallowing one of the fish.

Against a tree was a pair of tongs that Norma used for reaching leaves in the pond.

I picked up the tongs and grabbed the snake in the middle. It dropped the red fish, and to our amazement, regurgitated a second fish that as in its gullet, the white fish.

The snake was a Northern Water Snake. It was not venomous, but it had a painful bite. I didn't want to kill it, but just teach it a lesson. Gripping its mid- portion in the tongs, I walked toward the nearby lake, yelling all the time to scare the reptile. Then I flung it as far as I could out into the lake.

Two of our fish had been eaten, but miraculously, the fish that were rescued from the gullet of the snake survived. The white one seemed stunned for a few minutes, then swam off. But the red one had lost some scales from the experience with the snake, and within days a disgusting fungus began growing from its injured skin.

Norma netted the sick fish, then put it into a separate bucket to which was added an antibiotic solution. For several days the fungus increased in size and the fish weakened. The prognosis seemed bad. Then, the fungus began shrinking, and finally disappeared.

Delighted at her cure, Dr. Mckenzie-Schmitt reunited her patient with his friends in the pond. Because he came back from the dead, we broke our rule, and named it "Lazarus."

When Norma and I went kayaking later in the summer we spotted two grown water snakes sunning themselves on a branch overhanging the lake. This was likely our fish killer and its mate. When they saw us, they dropped into the water. I hoped I had taught them a lesson and they would stay away from our fish. After all, the lake was full of fish.

If we had driven in to our yard two minutes later, the goldfish would have been consumed by the snake. It seemed like Divine Providence had saved the fish.

One fall morning when I went out to look at the pond, I couldn't see any fish. "They are probably hiding." I thought. I threw in some fish food. Still no fish. "They are all gone." The water was muddy. Several plants were broken, as if the pond had been the scene of a titanic struggle. It could have been a raccoon, or a great blue heron, or maybe the snakes had returned. Eventually a few small fish came out of hiding, but the white one and Lazarus were gone.

Animals that you keep outside are just food for predators, not pets. When you live in Nature you get Nature.

Don't name fish who live outside.

When he was 6 years old, our son Brian got his first pet, a goldfish. Brian named him "Goldy".

The fish was kept in a small glass tank in Brian's room. At the bottom of the tank was a ceramic castle. A green plant that looked like a seaweed was rooted in the sand at the bottom of the tank. The fish happily swam around the tank, sometimes going in and out of crevices in the castle. Brian fantasized that the fish was living in the castle. He sprinkled fish food on the surface of the water every morning. "Don't give him too much." we cautioned Brian. We knew that overfeeding a goldfish could kill it.

One Saturday morning Norma was startled to see Goldy floating on his side on the top of the water. Goldy was dead. There had been little evidence that the fish was ill. "In retrospect he was a little listless yesterday." Norma remarked. "Maybe Brian fed him too much. Brian loved that fish. It was his first pet. Maybe he will think he killed it with too much food."

"He doesn't even know living things die. He thinks you go on forever." I added. Norma and I struggled for a few minutes as to how to deal with this tragedy.

"I have an idea!" I exclaimed. "Brian is at his friend's house. He won't be home for at least an hour. We can just buy another goldfish and replace it. He will never know the difference."

A few minutes later Norma and I were driving down Midlothian Turnpike to PetSmart, a nearby pet store.

We walked into the store expecting to find a tank full of goldfish. But our hopes were quickly crushed by the saleswoman. "We don't have any grown fish." she said. "We do have feeder fish to feed your grown fish. They are only 10 cents apiece." When we looked at the tiny fish in the tank, we realized they wouldn't do. We needed a dead ringer for Brian's fish.

"Maybe it is time for Brian to learn that all things die. He has to learn some time." Norma said. We thought for a moment.

"Let's go to Petco. They must have goldfish." I said. We drove to Petco, a nearby pet store. But Petco also had no grown fish. "Brian is 6 years old. He needs to learn about life and death sometime. Let's just go home and tell him that his fish died." Norma said with an air of resignation. I thought for a moment.

"Let's go down the road. There has got to be a store that has goldfish." I said. We were not ready to break the bad news to our 6-year old son.

Ten minutes away was The Pet Club. They had a few goldfish, their fish were orange and white, not pure orange like Brian's fish. "Brian would know that that was not his fish." Norma said. "Let's admit it. We won't be able to fool him. He is six. It is time to tell him that everything dies. It is time. Learning that everything dies is a rite of passage."

"I guess you are right." I said with resignation. "Let's go home and break the bad news to him. But wait, there is another pet store down the pike. Let's go there. Somebody has to have a pure orange fish."

We drove to another pet store. We were told that this store only sold warm blooded animals, like cats and dogs and guinea pigs, not fish. "Maybe your son would like a guinea pig." said the saleswoman who was trying to be helpful. A guinea pig wouldn't do.

"OK, that's it. unbelievable. No stores with the right fish, and goldfish are so common." I said with frustration. "I guess we have to go home and break the news." Norma and I got back in our car began driving home. We were not looking forward to our conversation with Brian.

"Wait!" I shouted. "There is a place called PJ Pets down on Cary Street. I have heard they have everything. Let's try them. Brian is probably still at his friend's. We can get a fish and put it in the tank, and he will never know the difference." I made a U turn and headed for Cary street.

Norma sighed, and gave me an uncomfortable sideways glance.

PJ Pets was about a half an hour away. In clean cages were every kind of animal, kittens, puppies, hamsters in cages running on wheels, canaries and parakeets. "We would like to see some goldfish." we asked.

We were taken to a large tank in the back of the store. There were koi and large goldfish, but no fish the size of Brian's.

"We could get a big goldfish and tell Brian that his fish grew overnight." I said hopefully. Norma gave me a disbelieving look and shook her head. "No".

Finally, we gave up and drove home. When we got home, Brian was sitting forlornly by his empty fish tank.

"What happened to Goldy?" he asked sadly.

"Brian, there is something I have to tell you." Norma said patting Brian on the shoulder. Then she explained the facts of life and death.

Brian became quiet as he digested his mother's words. At the tender age of 6 he realized that, some day, he would die. Finally, he spoke.

"Will you think of me?"

Don't name fish.

Brian's next pet was a cat. A feral cat had kittens in a woman's barn. The kind woman made it a point to gentle the kittens by petting them, having them neutered, and advertising to find homes.

Brian named his cat Tiger. Tiger lived to be 25 years old.

CHAPTER 30

OBSESSION

I was dreaming.

It wasn't a pleasant dream about some happy event in my life, like Christmas morning when I was a child, or catching a big fish when I went to the Berkeley Pier with my father.

I was floating above the ground in the dark, like a hovering ghost. I thought I was outside at night. In the distance the sky was becoming lighter. Perhaps the dawn was coming.

Then I realized that I wasn't outside. I was in a darkened room. I wasn't seeing the light of dawn, but the white walls of the room. I was in my office at the hospital where I worked.

The only source of light in the room was a glow coming from my desk top. Closer inspection revealed that the phosphorescent glow was coming from a piece of paper.

The piece of paper was a lab slip. The slip listed various clinical values including sugar, potassium, sodium, indices of kidney function, and a blood calcium level for a patient. They all were normal except the calcium level which was slightly elevated.

Calcium is necessary for contraction of the heart and skeletal muscles and for many other body functions including the activity of some enzymes. Blood calcium is maintained within a narrow range by parathyroid hormone which causes calcium to be released from bones.

A normal serum calcium level ranges from 8.2 to 10.4 mg/dL. This patient's calcium level was 10.7, just slightly above normal. It could be due to a lab error, or an overactive parathyroid gland or an elevated vitamin D level, or some other rare cause. But it was not an emergency.

"When I get around to it, I will have to get the patient in to get a repeat calcium level." I thought as I tossed the slip on my desk.

Each morning, when I went into my office, I glanced at the lab slip. The calcium level written on the slip was unchanged.

"I will have to get the patient in for a repeat test." I thought. Being able to call the patient at any time and get him in for a repeat calcium was comforting.

A week later I went on vacation in Disney World. In my hotel I remembered the calcium value on my desk. And that night I dreamed about it.

As I hovered over the lab test in the dark the calcium level took on a special glow. And as I watched it begin to increase. "10.8, 10.9, 11.2, 11.4, 11.6, 12. "

Now, the patient was beginning to feel lethargic and nauseated from elevated calcium. "12.4, 12.6. 13, 13.5, 14." I could see the patient becoming unresponsive in front of his wife. The Rescue Squad was called, and he was taken to the Emergency Room. In the Emergency Room he was unconscious, and his kidneys were shutting down. "16.1! The serum calcium is 16.1". the emergency doctor shouted. "The patient is unresponsive. We will have to intubate him "

Now the physician was inserting a tube into the patient's trachea. The patient was being admitted to the Intensive Care Unit.

If I had done something about the elevated calcium weeks ago this wouldn't have happened.

Maybe the patient would die. Maybe his wife would sue me.

I heard a woman's voice. It was my wife. "It will be hot today." The voice was coming from my hotel room. I awoke in a cold sweat. I was still in my hotel room and Norma was opening the drapes to let in the bright sun.

I reached for the phone. I called the Emergency Room at the VA hospital where I worked. Thank God that I remembered his name. There were three William Finchams who received care at the Veterans' hospital. One was dead. Another was only 30, too young. The last one was 66, the right age.

"Was Mr. Fincham admitted to the hospital recently?" I asked the clerk, half expecting to find that he had been admitted in coma from elevated calcium.

"No, he wasn't." She gave me the home phone number. I called it.

The phone rang, one time, two times, three times, four times. Why wasn't Mr. Fincham answering. Was he in another hospital in a coma from elevated calcium? Why didn't his wife answer? Maybe she was visiting him in the hospital. Or, maybe she was at a lawyer's office discussing a malpractice suit against me!? Six rings, seven rings, eight rings. Someone responded. "Hello" said a male voice.

"Mr. Fincham?"

"Yes"

"Are you OK? This is Dr. Schmitt."

"Yes, I feel OK." I was relieved to hear his voice. I tried not to sound concerned.

"I was just checking on you. Sometime in the next few days I need you to go to the lab. I need to check one of your labs again. Make sure you drink plenty water."

"OK. Thanks."

The next day Mr. Fincham came to the hospital to get a calcium level. His calcium was 10.6, still elevated, but lower than it was before.

I remember sitting in English class in college listening to a story. I don't remember where it came from.

It seems that an obsessive- compulsive burglar broke into a mansion at night. He exited the building around midnight carrying some pieces of expensive jewelry.

As the man walked away with his loot a thought occurred to him. "Did I touch the bowl next to the jewelry box? I might have left my fingerprints."

The burglar glanced up at the dark house, and after a moment's reflection decided to pick the lock on the back door and break in again.

Back on the second floor, he revisited the jewelry box in the master bedroom. Next to it was a large ornate bowel. He quickly wiped every inch of the bowel with his handkerchief. Then he hurried down the stairs and out the back door. Another thought came to him.

"Did I touch the door knob in the bedroom? I might have left my fingerprints." He stopped and ran back up to the bedroom. He quickly wiped the doorknob and again ran down the stairs and out of the house into the darkness. As he rapidly walked away, he happily thought of all the money they he was going to get when he fenced his stolen jewelry. Then another thought intruded.

"I might have touched the wooden bannister when I came down the stairs." An image of his fingerprints glowing in the dark on the wooden bannister intruded into the burglar's thoughts.

He hurried back to the house and again jimmied the lock. He breathlessly ran up the stairs and began wiping the bannister. While wiping part of it, he wondered if, during the process of wiping down part of the bannister, he had touched another part. For good measure, he wiped down the bannister, going down to the first floor, then back up to the second floor of the large house.

Again, the burglar exited the house. As he scurried away, he noticed a nearly full moon rising in the east. His car was parked three blocks away, too far away for anyone to connect to the robbery. He had thought of everything.

He thought of what he would do with the money. He had always wanted to go on a Mediterranean cruise. Maybe he would go on a cruise, a First- Class cruise with a room with a balcony that looked out on the water. He smiled at the thought. Then his smile vanished.

The house had three floors. He only went to the second floor. He wondered if he had touched the walls next to the bannister. He sighed and walked back toward the empty mansion. It was getting light in the East. He had to hurry.

The following evening the O'Learys returned from their vacation.

Mrs. O'Leary walked through the house to make sure that nothing was amiss, as was her routine when returning from a vacation. Everything seemed to be fine until she reached the third floor. She heard a noise coming from above her. She called her husband.

"I don't hear anything, Honey." her dentist husband replied.

"Well I did. Maybe it is nothing, a bird on the roof perhaps. Wait a minute there it is again."

A faint moaning sound came from above them. It was a man's voice coming from the attic.

"I'm calling the police." said the husband.

Fifteen minutes later two policemen were standing at the door of the attic, their guns drawn.

The mumbling was louder. The door was cautiously opened. The policemen looked toward the sound. They were stunned by what they saw.

The large attic was cluttered with cardboard boxes that were filled with memorabilia and discarded items. In the center of the room, hanging from the ceiling, was a large glass chandelier, its finely cut glass sparkling in the faint light. It had been placed there to prevent damage.

Standing on a ladder using his handkerchief to wipe each shiny reflector for finger prints was the burglar. He was exhausted and dehydrated, and he mumbled as he worked. He glanced down at the policemen and nodded. Then he resumed his work.

He was determined to get rid of every bit of evidence that he had been in the house.

Being obsessive can convey a survival advantage for the physician (and his patients).

During a physician's day his brain is bombarded with hundreds, even thousands of bits of data. Some of these bits can be lifesaving if acted on. A life can be lost if they are ignored.

A physician is paged by the lab to report that a patient is growing bacteria in his blood. This requires initiation of intravenous antibiotics to save the patient.

Before he can act, the physician receives another call that a patient has fallen out of bed. He runs to the bedside to examine the patient.

While examining the man, the doctor gets another call that a patient's serum potassium is critically low.

Then the patient in a room stops breathing. The doctor reaches down to check for a pulse. There is no pulse. The physician calls a "Code Blue" and cardiopulmonary resuscitation is begun. An AED is used to shock him back to normal rhythm and twenty minutes later the patient is moved to the Intensive Care Unit.

The physician receives an outside phone call. It is from a pharmacy. "Did you prescribe oxycontin for this patient?" the pharmacist asks. "It looks like you signed the prescription."

"No, I didn't!" the physician angrily states. "It is a forgery." The physician is angry that his name was used in this way.

Then a thought enters his mind, that positive blood culture. A special part of his brain stores critical information. Once he has a breather, that thought is injected to the forefront of his consciousness.

The physician runs to the ward and orders broad spectrum antibiotics for the old man with the infected blood stream.

Obsession over details is a part of medical education.

I took a course in college called Quantitative Analysis.

The student was given a jar that contained a mysterious liquid. First the student had to determine what the liquid was. If a wire was inserted into the liquid and a flame applied and the flame burned brilliant yellow, it meant that the liquid contained sodium.

Once it was determined what the liquid contained, you had to find out how much of the substance, say calcium chloride, was there. To accomplish this, you added something to the liquid that precipitated out the unknown substance as a fine powder. Then you transferred the precipitate to a beaker and weighed it on a supersensitive atomic scale.

The class was told that the weight of their fingerprints on the beaker could make the difference between an 'A' and a 'C' grade. The class, which had many premeds, became preoccupied with the weight of their fingerprints.

On some nights I lay in my bed wondering "Did I touch the beaker? Did I touch the beaker?"

Years later, when I was a medical resident, I lay in the dark thinking "Did I check the patient's potassium?"

And more years later I wondered "Did I log off the computer? Did I log off the computer?"

 Dr. Fredrika Lamb was a 30- year old mother of two who began work in the Outpatient Clinics after she finished her Internal Medicine Residency. She was perhaps 5 feet and ten inches, tall for a woman, and very thin. Her auburn hair was always pulled up from her neck in a tidy bun. Most of her dress was covered by a spotless and neatly pressed lab coat. But at the top of her dress, around her neck, she usually sported an old-fashioned ruff. Every few minutes she removed her rimless glasses and studied them for dirt. If she saw dirt, or even if she saw no dirt, she wiped the lenses.

On her first day of work she took twenty minutes to park. She drove around the lot for fifteen minutes looking for a place between two cars of the same make and color. Then she took another five minutes parking, driving into the place, then backing out over and over until she was satisfied that her car was precisely in the center of the space.

Dr. Lamb showed herself to be a caring physician who frequently stayed late checking labs and calling patients.   She seldom went to lunch. She spent the time in her office reviewing patients' labs.

 One day she went to lunch, closing her office door.

When she returned, she went into her office. The door opened abruptly, and Dr. Lamb burst out.

"Who touched my stethoscope?!" she shouted. "I left it on the desk, and it looks like someone touched it."

"No one was in your room." a smiling nurse reassured her.

"Well someone touched it. I can tell."

She walked back into her office and opened an alcohol pad and wiped her stethoscope down. Then she opened another alcohol wipe and cleaned one of the earpieces. She opened a third pad and vigorously rubbed the other earpiece, to remove any bacteria that might be present.

From then on, Dr. Lamb locked her office door whenever she left it.

A week later the agitated physician again bounded out of her room with an accusation.

Her green eyes opened wide as she spoke.

"Someone has been stealing my rectal jelly!" She paused and looked at the nurses standing nearby. They seemed puzzled but tried to look sympathetic.

"I know exactly how much jelly is in that tube, exactly 8 ounces. I use precisely a quarter of an ounce during each rectal exam, no more no less. That tube of KY Jelly was replaced at 3 PM on the 14th of October. It is now the 23rd of October. I have done precisely eleven rectal exams since 3PM on the 14th of October. This is two and three quarters of an ounce of jelly. I should have five and three-quarter ounces left in the tube. but there is only four ounces in the tube. I can tell I have sensitive fingers. There is only one inescapable conclusion".   The angry woman paused for a second.

 "Someone is breaking into my office. Someone has a key! Someone is stealing my KY Jelly!"

  Dr. Lamb picked up a phone and called the hospital Engineering Department. "I want my lock changed." she demanded. "Immediately!"

Fifteen minutes later two men from Engineering arrived.

As Dr. Lamb eyed them suspiciously and patients wondered why they hadn't been seen, the men from Engineering changed her lock.

As the year wore on Dr. Lamb became more compulsive.

This was the time of the paper record, before the electronic record. Her notes were so detailed that she could not complete them during the work day. She stayed late to write her notes, sometimes until midnight. Then she called the police to escort her in the dark out to her car.

When you looked at her patient's records you saw why her hours were so long.

They were elaborate essays, printed in small letters, sometimes almost novels on the life of her patient. The patient's history described not only why he had come to the hospital, and his past medical problems, but everything that had happened in his life including where he had grown up and even his school grades.

In the past medical history she described every aspect of her patient's life, including not only what his grandparents had died of, but what they did for a living and where they had lived. Sometimes there was even information on the great grandparents.

Almost every inch of the page was filled with an addendum. Arrows connected the addendum with a sentence or part of a sentence. It seemed that she had second thoughts about nearly everything that she wrote, and she went back and crossed out and added information.

Even more than this, to many of the pages she had added red and green posted notes to clarify what she had written about the patient. Her notes looked more like colorful graffiti than a medical record.

After she finished her notes, Dr. Lamb reviewed lab values. When she found an abnormality, often something minor like a slightly elevated blood sugar, she sometimes called the patient at home, even when it was after midnight. This is the reason the police had to escort her to her car in the wee hours of the morning. Her patients sometimes complained about being awakened by her late calls.

Dr. Lamb always seemed to be exhausted. She was losing weight and developed bags under her eyes. People around her noticed her plight.

"She has OCD." said a nurse

"She is going to die!" said a physician "You need to talk to her."

But before I could make an appointment with Dr. Lamb, she asked to see me.

"I am going to leave Primary Care." she said. "It is not my cup of tea. I am going to work for a drug company."

Dr. Fredrika Lamb went to work for a pharmaceutical firm monitoring research studies on normal volunteers who had normal lab values.

She gained weight, caught up on her sleep, became a good mother, and lived happily ever after.

CHAPTER 31

AN EMERGENCY ROOM CHRISTMAS

"There he is again!" shouted a nurse.

It was 7PM on the 23rd of December. It was already dark and there was a light drizzle.

The nurse had gone out to smoke under the awning in front of the Emergency Department. To her right was a "smoke box", a small, glassed-in room, where smokers can sit dry and warm as they inhale nicotine and carbon monoxide. Four men sat and joked and smoked. In the holiday spirit, one of them wore a green elf cap.

In front of the nurse was the Patient Parking Lot. Just beyond the lot on the other side of a chainlink fence were small houses. Even though the neighborhood was poor, many of the houses were decorated with Christmas lights.

"There he is. I see him." the nurse again remarked as she took a drag from her cigarette. She was watching someone in the parking lot. An orderly and I ran out to see what she was talking about. "What are you looking at?"

"There is someone wandering around the parking lot. I can't see him very well. But there is someone out there. I thought it was someone leaving the hospital and getting into his car. But I didn't see a car driving away. Maybe it is someone trying to steal a car."

I peered out into the dark lot. "I don't see anything."

"Well I did." replied the nurse as she took another drag of her cigarette.

I scanned the parking lot again. Suddenly, I saw a flash of light coming from the middle of the lot.

"I see it. It's a flashlight. Maybe somebody is trying to break into a car. We should call the hospital police."

A moment later two policemen arrived. They were both over 6 feet tall and built like fullbacks.

"There is someone wandering around in our parking lot."

The policemen looked toward the lot. Then, seeing nothing but the Christmas lights beyond it, they turned toward the nurse and gave her a patronizing smile.

"Well maybe it's gone." one of the men said. Just then there was another flash of light.   The policemen frowned. Then they drew their guns and walked slowly toward the light. The lead officer was carrying a flashlight.

A few minutes later the light went out. We looked for the policeman's flashlight, but it had disappeared too.

"We need backup." said a clerk who was standing next to me. As if in response to this, we heard a siren. A police vehicle with its lights flashing drove into the parking lot.

There were no patients in the Emergency Room. Patients don't want to come to the hospital during a holiday. Sometimes they are home with a heart attack, clutching their chests, because they want to spend time with their families.

The entire staff was huddling under the awning, staring toward the parking lot.

Even the inmates of the smoke box were observing the drama in the parking lot. They were all standing outside the box staring toward the lot. The line of glowing cigarette ashes looked like a string of Christmas lights.

We listened, trying to hear what was going on out there.

It was a violent neighborhood. Sometimes gunshots were heard. If someone was breaking into cars, he might have a gun. We listened for gunshots.

But we heard nothing.

Then a bright light came from the center of the lot. It was the lights from the police car. And we saw other lights, smaller lights near the bright light. Then small lights began slowly moving toward us. The police car, its lights no longer flashing, drove away.

We held our breaths as we watched the lights moving toward us. Perhaps the great "Parking Lot Mystery" would finally be solved. Had the police captured a carjacker? Would they be bringing him out in handcuffs?

 But what we saw was an old man driving a scooter. The man was quite obese. He wore a heavy down jacket and earmuffs. On either side was a policeman walking. The cops were smiling, and the gregarious old man was conversing with them.

"He thought he was in a used car lot. He thought car lots stayed open late around Christmas. He was driving his scooter around looking for price tags. He said around Christmas cars are cheaper. But he couldn't find a salesman. He was about to go home when we caught up with him. He thought he was in a used car lot!" said one of the policemen, almost unable to contain his laughter.

The old man gave us a number to call. He lived nearby. A half an hour later his wife arrived in a van and the scooter was transferred into the vehicle.

"He's getting a little demented." she said. As the old man got into the passenger seat, he shouted to us. "Merry Christmas."

With all the excitement I had lost track of the time. My twelve-hour shift was over at 8PM. I was looking forward to going home and watching a Christmas movie with my family, but my evening in the ER was just beginning.

I received an outside phone call. It was Dr. Autry, the person who was slated to relieve me at 8 PM.

"I'm sorry I am getting to you late. My father has had a heart attack. He was shoveling snow. We are in the Emergency Room now. They are admitting him. I am sorry, but I won't be there tonight." I expressed my sympathy and hung up.

"OK, who is the backup doctor? I asked.

A nurse brought me a cup of coffee. Another nurse began rubbing my neck. Without words, I had the answer to my question.

I was the backup doctor.

I would be working another twelve- hour shift. The nurses were trying to comfort me.

The silver lining to the situation was that in a few hours it would be Christmas Eve. This was usually a slow time in the Emergency Room. There was a good chance that I would be able to go to bed and sleep for several hours, maybe even all night.

"We have a man with chest pain." blared the radio. "ETA your facility 3 minutes."

The siren increased in pitch as it approached the hospital. A minute later the EMTs rushed a gurney through the door. The patient was grunting and gripping his chest.

Mr. Friend, a stocky man of about 45 years, was deposited in Bed 2. A few minutes later the man's ECG was handed to me.

I was feeling drowsy, but the ECG woke me up. The ECG shows the electrical activity of heart muscle. Mr. Friend's ECG showed a kind of heart attack called an "ST Elevation MI". This was an ominous finding. It indicated that a major artery to the heart was occluded, and that if this wasn't remedied, a large portion of the heart muscle would die.

I walked over to Mr. Friend. "Give him 2 mg of morphine IV" I instructed the nurse. I wanted to relieve his chest pain. "and give him a nitroglycerine and two baby aspirin."

"I was working on a house. I was breaking some drywall. I started getting chest pain." the patient told me.

"Mr. Friend, you are having a serious heart attack. The best treatment is to put a catheter in your heart to break up the clot. It is late at night. We are looking for someone who will do this. Maybe at Medical College of Virginia."

As it turned out, the cardiologists at MCV were working late on another case.

"Send him over." I was told.

Mr. Friend was bundled into a waiting ambulance and transferred to MCV where he was catheterized. The clotted artery was opened by inflating a balloon. The Emergency Room to balloon time was 77 minutes. This was my personal best time for a patient sent to MCV. Despite my exhaustion, I was thrilled.

It was now 1130. Working with me on the Night shift was Carol Hightower, my friend. She was a cheerful young African American woman who was always smiling. She wore her straightened hair in cute bangs. Mrs. Hightower seemed to believe in the inner goodness of people. She trusted people to be good. When they failed to live up to her expectations, she was surprised, not disappointed.

It was midnight, and the ER was again, empty.

"I guess I will go to bed." I said. Just as my head reached the pillow, the phone rang.

"An ambulance is bringing in patient in cardiac arrest." Mrs. Hightower said. I sprung out of bed and ran to the Emergency Room just in time to see the Rescue Squad bringing a patient to Bed 1.

"He collapsed at home. He has been down for 30 minutes." the female EMT remarked.

The old man was intubated and being ventilated by an "ambu" bag that was being rhythmically squeezed by a male EMT. Another EMT, an older woman, was compressing his chest.

"What is his rhythm?" I asked. The CPR stopped.

"Straight line." was the answer. This meant that the heart was showing no electrical activity-a very bad sign.

"Someone, please look him up on the computer." I asked.

A minute later we had the patient's medical record

"He's in Home Hospice. He has terminal cancer of the pancreas. He was DNR (do not resuscitate)." read a nurse.

The patient was a hospice patient. He had asked not to be resuscitated if his heart stopped, but when the rescue squad arrived at his house, they were not told this.

"OK, let's stop CPR." I said. I pronounced the patient dead.

The rescue squad retrieved their equipment and walked out of the Emergency Room to their ambulance. "Merry Christmas." said one of the women. The curtains were closed around the patient's bed. His family, which was in the Waiting Room, was informed of his death.

Then something occurred that I had never seen in the ER.

"His grandchildren want to come in to see their Grandpa's spirit leaving his body." said a clerk.

Children were not allowed in the Emergency Room. I assumed that this special request stemmed from their Christianity. After death, the soul leaves the body, and ascends to heaven.

It was Christmas eve. I decided to break the rules and let the kids see their Grandpa.

Two African American children, a boy of about 8 and a girl of about 6 walked into the ED and stood in front of Bed 1 that was behind a curtain.

The little girl wore a green sweater that was decorated with a Christmas tree. The boy wore a tee shirt that was embossed with a picture of Bat Man. They seemed to be frightened and awed at what was happening. They did not go behind the curtain. They stared at the curtain, then looked up at the ceiling. They were looking for their grandfather's soul. After a few minutes, the children retreated into the Waiting Room.

The Emergency Room was again empty. I went back to the Call Room to catch a few minutes of sleep. Over the years I have learned to sleep whenever the opportunity presents. Even a few minutes of rest can be refreshing.

 The phone rang. It was Mrs. Hightower again. "We have some patients for you to see." she said sweetly. I looked at the clock. It was 420 AM. I had slept for over two hours.

In the Emergency room in beds 1,2.3 and 7 were new patients. Since the problems were minor, and it took time to check the patients in, Mrs. Hightower had waited a few minutes before calling me, to allow me a few more minutes of sleep.

In Bed 1 was an old man who had an indwelling catheter in his bladder. The catheter had become plugged and the old man came to the Emergency Room. The nurses, anticipating my order, had already changed the catheter and his urine was once again filling his leg bag. I quickly discharged the smiling senior citizen.

In Bed 2 was a fifty -two- year old man with a cough. I pulled his hospital gown up to listen to his chest and was greeted by a shocking sight. Folds of flab hung from his chest and abdomen. Almost every inch of skin was covered by a tattoo.

 "Oh that." he said with a smile. "I was really fat, and I had diabetes. I had gastric bypass surgery and I lost a lot of weight, and my diabetes went away. I was so happy that I celebrated by tattooing my body. See, I even have a Navy insignia." He pointed to his right shoulder. "But I gained all the weight back."

 The folds of flab created an interesting visual effect. A wolf on his abdomen had been decapitated by a skin fold. Fat had destroyed most of the designs on the rest of his body and had created an amorphous blob of color. He looked like a human Christmas tree. I ordered an antibiotic and discharged the patient.

I turned my attention to Bed 7.

Mrs. Hightower whispered in my ear. "This is sort of an odd situation. You will see when you get there."

In Room 7 was a table with stirrups for performing a pelvic exam. An African American woman aged about 40 was sitting on the bed. Sitting on the stool next to her was an African American man, somewhat younger than her, maybe as young as 30.

"He did this to me." she with a smile. She pointed to the man. "I have something... down there. He did it." I asked the man to leave so that I could do an exam.

"No, I want him to be here. I want him to see what he did. I want him to stay." The woman declared.

Mrs. Hightower laid the woman down and put her feet in the stirrups. I spotted a lump on her labia. When I touched it with my gloved finger the patient winced.

"That's it. He did it to me. I wanted him to see." She smiled alluringly at her sex partner. "You did it. I want you to see it. See how powerful you are." Her male friend seemed to be embarrassed.

Mrs. Hightower and I were both uncomfortable with this situation. She empathized with me and was aware of the awkward situation, but she was nonjudgmental. Mrs. Hightower was a better Christian than I was. I was angry.

"They woke me out of a sound sleep for this." I thought.

It seemed that a pelvic exam in the Emergency room had turned into a pornographic event. The woman smiled gleefully. She was obviously thrilled at such a public display of what she thought was the man's potency.

The lump on the vaginal opening was a Bartholins cyst, an abscess that forms when mucus glands are plugged, and not the result of sexual prowess.

"You have an abscess. Soaking it with warm compresses will help. I am prescribing an antibiotic. And, Oh Yes. No Sex. Not till you are better." Mrs. Hightower smiled sweetly at the couple. "No Sex."

The gleeful smile on the woman's face dissolved. "No sex?"

"Yes, no sex." She frowned and looked at the man. It was if this visit to the Emergency Room was foreplay for sex. She planned to go back home and have passionate sex. Now I was banning sex, at least for a while.

It was now 5 AM on Christmas Eve morning. I walked toward the Call Room to get a few more winks of sleep before my shift was over at 8AM.

"Don't forget Bed 3." reminded Mrs. Hightower. In my desire to sleep, I had forgotten Bed 3.

Behind the curtains was a huge man lying on the bed. He wasn't just fat, he was tall, six feet six at least. His jeans were held up by suspenders. His chest was covered by the top of a suit of long underwear. On his feet were combat boots which had soiled the sheets.

But the most noticeable aspect of the old man was his hair. His head was covered with a shock of white hair which extended down past his ears until it became a long white beard that stretched down to his mid chest.

"I hurt my hand while I was cutting firewood." He said as he pointed to his right wrist.

I examined the wrist. It was tender, but it moved normally. "It is probably not broken, but I will get an X-ray." Mrs. Hightower put the man in a wheelchair and took him to X-ray.

Fifteen minutes later the man was brought back. I pulled the X-ray up on the computer. "There is nothing broken." I said to the patient. "It is a sprain. We will give you a splint." I ordered a splint, and Mrs. Hightower walked over to Prosthetics, the part of the hospital where movable equipment is kept, to retrieve it. Within twenty minutes she had applied the splint.

"I will give you a narcotic for a few days if you need it." I said.

"No. I am fine. I will take Motrin. I have one question. Will I be able to hold children on my lap tonight?"

This last remarked piqued our curiosity.

"Are you Santa Claus?" Mrs. Hightower asked.

"Yes. I am Santa Claus."

We were both relieved that near the end of a stressful evening, we could turn our attention to lighthearted banter about childhood memories.

"Do you remember me Santa? I was Curley." The old man smiled at Carol Hightower.

"Yes Curley, I remember you very well. I brought you a doll for Christmas one year."

Mrs. Hightower seemed pleasantly surprised. She winked at me. "Yes, you did bring me a doll one year."
"Do you remember me. I was Jimmy. I lived in Berkeley, California."

"Yes, I remember you, Jimmy. You usually were a good boy. You had a small chimney. It was hard to get down."

"Do you remember what I wanted for Christmas when I was nine?" I was testing the old man. He thought for a second. "You wanted a cap gun in a holster."

He was right. As I recalled when I was about nine or ten, I had received a cap gun in a leather holster. It was, specifically, two guns in leather holsters, genuine Roy Rogers holsters.

"You are right. I did want a cap gun." I smiled at Mrs. Hightower in mock amazement. It was Christmas eve, and we were finally enjoying the season.

The old man slowly walked to the exit and out into the parking lot. "He forgot something." said Mrs. Hightower. On the bed was a cell phone that had fallen from his pocket. I picked it up and ran out into the parking lot that was showing the first light of dawn. The old man was about to get into his pickup truck.

"Santa, you forgot this." I said.

"Thank you for the cell phone." he said.

"And Jimmy, when you were ten years old, you got a Roy Rogers two gun set with genuine cowhide holsters. Merry Christmas."

CHAPTER 32

WHY DOESN'T THE VA GIVE MORE VIAGRA?

There is an adage that "There is Somebody Out There for Everyone".

The truth of this is brought home to me by my prescribing of Viagra.

When I was a teenager, I had trouble getting a date. I was awkward, had acne, didn't know how to dress, and probably most important, didn't have a car.   I developed the impression that a woman was extremely hard to come by.

 My belief that for many men, a sexual partner is out of reach, was shattered, when I began working at the VA Hospital. The most unappealing of men have asked me for prescriptions for Viagra.

This told me immediately that there was a woman in the man's life who was willing to have sex with him.

Bob Roberts was a 63year old retired septic tank salesman. As far as I knew, he had never been married.

 He lived in a Honda Odyssey Van. He was morbidly obese and looked like a huge ball. The spindly legs and arms sticking out from the ball seemed to almost be an afterthought. He had type 2 diabetes mellitus. He sweated a lot. Yeast, that love a moist, sweet, environment, had taken up residence in his armpits and groin causing an infection that gave him a foul odor. There was even a faint odor of urine.

 The fact that he lived in an automobile and couldn't shower didn't help the situation.

Mr. Roberts was an awkward little man who bombarded me with questions every time I saw him. He seemed to have trouble understanding instructions and needed things repeated over and over.

When he complained of painful hemorrhoids, I prescribed soothing suppositories to be inserted into his rectum.

The next morning Mr. Roberts called me.

"Doctor, those pills are kind of big. I grew up on a farm where we raised horses. Those are like the pills we gave horses. Should I just swallow them, or wash them down with water? Can I mix them with food?"

"No, Mr. Roberts, those are suppositories. You put them in your rectum! You don't swallow them." I was horrified at the thought he him trying to swallow one of the suppositories. He might end up in the Emergency Department with one of them stuck in his esophagus.

"So, I don't eat them?"

"No."

"They are not pills?"

"No, Mr. Roberts. They go in your bottom."

"So, they go in my bottom. They really aren't pills at all."

"No. They are suppositories, not for swallowing."

"Suppositories, not pills. They go in my bottom not in my mouth. Thank you, Dr. Schmitt."

The next afternoon I received an outside page. It was Mr. Roberts again.

"I hate to bother you Dr. Schmitt. But you said that suppository only went in my rectum?"

"Correct."

"But that is the only thing that goes in my rectum. Everything else, all of the rest of my pills go in my mouth?"

"Yes."

"That is of course excluding my creams. They don't go in my rectum or in my mouth. They just go on my skin."

"Correct."

"My friend has hemorrhoids too, and he puts creams on them. But none of my creams go on my bottom. They just go on my skin for rashes. Is that right?"

"That is correct."

"Thank you, Dr. Schmitt."

I wondered if he was mentally slow, or just liked talking on the phone. Living in a minivan, he couldn't have much of a social life. Perhaps his major social interaction was talking to me about his medical problems.

That is why his next phone call surprised me.

"Dr. Schmitt, I hate to bother you. ah, ah, I would like some Viagra."

At the time of sexual arousal, a part of the nervous system called that autonomic nervous system is activated. This results in blood rushing into the penis causing an erection. Chronic elevation of the blood sugar, such as occurs in diabetes, can damage the nervous system, causing erectile dysfunction.

Mr. Roberts had diabetes, so it was not surprising that he had ED.

What surprised me was that he had a partner. How could such an unappealing man have found somebody that would have sex with him? And where would they have it? In his Honda minivan? Well, at least he had a car, something that I didn't have when I was trying to attract women.

I wanted to ask more questions, like "Who is your partner?" but it was none of my business.

I ordered the Viagra.

Viagra is a type of drug called a PDE Type 5 inhibitor that increases blood flow to the penis, thereby reversing erectile dysfunction. The Veterans Administration dispenses two 100 mg pills per month. Breaking the pills in two provides 4 doses per month.

A few days later Mr. Roberts called me again.

"Dr. Schmitt, I hate to bother you. Dr. Schmitt, I haven't had sex for two years. Will my penis remember when I take Viagra?"

"Yes, Mr. Roberts. Your penis will remember. It's like riding a bike. Your penis doesn't forget."

"Thank you, Dr. Schmitt. And one more thing. If I take a Viagra, but I don't have sex, will my penis go down anyway?"

"Yes, Mr. Roberts. Your erection will go away, even if you don't have sex."

"Thank you, Dr. Schmitt."

A week later I received yet another call from Mr. Roberts.

"Dr. Schmitt. I hope I'm not bothering you. But I have another question. Why does the VA give only four Viagra per month? Actually, you have to break the pills in two. You only get two pills. Some people take a whole pill. That would be only two doses per month. Why does the VA give only two doses per month?"

"I don't know, I have a patient right now. But I promise I will get the answer for you."

The next morning, I received another call from Mr. Roberts.

"Dr. Schmitt, I hate to bother you. I know a woman who gets two Viagra every day. She gets sixty pills a month. But men only get two pills. And women don't even have penises. I think that is strange. Why do women, who don't have penises, get two pills every day, and men like me, who do have penises, get only two pills a month?"

"Mr. Roberts, there is a condition called pulmonary hypertension. The heart has to work against high pressure in the arteries in the lungs. Viagra decreases the pressure in the lungs. This is a special use. That is probably why that woman is getting Viagra."

"Thank you, Dr. Schmitt."

The next afternoon, while I was seeing a patient, I received another call from Mr. Roberts.

"Dr. Schmitt. I hope I'm not bothering you. But did you find out why the VA gives only two Viagra a month…to men?"

"Mr. Roberts, I have a patient." I sighed. "But I promise I will find the answer and get back to you."

I needed to find out the answer to Mr. Roberts' question. Otherwise I would have to put up with his phone calls for the rest of my career.

"Where does VA Viagra policy come from? Where does that number, two pills a month come from? It seems random. Somebody has declared how much sex somebody should have." I asked a pharmacist.

"Drug prescribing policy is written in the PBM, the Pharmacy Benefits Manager. That would include prescribing of Viagra." was the reply. He handed me a copy of the policy.

Here it was. "Sildenafil (the generic name for Viagra) is limited to two 100 mg pills per month."

"But who decided on that policy? Who decided on two pills a month?"

"It was probably some committee in Washington."

I called the VA Central Office in Washington DC. After three transfers I found somebody who was supposed to know about Viagra.

"Where does the policy that a veteran gets only two pills a month come from?"

"I will transfer you to that office."

The phone was answered. "Where does policy on prescribing of Viagra come from?" I asked

"I will put you on hold." said the young man. After several minutes the man picked up again. "I will transfer you to that office." This time a woman picked up.

"This is Dr. Schmitt from Richmond, Virginia." I began. "I am investigating policy on prescribing Viagra. I promised a patient I would check this out. Why does the VA give only two 100 mg Viagra pills per month?"

I could hear the woman breathing as she thought about my question. "That is an unusual question. The person that you should talk two is Dr. Carlson. He deals with that. Let me transfer you. The phone rang eight times. Just as I was about to hang up, it was answered.

I had reached Dr. Carlson.

"Dr. Carlson. I hope I am not bothering you. I am investigating VA policy on prescribing Viagra. Why do we give only two pills a month? Is this determined by a committee? Is it because Viagra is expensive? Patients want to know."

"I am doing something right now. But give me your number and I will call you back with the answer."

Two hours went by. I began to think that Dr. Carlson was ignoring my call.

Then the phone rang.

Dr. Carlson had returned my call. "Dr. Schmitt, I have the answer to your question. You asked where the VA policy for the prescribing Viagra came from. I have the answer. Do you have something to write this down?"

"Yes."

"Dr. Schmitt. Our policy for prescribing Viagra is in the **Pharmacy Benefits Manager, the PBM.**"

I sighed." Thank you, Dr. Carlson." Then hung up

I knew that if I didn't give Mr. Roberts a reasonable explanation, he would be calling me forever. I thought for a few minutes.

Then I picked up the phone and called him.

"OK Mr. Roberts, I did extensive research on your question. Why does the VA only give you only two Viagra a month? I will tell you why the VA gives only two pills a month. You have heard about those lobbies in Washington. People lobby for everything, less guns, more guns, eat more chicken, don't eat chickens.

People lobby for absolutely everything, even sex. Some people like sex. Some people think sex is bad, sinful, evil. Some people say sex is bad because it produces children. The Earth has too many people.

 I discovered a lobby that is against sex. Viagra helps sex, sex makes babies. The lobby is paid by a group of religious fanatics.

 It is called the 'Lobby to Impede Marital Pleasure'.

Otherwise known as **LIMP.**"

CHAPTER 33

THE ATHLETE AND THE BEEKEEPER

The moving van seemed to come out of nowhere.

Cassandra Gentry was late for a job interview. She had stopped for a school bus which was loaded with children. The driver waited for a little boy who came running up just before the door closed. When the door of the bus closed, Ms. Gentry gunned her Honda Civic's engine, hoping that she could make up for lost time.

She looked down to text her interviewers that she would be late. She crossed over the line into the oncoming lane. When she looked up, the van was almost upon her. She slammed on her brakes. The van driver also hit his brakes, but too late.

The two vehicles collided at a combined speed of 70 miles an hour.

Cassandra's obese body lurched forward, restrained only by her seat belt. Her lower abdomen bore the brunt of the force of the collision. Her body and her spinal cord pivoted on the seat belt. In an instant she became a paraplegic, unable to move from the waist down.

In the Emergency Room a catheter was inserted into her bladder. She soon learned that she would never again urinate normally and that she would have to rely on catheters for the remainder of her life. After a week in the Intensive Care Unit, Cassandra was transferred to a rehabilitation hospital.

In the rehab hospital it was confirmed that Cassandra was a T10 paraplegic, complete. This meant that she her spinal cord had been injured at the level of the tenth thoracic vertebra. She had no sensation or motor function below her lower abdomen, and it was highly likely that this would be permanent.

Cassandra had been overweight for most of her life. In her late teens, her obesity accelerated, and now at age 35 she was 80 pounds overweight. She was made fun of in school and had never had a real boyfriend. This made her depressed, and when she was depressed, she ate more. Her obesity had caused hypertension and type II diabetes.

Rehabilitation concentrates on helping weak muscles recover and helping normal muscle adapt to the disability. Cassandra would now have to rely on her normal arms to compensate for her paralyzed legs. She would have to transfer from place to place, from bed to chair, from wheelchair to toilet, using just the strength of her arms. And she would have to operate a wheelchair using the power of her arms on the tires.

In rehabilitation the muscles of her arms became stronger and she noticed that when operating her wheelchair, she had more stamina than she had when she walked. And she began losing weight. She reveled in her newly discovered fitness. She forgot her paralyzed lower body and became obsessed with her healthy upper body. She began playing wheelchair soccer and entering in wheelchair races. She bought a special wheelchair where the large wheels are bent inward for stability in athletic events. Cassandra became a very fit woman, from the waist up.

At the Special Olympics Cassandra met a paraplegic man. They soon married. The couple wanted to have a child.

Women with spinal cord injury have almost normal fertility. Not so with the men. Although they usually can have erections, they have trouble producing normal semen. There is something in the semen of men with spinal cord injury that impairs the motility of sperm.

A relatively new technique of harvesting a single sperm from the testicle and uniting it with a single egg has given new hope to infertile couples. Using this technique, Cassandra and her husband became the parents of a healthy baby girl.

One afternoon, Cassandra came to my clinic in her wheelchair. In a baby carrier on her lap was a sleeping infant whose head was covered with a large thatch of black hair. The muscles of Cassandra's shoulders were hypertrophied from frequent exercise.

I noted that Cassandra's blood pressure was an athletic 100/60 and that her random blood sugar was only 80.

"You have cured your hypertension and diabetes." I said.

"Dr. Schmitt, the best thing that ever happened to me was my spinal cord injury. I wouldn't change a thing."

Steven Hatcher missed his clinic appointment. He missed his appointment because he was in jail.

Steve was a former Marine. In a local pub he got into an argument about who was tougher, the Marines or the Army. The argument escalated, and Steve punched the soldier in the face.

He was sentenced to three months in jail for assault.

Steve had bipolar disorder.

There was a cycling of the chemicals in his brain that sometimes produced a moody depression, and other times produced an agitated mania. These symptoms were controlled by lithium, but often Steve forgot to take his lithium. When he was manic, he got into fights.

When Steve did keep his clinic appointments, I saw a disheveled, unshaven, overweight man, aged about 50. His blood pressure and cholesterol were always elevated even though he was on meds for this. When I inquired, he informed me that he was not taking his medication. He stared at me with a blank expression and seemed not to care what happened to him.

"For your health you need to take your medication." I chided him.

He nodded weakly seeming not to care what I said.

I worried that Steve would die of some medical complication such as a heart attack or be beaten to death in a bar fight.

But this changed.

When Steve returned for a clinic appointment, I noticed that he was different. He had lost weight. His blood pressure was normal. He was wearing a clean dress shirt and he was shaven. He had a pleasant smile.

"What has happened Mr. Hatcher?" I asked, amazed at his transformation.

He looked down at the ground as if in deep thought, then looked up at me.

"Doc, I keep bees."

I was stunned by this revelation.

"Doc, bees have an incredibly organized society. They are fascinating. They all work for the hive. They cooperate. They are peaceful little creatures. This taught me something. I have to take care of them. I now have something to live for. I have six hives now. I have to take care of myself. I take my medication now."

To emphasize his point, Mr. Hatcher opened his shirt. Underneath he was wearing a tee shirt which was embossed with the words. "Bee Happy". Next to the words was a smiling honeybee.

Mr. Steve Hatcher continued to do well. He never again was incarcerated or missed an appointment.

Often, when he came to see me, he brought me a jar of honey.

Sometimes, unexpected events in patients' lives have a greater impact than medications

CHAPTER 34

THINGS LEARNED WHILE RIDING IN A TUKTUK

The tuktuk driver turned around and smiled at me as we drove down the road from Kampot to Sonya Kill Memorial Hospital. I noticed that his right eye was missing. It was probably an injury from one of Cambodia's wars. It was March of 2015, and I was on my way to spend 3 weeks as a volunteer in the hospital.

A tuktuk is a common form of transportation in Cambodia. It is a three- wheeled cart that is pulled by a motorcycle. The unemployment rate in this area exceeds 60 per cent. Driving a tuktuk is the only way for many of the men to make a living. For some, the little cart is their only home, and they sleep in it at night.

We passed people's homes. Some are substantial houses on stilts to protect them from floods. But many buildings are little more than shacks built from scrap wood. In front of many houses are large urns. These catch rain water which is used for both cooking and washing.

Everywhere I looked I saw chickens running and scratching. They converted bugs into eggs and meat, an efficient way of producing protein for a poor country. Among the chickens you occasionally saw a scrawny animal with a pointed nose. They looked like coyotes, but these were Cambodian dogs.

In fields grazed cattle. They were different from cattle usually seen in America. They were Brahma cattle, with a characteristic tan color and large humps. The bulls are used in American rodeos. Perhaps because of the cattle, some Americans call this part of Cambodia "The Wild West."

Along the road were small stores, some just shacks with Pepsi Cola signs. Many of the stores sold gas. The gas was measured into empty one-liter Pepsi bottles, then poured into the cars.

The tuktuk slowed. "Sonya Kill" said the driver. He drove past a large number of motorcycles and scooters that were parked in front of the hospital.

The front of the hospital was a large "A" frame structure. Beyond this was a courtyard that was surrounded by offices. A sign at one of the rooms read "CAT Scan", but the room was empty. Maybe, some day they would have a CAT scanner.

A large hallway led past one- story buildings that housed the hospital wards. After this you came to an open area where the two-story guest houses were situated. Towering over the hospital was a mountain that was a few miles away.

Sonya Kill Memorial hospital was built to care for poor people, especially children, in this very needy part of Cambodia. I read that Sonya Kill was a German girl who was killed in a tragic accident. Her parents founded the hospital in her memory.

The chief executive of Sonya Hill is Dr. Cornelia Haener, a Swiss woman trained as a surgeon. At Sonya Kill doctors were called by their first name. She was Dr. Cornelia, and I was Dr. James.

Dr. Cornelia was a fit woman, aged about 50, who wore brown rimmed glasses. She had short cropped brown hair and usually wore the blue scrub suit worn by surgeons. She was a micro-manager who kept track of everything that happened in the hospital, and addressed problems with carefully worded memos.

"Employees who ride motor bikes or scooters must wear helmets." read one memo. Dr. Cornelia was aware that the number one cause of death in young people in this country was from motor vehicle accidents.

Another memo read. "A venomous snake was found in Dr. Cornelia's house. Snakes and insects want to come inside your house, especially during the wet season. Please keep your doors closed at all times."

Rounds began at 730 am on the pediatric ward. The team consisted of staff physicians, nurses, and residents in training.

One patient was a 6 year -old boy who had been scalded by hot water over 30 per cent of his body.

Dr. Haener talked to the boy in Khmer (the language of Cambodia), then she talked to his father, smiled and said something to him. I was surprised to see what the boy's burns were being treated with. They were covered with honey. In my career I had never seen honey used for this purpose. But when you thought about it, it was logical. Honey is soothing, and has antibiotic properties. When I looked it up on the Internet, I found a journal article that compared honey to Silvadine, an ointment commonly used in the US to treat burns. The paper found that honey was superior to Silvadine.

After the children's ward the team visited the adult ward. Each patient's record was protected by a metal cover. The records were placed on a cart and the cart pushed from room to room. Many of the patients had complications of diabetes mellitus. In one woman an ulcer had eaten into the sole of her foot causing osteomyelitis, an infection of the bone. This would require six weeks of intravenous antibiotics to cure.

An old man had abdominal pain following removal of his gallbladder. An X-ray showed the cause of the pain. During the surgery a sponge was left behind in the abdominal cavity. He would have to have surgery to remove the foreign body.

At almost every bed was one or more family members. Often, they fed the patient with food they had brought in. The family was important in the patient's care.

I was told that a few years earlier a comatose patient was not breathing. There was a breathing tube in his trachea, but no respirator. For hours members of his family took turns squeezing the rubber bag that was connected to the breathing tube, and they kept him alive.

Dr. Haener read the record of each patient carefully.

A fifty- year old smoker developed a pneumothorax, a collapsed lung. A rubber tube, called a chest tube was inserted between the ribs into the space around the lung. It was hoped that each time the patient took a breath air would be pressed out of the chest cavity and the lung would eventually expand. Dr. Cornelia studied the man's record.

Something caught her eye. She walked over to the patient and smiled.

"Sua" she said (the Khmer word for "Hi"). Then she asked "Chewe?" (the word for "pain"). The man grimaced and nodded. Dr. Cornelia listened to his chest with her stethoscope, then studied the tube coming from his chest. She motioned to a young man standing near the patient. He was wearing a lab coat.

"Are you the patient's physician?" The thin young man in glasses nodded. The medical language of Cambodia is English. Patients are discussed in English. Since most patients don't understand English, privacy is maintained even when physicians discuss patients in an open ward.

"He has a chest tube in. You aren't giving him anything for pain." The young physician nodded nervously. Dr. Cornelia continued, her voice growing in amplitude.

"Do you know how painful a chest tube is?" I could see a thin line of perspiration on the physician's upper lip. "If I ever again catch you putting in a chest tube without giving the patient pain medications, I am going to put a chest tube in you!"

Then Dr. Haener smiled and relaxed. "You know one of my favorite movies is 'The Doctor'. In the movie is a doctor who is insensitive to his patients' suffering. He doesn't answer their phone calls. He doesn't treat their pain. He doesn't treat their feelings. Then the doctor gets cancer. He becomes a patient. He learns what it is like to be a patient. He mends his ways. When new interns come into the hospital at the beginning of the academic year, he gives them hospital gowns. 'Put them on. You are going to wear them for a week. You are going to see what it is like to be a patient.' the surgeon tells the group, having learned what it is like to be a patient."

She smiled at the patient and spoke. "Ah Kunh." she spoke the Khmer phrase for "thank you."

I admired this matter- of- fact woman. She could be spending her career in some pleasant place making a lot of money, but she had chosen to come to Sonya Kill in the tropical heat, to help poor people.

After we finished with the Medical wards, I went to the Clinic where I supervised resident physicians.

The amount that the patient paid for services was prorated based on the patient's income. The poorest echelon of patients paid nothing. Patients who had more money paid more.

A woman was being treated for an overactive thyroid gland with methimazole, a medication which turns off the thyroid. For labs we ordered several tests including tests of thyroid function. When the woman reviewed the cost of the tests she protested. "The tests will cost $16. I only have $20. If I get all of those tests, I will have only $4 left." We reconsidered and decided to just order the thyroid test which cost $4.

Diabetes mellitus is common in Cambodia.

"There are two times a year when the sugar is high." Dr. Akra, the young resident physician, remarked. "During the wedding season which begins in October, and the when the durian fruit ripens in March." This fruit apparently contained a lot of sugar.

Starting patients on insulin was problematic. Insulin had to be refrigerated. Many of the patients were too poor to own a refrigerator. This sometimes resulted in a delay in initiating insulin therapy, or not starting it at all.

In Cambodia the attitude toward pain is different than in the United States.

In America pain is regarded as the enemy. When a patient sees the doctor, a pain scale is completed showing the degree of pain from 0-10. The physician feels obligated to treat the pain number, just as he is obligated to treat an elevated blood pressure. This pain score is one of the reasons that there is rampant use of opioids in the US. This results in addiction, illegal trafficking of narcotics, and death.

In Cambodia pain is regarded as a friend, not an enemy. "Pain tells you where the disease is." one Buddhist monk told me.

"Painful ordeals, such as climbing a mountain to get to a holy place, increase karma which help you reach Nirvana."

None of my patients at Sonya Kill were on chronic narcotics. When pain did occur, it was treated with Motrin and Paracetamol (a drug related to Tylenol). Whether or not the Cambodian is benefited or harmed by this approach to pain is uncertain. What is certain is that there is far less addiction and abuse of opioids than in the US.

A white-haired old lady complained of chest pain which she had for days. The symptom of chest pain in a person her age was ominous and could mean a heart attack. Her EKG showed changes which could be consistent with ischemia (lack of oxygen) of the heart.

In the US, the woman would probably have had an immediate heart catheterization to look at her coronary arteries. At that time a narrow coronary artery could be opened with a balloon. But the nearest catheterization lab was in Phnom Penh, two and a half hours away, and she had no way to get there, and probably couldn't afford to pay for it. I had to work with what I had.

"Let's give her an aspirin." I said. This would prevent further clotting in her arteries. I scanned the hospitals limited formulary to find something that could help the woman. The pharmacy had nitroglycerine patches. We put a nitroglycerine patch on the skin of the woman's arm. Nitroglycerine opens narrowed coronary arteries, increasing oxygen delivery to the heart.

Then we ordered an ultrasound of her heart. This would give us information on the heart's pumping activity. Ultrasounds were performed by a Ukrainian cardiologist who had moved to Cambodia with her young son.

Two hours later the old woman returned to the clinic. Her heart ultrasound showed that the heart was pumping with slightly reduced activity. Her chest pain was gone. She was smiling. Convinced that the woman was not having a myocardial infarction, we put her on aspirin, and a statin to lower her cholesterol, and sent her home.

When western physicians go the work in the Third World, they must accept the fact that they will sometimes be committing what would be considered malpractice in their native countries.

Just past the medical wards were the two- story guest houses. For 15 dollars a day I got a room and a meal. Next door to the hospital was a large farm where chickens and geese and dogs ran. Each day the farmer drove his ducks over to feed in the nearby pond. Every morning, at 5 AM a rooster crowed and woke me up.

Lunch was served under an awning on a concrete walkway. At about noon, women brought tubs of rice, fish, boiled vegetables, eggs from the farm next door, and crabs from the nearby Gulf of Thailand. Beef and chicken were sometimes part of the menu. Cattle were not eaten until they had outlived their usefulness as sources of milk, dung, or to pull plows. If you got beef, it was usually tough. Hens were eaten only when they stopped laying eggs.

For dessert there was often a strange fruit, the durian fruit. The skin was prickly and leathery. Inside was a sweet pulp that some people thought had a foul smell. At the center was a crunchy seed.

One morning I awoke at 6 AM.

I felt uneasy. Something was different. Something had happened. Had I forgotten to do something? Had the weather changed? I couldn't place it, but something was wrong, different. All morning, as I saw patients I struggled with my feelings. Maybe it was a premonition of something that was going to happen. Maybe someone was sick or in trouble. Perhaps I should call home.

At noon I went to lunch. In addition to the rice and vegetables and fish and fruit there was a welcome addition to the meal, chicken. Then I realized what was different about today.

This morning the rooster didn't crow.

Kampot is only 40 miles from the Vietnamese border. I decided to take the bus to Ho Chi Minh City, previously called Saigon, for the weekend.

The bus left from a tourism company in Kampot.

While I was standing in front of the agency waiting to board the bus, I observed an amazing sight. A feral cat strolled past me. The cat was carrying a huge rat it its mouth. The rat was almost as large as the cat. The rat was dead.
"We need cats like that in America!" I shouted with admiration.

"And in New York!" exclaimed the American woman who was standing next to me. She too was impressed with the cat's exploit.

The bus took us to the Vietnamese border. On the Cambodian side a man in a small building looked at our passports. The passengers walked a hundred feet or so through a "No Man's Land" to the Vietnamese side.

On the Vietnamese side was as sign with the huge word "EBOLA". At the Cambodian -Vietnamese border, the script changed from the Cambodian alphabet, which resembled

Sanskrit, to the familiar English letters. Under the word, written in smaller print, was an admonition that you should tell the officials if you had been in an area where there was Ebola. In a small building, an immigration agent took my temperature with a digital thermometer.

Perhaps the Vietnamese caution about Ebola was a statement that "Viet Nam is a major power that is involved in the industrialized world and we have the same concerns as the other industrialized countries such as the US."

We paid an entry fee into Viet Nam.

During the Viet Nam War, I was on active duty in the Air Force. In that war many thousands of Vietnamese were killed. For many years they were our enemy and Americans couldn't enter Viet Nam. I was happy to see that they took American money. This was a good sign.

We passed through a rural countryside. Farmers in hats that looked like overturned baskets pushed plows pulled by water buffalos. There was a seemingly endless number of canals. On the edge of the canals were small houses. The canals eventually ran into the mighty Mekong River that connected Cambodia with Viet Nam.

We came to a rest stop and were told to get off the bus.

At the stop was a large restroom.

I walked in went to the urinal. As I stood at the urinal, someone brushed past me. I was startled to see that this was a woman. Then more women came past me. This was my first experience in a unisex restroom. The line of urinals was placed in front of stalls which were used by both men and women. Men and women seemed to be totally oblivious to the fact that they were eliminating in the presence of members of the opposite sex. The possibility that someone might, for an instant, catch a glimpse of the genitals of another person was irrelevant.

Within a year the US was embroiled in a controversy about transgender people using the rest room of their reassigned gender. In Viet Nam the process of elimination was not a sexual event. The only individual who was uncomfortable in the Vietnamese restroom was me.

As our bus drove toward Ho Chi Minh City, it grew dark. At every stop I asked hopefully "Ho Chi Minh City? Ho Chi Minh City?"

"No Ho Chi Minh." the driver said each time.

The projected time for arrival was extended from 8 PM to 10 Pm. Then it became 11 PM. My plans to visit Ho Chi Minh City on a shoestring began to unravel. I had thought that I would arrive in the early evening and see a few of the sights before finding a hotel. That was all gone.

Finally, at 1130 PM we drove into a huge yard.

"Ho Chi Minh" said the driver glancing back at me.

When I got off the bus my heart sunk. I was in the middle of a huge bus terminal. In the dark I could see bus after bus lined up. The trip from Cambodia had taken longer than I thought. I worried that it would be equally difficult to get back to Cambodia. I was in a Communist country where I didn't speak the language, and I wasn't sure how or when I would be able to get home.

If I didn't show up on the hospital ward on Monday morning Dr. Haener would be worried. She would call Health Volunteers Overseas, and they would call my wife. Health care providers had sometimes disappeared in Third World countries never to be seen again. My plans for seeing Ho Chi Minh City dissolved. I just wanted to get home.

"Kampuchea?" I asked my driver. (Kampuchea is the Vietnamese word for Cambodia.)

The driver pointed to the terminal.

I walked into the terminal and up to a window. "I want to get to Cambodia." I told the agent.   The man didn't understand me. He shook his head. "Cambodia, Kampuchea" I repeated in a loud voice. The man looked puzzled and shook his head again.

I walked to another window. "Kampuchea?" I said to the agent who was middle aged woman.

The woman said something in Vietnamese. I shrugged my shoulders.

I turned to nearby customers. "Kampuchea? Kampuchea?" I asked frantically.

I was the only white person present. The people stared at me indifferently. I was an American. Perhaps they remembered the war and resented me. I was stuck in the dark in a bus terminal in a Communist country and I couldn't communicate with anyone.

"Kampuchea? Kampuchea?" I asked to everyone who passed me. People shook their heads.

I stared anxiously out into the darkness of the bus yard wondering when I would get home.

"I speak English." said a voice.

I turned to see a heavy-set Asian man in a dress shirt. "I speak English. I lived in Canada for twelve years."

The man asked one of the agents something.

"Haitan." the agent said. "Haitan."

"You need to get a ticket to Haitan." the Canadian man said. "The bus leaves in ten minutes." I looked at the agent.

 "Kampuchea? Kampuchea?" I asked, as if the Canadian wasn't there. Perhaps I didn't believe that the Vietnamese wanted to help me. Maybe they remembered the war and knew that I was an American. Keeping me trapped in a bus terminal forever was their revenge.

"Haitan! Haitan!" repeated the Canadian. "I lived in Canada for twelve years. You can trust me." The man seemed miffed that I was ignoring him.

"Thank you." I said. I bought a ticket to Haitan.

A small man came up to me and motioned me to follow him. He led me through the maze of buses to a bus whose door was open. "Haitan" the little man said pointing to the open door.

 There was no devious plot against me. The people in the station were just trying to help a fellow human being, who seemed a little strange. The bus headed off toward the West. I was the only American on board.

Each time the bus stopped I anxiously asked "Haitan?"

"No Haitan." I was told at every stop.

Finally, when the bus stopped, a young Vietnamese man turned to me and smiled. "Haitan".

Haitan is close to the Cambodian border. When I got off the bus it was 4 AM. I knew that in several hours another bus would arrive and go to Cambodia. I was elated to be so close to home.

I walked toward the only source of light that I could see. It was a bar. Sitting at small tables were a collection of rough looking men. Maybe they were criminals waiting for their next heist, or so

I imagined. It reminded me of the "Cantina" scene in the first Star Wars movie.

I sat down at a table and asked the waitress for a cup of coffee. "When does the bus for Cambodia get here?" I asked the waitress. She shook her head.

A slight, balding man, of about 40 years of age came to my table. "Kampuchea?" he asked. "Kampuchea?"

"Yes. Kampuchea. How much?"

The man showed me all ten fingers, then lowered them and raised them again. Twenty. He wanted me to pay twenty dollars. I nodded my head. The man pointed to his watch. Five O'clock. We would leave at 5AM.

A heavy man who had been sitting at one of the tables got up and spoke to the bald man. They began arguing in Vietnamese and pointing at me. I guessed that the fat man was upset that the bald man had taken a client. Finally, the fat man smiled, and walked away with the bald man following him. I ordered another coffee and waited.

The bald man returned and wiggled his fingers to imitate walking. I followed him. It was still dark. I was led to a small motor scooter. He was going to take me to Cambodia on the back of a scooter.

The scooter started with a lurch that made me fall backwards. As we accelerated, I worried about falling off. I felt uncomfortable hugging a man.

If I fell backwards, the back of my head would hit the ground, causing extreme flexion of my neck. My spinal cord would be severed, paralyzing me from the neck down. I would be lying on the road in the dark, in Viet Nam, unable to move my body, and possibly unable to breathe. I would die.

My survival instincts overcame my homophobia. I gripped my driver around the waist. He didn't seem to mind.

The sun was beginning to rise when we reached the border. In contrast to the Vietnamese border, the Cambodian border had no Ebola sign. I walked across the border without my temperature being taken.

Monday, I reported to the hospital for work as usual.

Although it was March, it was hot and muggy. After all, this was the Tropics.

I frequently walked out to the water cooler in the courtyard. During one of these trips, I was accosted by a large white woman. She was about sixty, tall for a woman. She wore glasses, and her head was covered by a krama, the traditional Cambodian scarf. "Are you a doctor?" she asked. "I need a doctor." Her accent was Australian.

"I am a doctor."

"I am Janine Judd. I am from Australia. I need I doctor to talk to my women about women's issues. One of my women went through menopause and she thought she was going to die. She didn't have a clue what was happening. Could you come out to Kep Gardens and talk about women's health?"

The following Wednesday at noon a tuktuk drove up to the front of the hospital. The smiling driver pointed to the cab and I got in. Sitting in the cab was Mrs. Judd. I sat across from her. As we drove, she told me her story.

"Our only child was killed in a motor vehicle accident when he was nineteen. My husband and I were devastated. We sold everything we had and came to Kampot, and bought four rice fields and built a school. We call it Kep Gardens. The women need someone like you to talk to them about menopause and birth control."

We passed what looked like a small mosque.

"Are there Muslims in Cambodia?" I asked.

"Yes. They are the Cham Muslims. The Khmer Rouge slaughtered them in the 70s. They hated religion of any form. Now there are about 200,000 Cham here. They like their beer. An old Cham man was talking to me about the pilgrimage to Mecca. 'Before you go to Mecca you can't drink beer for a month. Then after you come back you can't drink beer ever again. I love my beer. I won't go to Mecca until I am so old that I'm not interested in beer or anything else.' The woman sitting across from me smiled. "Isis won't get very far trying to recruit **our** Muslims!"

We passed the river that ran past the town of Kampot. Kampot is a tourist town. There are bars and restaurants along the river. Then we drove through a rural area.

Men and women stood in front of houses that often were little more than piles of boards and sticks thrown together. In this area the unemployment rate is above 60 per cent. Children played in front of the hovels. I thought it would be nice to buy a toy for each of these deprived children, but that would be many thousands of toys.

The tuktuk arrived at a sign that said "Kep Gardens." Just beyond the sign was a playground-a jungle gym, a slide, a monkey bar, where smiling children played. It was all made of stainless steel. The Judds had solved the dilemma of toys for poor children. They made an eternal toy where countless children would play.

"We had a problem with the trees." Mrs. Judd's voice interrupted my thoughts. She motioned toward the trees surrounding the playground. "The witch doctors said that the trees had evil spirits and that the spirits would harm the children. The men refused to plant the trees. But we talked to the monks. They said that there were spirits in the trees, but they were good spirits, and would not harm the children. So, the workmen planted the trees."

Beyond the playground were rice fields and fields planted with vegetables such as corn and tomatoes. "We only got one rice crop this year." my hostess said. In a good year we can get at least two, maybe three crops. But it was so dry we got only one crop." We came up on a group of small one -story buildings. "That is mine and my husband's place." she said, as she pointed to a modest structure. It was only a single room.

Lunch was served on a small patio that was covered by an awning. Mrs. Judd continued to talk about the "witch doctors."

"I sprained my ankle and got a witch doctor. He burned incense near my ankle and blew water on it. It got better. I got up and walked right away." She was guileless, almost innocent. When she described an event. she was totally matter of fact and nonjudgmental.

The lunch was served. It was pot stickers, corn and coleslaw. "The corn and cabbage came from my garden. If you want to compliment the cook, say "La O!" (This means 'good' in the Khmer language). "La O!" I said to the cook as I gave a "thumbs up." Mrs. Judd reached down and patted a little pointy nosed Cambodian dog.

335

"He got a snake. He broke its neck. He is the puppy and he got the snake." she said proudly. "We also have geese. Snakes don't like the smell of geese. Dogs and geese protect you from snakes." Then Mrs. Judd changed the subject.

"There was a Khmer Rouge watch post over in the next village right over there through the trees. One of my women's father was killed by the Khmer Rouge. She still has nightmares. One of the Khmer Rouge men still lives there. People know he killed men in the village, but they don't do anything about it. 'What happened in the past is in the past' they say".

My lecture was held in an open area that was covered by a roof. At one end was a blackboard.

Mrs. Judd introduced my interpreter, a young Khmer woman. Women began arriving. Some were dressed in neat dresses. Others wore sarongs. Some of them wore head coverings. These were the women who lived in homes that were made of piles of boards and sticks thrown together. I wondered where these nice dresses came from. Many of the young women held children.

My interpreter stood at my right. Mrs. Judd sat to my left. I was not quite sure how to begin.

I picked up a piece of chalk and began drawing on the board. I drew two oval shaped lumps to represent the ovaries. Tubes ran down from the lumps to a structure that was wide at the top and narrowed at the bottom. This was the uterus. Then I drew what looked like a bull's eye. This was a cervix as seen during a pelvic exam.

"These are the ovaries. Every woman has ovaries. They make eggs." I began. My interpreter said something in Khmer. The women tittered at this information. "Every month an egg comes

336

from the ovary. It goes down the tube and stops in the uterus. If it is fertilized it can grow into a baby." My interpreter translated. The women tittered again.

"They don't understand about fertilization." my interpreter said. I sighed and picked up the chalk. I drew two lines extending down from the cervix. "This is the vagina." My interpreter said a few words. More titters from my audience. I picked up my chalk again.

I drew an object that could have been several things. It was long and cylindrical. Two round objects hung down from it. It could have been an airplane with landing gear. "This is the penis. The man's sex organ." I said. When my interpreter explained, the audience erupted in laughter.

At least I was entertaining them.

"When you get older your periods will stop. This is normal and nothing to worry about. You will eventually become infertile. You will have no more babies."

"Thank goodness for that!" chimed in Mrs. Judd. "Menstrual periods are terribly messy."

The women smiled and talked among themselves, seemingly enjoying their lecture. It was as if the President of the United States, or the Dalai Lama had come to visit.

"How many of you have children?" I asked. Nearly all the women raised their hands. "How many of you want to have more children?" A few hands went up. The best form of contraception for these women was probably Depo-provera, a shot that prevents pregnancy for a month.

I pointed at the blackboard to the circle that represent the cervix. "Cancer can occur here. A Pap smear is a way of finding cancer early before it spreads. How many of you have had a Pap smear?" No one raised their hand. I knew that in Cambodia over a thousand women per year died of cervical cancer, something that could be prevented by Pap smears.

 I thought that my lecture was over, but this it was only Part 1. Mrs. Judd brought me a bottle of water and I petted one of her dogs.

The room began filling up with teenagers, teenagers of both sexes. I shuddered at the task that was before me. It was possibly the most difficult job of my medical career.

I was going to discuss the facts of life to a group of teenagers through an interpreter. I reached for my Cambodian dictionary and quickly looked up some words.

I asked the children their ages. The youngest was 11 and the oldest was 14. I pointed to my drawings on the blackboard and began explaining the process of reproduction.   I pointed to the vagina. "Gorduoy" I said, proud of my use of a foreign language. The teenagers chuckled.

 I pointed to my airplane- turned- penis. "Kadorth" I said. The audience roared with laughter.   Then I discussed sex in teenagers.

 "At your age you will really want to have sex." My interpreter translated. Mrs. Judd still sitting to my left commented. "Yes, that is right. Listen to this man".

"But if you have a child your life will be affected. Kone." I was using the word for baby. "It will be harder for you to go to school and learn things and get a job and make a living. It is better that you don't have sex until you are married. "

"Yes, listen to him." said Mrs. Judd.

"If you have sex, you should use birth control." When I pointed to my drawing of a penis and discussed condoms the audience laughed. My lecture was at an end. "Are there any questions." A boy raised his hand and spoke in Khmer. My interpreter turned to me. "He wants to know if men go through menopause."

That night I was going to a movie in Kampot. The movie was "The Killing Fields", which was about the genocide that occurred in the 1970s when Cambodia was controlled by the Khmer Rouge. Mrs. Judd took me to her tuktuk and told the driver where to go.

As we drove, I thought of the day's events.

Regardless of their poverty, the poor people were happy. Any event, a lecture on women's health, or just swinging on a swing in a playground was a reason to be joyful.

One of my favorite actors was Heath Ledger, who won the Oscar posthumously for playing the Joker in Batman. His economic assets were literally a million times those of one of the women at Kep Gardens. Yet, they were happy, but he needed something more. He overdosed on a drug that killed him.

Perhaps someday I will come back to Kep Gardens and live in Mrs. Judd's guest house and do Pap smears on Mrs. Judd's women and show them the moon and stars with my telescope.

I thought of how Sonya Kill and Kep Gardens were founded. Both were created because of the death of a child. These institutions had improved the lives of thousands of people and saved the lives of many more.

Perhaps God does work in mysterious ways.

CHAPTER 35

JOURNEY'S END

"The fear of death follows from the fear of life.   A man
who lives fully is prepared to die at any time."
Mark Twain

I was looking down into a huge sunken living room. At one end
was a majestic stone fireplace. A few glowing embers added their
light to the darkened room. The major source of light was a
spotlight that highlighted the oversized portrait above the
fireplace. The subject of the painting was a smiling couple, a
beautiful blond woman and a tall balding man. They were
standing, each with an arm around the other's waist. They were
apparently the owners of this magnificent mansion. The opulent
room testified to their success.

As I looked around the great room my eye caught something on
the right. The object was dwarfed by the interior of the room,
almost an afterthought.

It was a woman sitting on a couch. It was the pretty blond
woman on the portrait. On her lap were two children. They were
boys. One was about 18 months old. The other was older,
perhaps three.   Even in the dim light I could see that the boys
were not normal. They both were victims of cerebral palsy. Their
mother talked to them and moved their arms. She was intent on
stimulating them, perhaps to heal suffered birth defects. Their
heads moved uncontrollably on their necks as they smiled at their
mother.

"They had everything, and they wanted children." I surmised.
"They had a child, and he had cerebral palsy. Bad luck. They

quickly tried for another child so that they could have a normal child. And he had cerebral palsy. More incredible bad luck. I will wager that they would give up this wealth for normal children".

I was visiting the home of my patient, Mr. Clarence Sheffield. Mr. Sheffield was a retired Navy captain.

His last duty assignment was as commanding officer of an aircraft carrier. He hoped that he would soon make admiral. But one day, while climbing the stairs to the bridge of the carrier, he developed chest pain. An EKG performed in the sick bay showed a massive heart attack

Captain Sheffield was taken by helicopter to a military hospital. There, in addition to his myocardial infarction, it was discovered that his aortic valve was critically narrowed. The calcified valve obstructed blood flow to the body and placed an additional strain on the heart.

Open heart surgery bypassed his diseased coronary arteries and replaced his valve with a mechanical valve. His hopes of making admiral were dashed, and he received a medical discharge from the Navy.

Captain Sheffield's already damaged heart began to fail. Each year the ejection fraction, which is the relative amount of blood that the heart expels during a contraction, decreased. Whereas in a normal person, the amount of blood that is ejected is at least 45 per cent, Captain Sheffield's feeble heart pumped out less the twenty per cent with each beat. He was chronically fatigued, his ankles swelled up with fluid, and the slightest exertion made him short of breath. He had developed congestive heart failure.

The 76- year old man was living in a small portion of his daughter's home with his wife.

He had been slightly overweight before his heart attack, but in an effort to reduce the work of his heart he had intentionally lost 30 pounds. He now was a scrawny old white man.

His wife, who was 20 years his junior, had been his executive officer when he served on the carrier. This vivacious woman bore a close resemblance to the young woman in the portrait above the fireplace. The major difference was that her hair was black, rather than blond

Captain Sheffield was on several drugs. Most important was lisinopril, a drug which decreases levels of angiotensin II, a substance which makes the heart work harder. He was on Carvedilol, a beta blocker, which slows the heart. This protects the diseased heart, and by giving it time to fill, increases its output with each contraction. And he was on furosemide, a diuretic which removes excess fluid from the body. He was also on warfarin to keep his mechanical aortic valve from clotting off.

This well- educated and articulate couple bonded with me. Every few weeks I stopped by their home for dinner, which was heart healthy food and wine. After my earlier shadowy glimpse of the daughter, I never again saw the mysterious couple who owned the mansion.

I enjoyed talking to the Sheffields about their lives on the aircraft carrier and my life as a doctor. We also talked about astronomy which had been my passion before I went to medical school.

In the beginning we didn't discuss Captain Sheffield's failing heart. My visits were just social.

The couple was fully aware of the falling number which was the ejection fraction of the captain's heart. I believe that this close connection with their doctor helped relieve their anxiety, even though my eating dinner with them did nothing to help the dying heart.

Over the next 6 months the ejection fraction fell to 10 per cent. Walking required tremendous effort. Someone who has an ejection fraction this low has an average lifespan of 6 months. The patient could qualify to enter a hospice.

"What you need is a heart transplant." I declared one day in my office. I knew he was too old for a transplant, but that was the only treatment that would save his life.

"I don't care how old he is. I love him. I just want him with me." declared Mrs. Sheffield in anguish. She had read my mind.

I looked upon marriages between young women and older men somewhat suspiciously. I wondered if the woman was just marrying the man for his money, for security, but at this moment I realized that Mrs. Sheffield truly loved her husband.

I began bringing my telescope to their house when I came to dinner. At that time, the planet Mars was making the close approach to the Earth that it made every two years. The bright orange ball dominated the evening sky.

Fifty years earlier, at another close approach, a view of Mars through a neighbor's telescope ignited in me an interest in science. I majored in astronomy in college, but switched to medicine, another branch of science. At that time, I never imagined that, years later, I would be using astronomy in my medical practice.

I hoped that showing the couple a world that was forty million miles away would distract them from Captain Sheffield's medical condition.

As we stood on the grass looking up at the sky, I began a kind of lecture.

"See that red star over there. It is Antares, the brightest star in the constellation of the Scorpion. It is a red supergiant star. In 5 billion years the Sun will expand and become like Antares. Do you know where Antares gets its name?" The couple looked at each other, and shook their heads.

"Well, Antares means 'Rival of Mars'. Ares is Mars. Both are red. Get it?" The couple smiled at this lesson.

"The Big Bang Theory tells us that the Universe began in a kind of explosion ten billion years ago. Every particle in our bodies was made in that event. When we pass away, the atoms persist, so we continue to exist, just in another form. The Universe is expanding. The galaxies are all moving apart. The Catholic Church likes this idea. It agrees with the story of Genesis, that the Universe began in a burst of light. One theory is that eventually the Universe will stop expanding, and collapse. Everything will come back together, and another Bing Bang will occur and, who knows, maybe we will be created again."

The couple looked at each other and smiled. They seemed to like what I said. Cosmology gave the captain hope for reincarnation, or resurrection.

 As I drove home, I thought about human mortality and fear of death. As life evolved, reproduction of the species became the primary goal. Fear of predators became imperative for the survival of the gene. The "fight or flight" reflex, which involved release of adrenaline, caused anxiety and increased pulse, and became a part of physiology. Man is probably the only species which is aware its mortality.

I have seen death many times. The heart stops. Blood flow to the brain stops, and the brain dies. All awareness of the Universe, algebra, the taste of macaroni and cheese, is gone.

Christian Heaven, as I was taught, was a place where you were close to God. Would you carry he information that you acquired in life to Heaven? Knowledge is stored in the brain. I wondered if what you learned in life would be carried with you to Heaven. Or would you have to start learning again?

Would college credits achieved in life be transferred to Heaven?

I have worked in Buddhist countries. Buddha preached that a good life produced Karma. Good Karma allowed someone to achieve Nirvana, oneness with God, when he died.

I was never quite sure what Nirvana meant. Was it total forgetfulness? Or was it some form of consciousness, perhaps the taste of chocolate, that separated the departed person from total oblivion?

When I stood over the corpse of someone who had just died, I thought that from what I know about brain function, he had achieved something close to Nirvana.

Captain Sheffield was acutely aware of his mortality. He wanted the shortness of breath and fatigue to go away. But he was also aware that his failing health was taking him to his death. This produced as much, or more pain. than his physical condition.

Eventually he would reach death, and fear would be gone.

Someone once asked Chuck Yeager, the test pilot, the first man to break the sound barrier, if he feared dying.

"No" was the reply. "When you are dead you don't know you are dead."

Mr. Sheffield was followed by a cardiologist. Several times he received what is known as a "dobutamine tune up". Dobutamine is a drug which makes the heart pump harder. The medication is infused for several days or even longer to help the heart pump the excess fluid out of the body. This was only a temporizing measure, and the retired captain deteriorated further. He was placed on Home Hospice care.

The last time I saw the captain he was in a hospital bed in his home Most of his medications had been stopped. Since he was near death, medications, such as his statin to lower his cholesterol, had no purpose. Even his blood thinner was stopped. It was irrelevant if he got a clot on his aortic valve.

A very heavy African American woman, dressed in a floor length white dress, stood by the bed. She was his Home Hospice nurse. Standing nearby was his wife looking depressed. The frail old man was lying with his head cranked up to a 30- degree angle. The nurse injected morphine into his IV line. This was to treat the shortness of breath attendant with his heart failure.

"You are lucky." I joked. "I have never had the morphine experience. I will have to wait until I am on Home Hospice before I get it."

Mrs. Sheffield disappeared. A minute later she returned with a tray that held 4 glasses of white wine. We all took one, including the nurse. I looked at Mr. Sheffield.

"We will remember today when we pass away. One of my favorite actresses was Katherine Hepburn. When she talked about her death she said. "Death is like sleep. I love sleep.""

It was if we were giving the captain a bon voyage party for a cruise he was going to go on. We all clinked glasses. When the other people in the room passed on, we would remember this moment. The patient managed a faint smile.

Captain Sheffield's life came down to his last thoughts. I hoped they were pleasant, like his life in the Navy, or the birth of his daughter, or maybe hitting a home run in a school yard baseball game.

Mrs. Sheffield, who had been silent, suddenly spoke. Her voice was anguished. "If I had given him more vegetables and less meat, maybe this wouldn't have happened."

Their dog, an ugly, but friendly, English bulldog nuzzled my knee. "Too bad. He will be losing his master." I thought as I petted the dog.

The next day I receive an email from the Home Hospice agency. Captain Sheffield had passed away, free of anxiety, in a morphine induced state of euphoria.

About a mile away from the home of Captain Sheffield was the home of Bobby Harper. Mr. Harper was a tall, handsome, man with shoulders like an ox. He reminded me of the late actor John Wayne who appeared in many westerns. Like John Wayne, he had been a heavy smoker. When John Wayne died of lung cancer, Mr. Harper stopped "cold turkey". But he still had a craving, and admitted that he sometimes sneaked a cigarette.

The 84- year old man was a retired attorney. When something didn't agree with him, he let his feelings be known. He was a vocal advocate of veteran's rights and had helped get legislation passed that improved veterans' benefits. In a way, I felt lucky to be the physician for such a powerful and aggressive man.

The down side was that Mr. Harper was a "control freak". When he had a medical issue, he showed up at my office unannounced. "You're a good man Dr. Jim and they ain't too many of us left." he charmed me into seeing him.

When he was 82 years old, he noted that his eyes were becoming yellow. His stool turned clay white and he had abdominal pain. A CAT scan made an ominous diagnosis. He had cancer of the head of the pancreas. The cancer was pushing on the bile duct that drained bile from the liver. The bile pigment was piling up in the blood. That was why his eyes were yellow.

An operation called a Whipple Procedure was performed. The cancerous head of the pancreas and part of the intestine and stomach were removed. The bile duct and pancreatic ducts were reconnected to the small intestine. It was hoped that this would provide a cure.

Mr. Harper did well for several months. He looked up everything that he could about cancer of the pancreas. He was optimistic that he had been cured, even though the cure rate from pancreatic cancer was less than ten per cent.

He again developed abdominal pain and he lost weight. A CT scan revealed that his cancer had recurred and had spread to his liver. Chemotherapy was started, but he continued to deteriorate.

Mr. Harper read about certain herbs and vitamins that helped cancer.

When the body is sick and dying, various processes shut down. Sex and reproduction are not necessary. Testosterone decreases, resulting in anemia and decreased muscle mass

One afternoon Bobby Harper barged into my office. "I need to see you right away." he said. He carried a small bottle that contained testosterone. "I need you to shoot me in the butt with this stuff." he said. He was determined to fight the "dying" process everywhere he found it. I injected a cubic centimeter of the clear liquid into his buttock. He returned every two weeks for a repeat injection.

But Mr. Harper's efforts to keep his life afloat on the sea of mortality failed. There were too many holes in the boat to plug,

He finally realized that he was dying, and there was nothing more that he could do about it.

He became preoccupied with his legacy. He gave me some DVDs of him playing banjo music. This was something he had accomplished, and he wanted me to know about it.

Like Captain Sheffield, Mr. Harper used his Medicare Home Hospice benefit.

I visited his sprawling one-story home that was situated at the edge of a wooded area. I met his nurse and his wife in the living room.

His wife was also much younger. She was a senior administrator in a federal agency before she retired.

"He's stubborn like my two -year old grandson." remarked the nurse, a grey- haired woman in a two- piece dress. Mrs. Harper and I laughed. She was telling us something that we knew only too well.

Mrs. Harper was totally accepting of the impending death of her 84- year old spouse. The nurse looked at the process of easing someone's transition to death as a privilege. The two women chatted happily, as if they were planning a daughter's wedding.

I walked down the narrow dark hall to Mr. Harper"s bedroom. In the dim light I could barely see his gaunt body. A bedpan rested on the bedside table. He nodded weakly.

Some patients look forward to death. This is when they are religious.

"Getting ready to see Jesus!" exclaimed an old man who was near death in a hospice. I hoped that such feelings might give comfort to Mr. Harper. But no.

"I don't mind religion too much." Mr. Harper remarked. "But I can't stand religions that dispense guilt." I was surprised at this remark coming from a conservative old man.

Then he changed the subject. "That narcotic is constipating the hell out of me. Can't you do something about it?" I prescribed a laxative.

I had just completed a book about my medical career. In it, I described some iconic patients, including Mr. Harper. For decades he and his friends gathered dead wood to give to poor people to heat their homes in the winter. I called him the "Woodchopper".

I gave him a copy of that book so that he could read about his service to Humanity.

Two weeks later Mr. Harper called me. "You say "had" too many times." he said critically.

His controlling personality had returned. As sick as he was, he had read the book cover to cover, and edited it.

I went through the book deleting the word "had" whenever I could. To this day, whenever I think of writing that word, I hear Bobby Harper's voice in my head.

The last time I saw Bobby it was at the Virginia War Memorial. The wasted, weak, old man was slumped down in a wheelchair. He was obviously in pain, and seemed to be oblivious to the ceremony.

The occasion was the dedication of a peace garden that my patient and his wife had endowed. Following the invocation by a minister, a congressman came to the podium and thanked Mr. Harper and his wife for their gift.

Two days later Bobby Harper passed away at home.

I thought of my own mortality. Perhaps I would be able to experience, first -hand, one of the diseases that I studied in medical school.

And what about the end? I remembered a young man who was dying of AIDS. The poor man's lungs were filling up with fluid from an incurable infection. He knew the end was near. "This should be interesting." he gasped.

Sergeant Henry Gupton was on Omaha Beach on D Day.

As he stood talking to his friend Joe, a sniper's bullet struck his friend between his eyes and killed him instantly, spattering blood on Henry's face. Henry got through the war uninjured. Perhaps his war experiences told him that he was living on borrowed time, and he didn't need to worry about his mortality.

I saw Henry in my office every three months. When patients make it to 90, I see them frequently. The chipper old man spent most of the visit talking about his experiences in the War and making veiled sexual references to the wife of his caretaker. "You stay away from my wife!" shouted the caretaker in mock annoyance. Then he smiled and winked at me.

Henry's chest X-ray showed congestion consistent with early heart failure, but he never complained of shortness of breath. I had him on lisinopril, a medication that protects the heart from further damage.

"I pee a lot at night." Henry told me with his ubiquitous smile. I did a bladder scan to check out the cause of the urination.

If the bladder was enlarged it would mean that he had a problem emptying it, such as occurs when the prostate is large. This is the most common cause of frequent urination in an elderly man. If this was the case, I could start him on tamsulosin, a medication which opens the sphincter between the bladder and the urethra.

However, Mr. Gupton's bladder was small. He had an overactive bladder. I started him on oxybutinin, a medication which decreases the strength of bladder contractions. This medication can worsen dementia in the elderly. I was relieved that the medication had improved his urinary symptoms without producing any effect on his thinking.

One evening, while singing Karaoke, Henry stopped singing in the middle of a word. With the impish smile still on his face he collapsed. CPR was attempted but he could not be revived.

Sergeant Henry Gupton went to Eternity at age 96 with no awareness of dying and no fear of death.

As a medical student I thought that it was a privilege to be present at the time of birth.

Many years later, I concluded that it was also a privilege to be present at the time of a patient's death.

Printed in Great Britain
by Amazon

69466131R00208